T0329962

The Economic Surplus in Advanced Economies

NEW DIRECTIONS IN MODERN ECONOMICS
Series Editor: Malcolm C. Sawyer,
Professor of Economics, University of Leeds
New Directions in Modern Economics presents a challenge to orthodox economic thinking. It focuses on new ideas emanating from radical traditions including post-Keynesian, Kaleckian, neo-Ricardian and Marxian. The books in the series do not adhere rigidly to any single school of thought but attempt to present a positive alternative to the conventional wisdom.

Post- Keynesian Monetary Economics
New Approaches to Financial Modelling
Edited by Philip Arestis

Keynes's Principle of Effective Demand
Edward J. Amadeo

New Directions in Post-Keynesian Economics
Edited by John Pheby

Theory and Policy in Political Economy
Essays in Pricing, Distribution and Growth
Edited by Philip Arestis and Yiannis Kitromilides

Keynes's Third Alternative?
The Neo-Ricardian Keynesians and the Post Keynesians
Amitava Krishna Dutt and Edward J. Amadeo

Wages and Profits in the Capitalist Economy
The Impact of Monopolistic Power on Macroeconomic Performance
in the USA and UK
Andrew Henley

Prices, Profits and Financial Structures
A Post-Keynesian Approach to Competition
Gokhan Capoglu

International Perspectives on Profitability and Accumulation
Edited by Fred Moseley and Edward N. Wolff

Mr Keynes and the Post Keynesians
Principles of Macroeconomics for a Monetary Production Economy
Fernando J. Cardim de Carvalho

The Economic Surplus in Advanced Economies
Edited by John B. Davis

Foundations of Post-Keynesian Economic Analysis
Marc Lavoie

The Post-Keynesian Approach to Economics
An Alternative Analysis of Economic Theory and Policy
Philip Arestis

The Economic Surplus in Advanced Economies

Edited by John B. Davis

Associate Professor of Economics
Marquette University

Edward Elgar

Published by

Edward Elgar Publishing Limited
Gower House
Croft Road
Aldershot
Hants GU11 3HR
England

Edward Elgar Publishing Company
Old Post Road
Brookfield
Vermont 05036
USA

A CIP catalogue record for this book is available from the British Library.

A CIP catalogue record for this book is available from the US Library of Congress.

ISBN-13: 978-1-85278-555-0

Printed and bound by CPI Group (UK) Ltd, Croydon, CR0 4YY

Contents

List of Contributors

Keith Cowling, Professor of Economics, University of Warwick

John B. Davis, Associate Professor of Economics, Marquette University

Michael Dawson, Instructor in Sociology, University of Oregon

Amitava Krishna Dutt, Professor of Economics, University of Notre Dame

Leslie Fishman, Emeritus Professor of Economics, Keele University

John Bellamy Foster, Professor of Sociology, University of Oregon

Victor D. Lippit, Professor of Economics, University of California, Riverside

Tracy Mott, Assistant Professor of Economics, University of Denver

Joseph D. Phillips, Late Professor of Economics, University of Illinois

James Ronald Stanfield, Professor of Economics, Colorado State University

Paul M. Sweezy, Co-Editor, *Monthly Review*

For Joseph D. Phillips

1. The Monopoly Capital Approach to the Concept of the Economic Surplus

John B. Davis

In the century that followed the appearance of Adam Smith's *Wealth of Nations* (1937 [1776]) and saw the beginning industrialisation of the European capitalist market economies, the concept of the economic surplus – the difference between the value of a society's annual product and its socially necessary costs of production – was central to an economic thinking whose chief subjects were growth and production, income distribution and class, and power over disposition of the surplus. By the end of the nineteenth century, however, the focus of economic thinking had shifted to marginalist analyses of free market exchange between autonomous individuals, and economists were to argue that were every factor of production paid according to the value of its marginal contribution to production, the value of the entire product created would be fully exhausted by these factor payments. On this view, firms retained no residual value or surplus product that might be thought to function as an accumulation fund, income distribution was determined by the technical properties of the factors of production, and growth reflected the virtue of thrift exercised by savers. More generally, the economic process was said to be driven by a logic of gains from trade and comparative advantage that twentieth century economists were to argue produced a Panglossian world in which competitive markets generated optimal results.

This fundamental shift in vision and understanding of the economic process had the effect of displacing for a time many if not most of the paradigmatic themes of Classical political economy. Neoclassical marginalism, however, did share one significant assumption in common with Classical economic thinking: both assumed that the economy was essentially a competitive one populated by a large number of small firms none of which possessed significant market power. Ironically, then, it was in precisely this connection that the Classical notion of the economic surplus was re-introduced (if in somewhat different form), and the marginalists exchange-based paradigm was first seriously contested, when in the 1920s and '30s the modern reality of large monopoly firms exercising significant market power could no longer be ignored by economic theorists. Joan Robinson (1933) and E.H. Chamberlin (1946 [1933]), both academic economists traditionally trained in Neoclassical price theory, each separately demonstrated that firms exercising market power could earn monopoly profits while remunerating factors at rates less than their marginal value contributions to production. The resulting profit and factor exploitation residuals, as Robinson termed them recalling Karl Marx's surplus value concept, were not eroded by price competition, so that questions regarding the disposition and authority over the economic surplus once again emerged as deserving attention. The difference with Classical thinking, moreover, was important. In its twentieth-century guise, the economic surplus was closely related to the advent of market power and the rise of large, monopolistic firms, as had been given special emphasis by V.I. Lenin (1970 [1914]) and Thorstein Veblen (1904 [1935]). This gave the theory of the economic surplus a distinctly firm-based emphasis, as opposed to the class-based view of the surplus that was present in the thinking of Smith, Marx, David Ricardo and Thomas Malthus, and this was later to have important implications for the Monopoly Capital theory approach to the question of economic policy.

At about this same time, independent developments in the analysis of the economic system as a whole produced the important conclusion that – contrary to the then prevailing Say's Law wisdom that supply created its own demand – an understanding of the demand for invest-ment goods and the investment process were central to an explanation of both the general functioning of the capitalist market economies and the particular relationship between commodity and labour markets. John Maynard Keynes (1936) from the Marshallian tradition and Michal Kalecki (1971) from the Marxian both recognized that, given a population's saving propensities, output and income increased when investment increased, and the level of saving adjusted to the level of investment through changes in output and income. Moreover, since increased saving could paradoxically produce lower levels of output and income, and since it was firms that were responsible for investment decisions, the principal question in what was later to emerge as macroeconomics became how might high levels of investment spending be sustained so as to permit full-employment levels of output. This focus effectively re-linked the issue of economic growth and the question of the disposition and authority over the surplus, since firm's investment funds constituted a surplus account upon the necessary wage costs, materials costs, etc. of production. Like the Classical thinkers, Keynes and Kalecki saw that the central issues involved in explaining the functioning of the capitalist market economies turned on understanding the discretionary use of the economic surplus.

Keynes, however, avoided associating these issues with the development of monopoly, arguing that even a competitive market system with considerable money wage flexibility would tend to produce levels of effective demand insufficient to maintain full employment levels of output and income. Asserting in the last chapter of *The General Theory* that the outstanding faults of modern economic society were its failure to provide for full employment and its inequitable distribution of wealth and income, he recommended a redistribution of income from the rich to the poor to enlarge consumption expenditure and enhance the living standards of the less fortunate, and a significant socialization of investment to bring about a better adjustment between the propensity to consume and the inducements to investment. As a result, he brought into question the capacity of the private market system to make effective use of accumulated surpluses, and also challenged traditional thinking about the customary social relationships underlying the economic process.

Kalecki, on the other hand, proceeded directly to the integration of macroeconomics and the theory of noncompetitive markets by arguing that the degree of monopoly (or the profit mark-up over unit prime costs) was directly related to the rate of growth of the macroeconomy via the social or class composition of demand. Using Marx's (1967 [1893]) reproduction schemes and emphasis upon the centralization and concentration of capital, Kalecki developed an underconsumptionist explanation of deficient effective demand deriving from the overaccumulation of capital under monopoly. In a number of important respects Kalecki's analysis of deficient effective demand anticipated Keynes's own thinking on the subject. In other respects it reflected Kalecki's very different interest in Marx's account of realization crises associated with the translation of commodity capital into money capital subsequent to production, especially as had been developed in the work of Rosa Luxemburg (1913 [1951]). Importantly, Kalecki showed that accumulation and the distribution of income were closely connected, thus restoring a principal focus of Classical thinking about the economic surplus.

However, these beginnings of a new approach to the concept of the economic surplus were, except for the work of a small number of individuals, interrupted by the Second World War and the tendency of the postwar prosperity of the 1950s and '60s to undermine investigation into the issues surrounding the role of monopoly power in the economy. Keynesian growth theory in the works of Roy Harrod (1939), Evsey Domar (1946), and Robinson (1956) maintained an emphasis on the analysis of an underlying tendency towards stagnation in the capitalist market economies, but more economists were ultimately attracted to Neoclassical full-employment growth models of the sort developed by Robert Solow (1956). Kalecki's subsequent work (e.g., 1972) focused more on the application of his earlier ideas to a diagnosis of the postwar capitalist political economy and also upon the problems of planning in the socialist world with which he became closely involved. Keynes's moderately conservative social views were more palatable to a postwar political climate hostile to socialism, and his emphasis on effective demand was successfully translated into a Neoclassical Keynesianism that took short-run demand management as its chief priority. This undermined concern with the question of whether capitalist market economies were chronically stagnationist, and also postponed further consideration of the relationship between the economic surplus, growth, and income distribution.

There were, none the less, important exceptions to this general trend of thinking. One was Josef Steindl's *Maturity and Stagnation in American Capitalism* (1952). Extending the insights of Kalecki (with whom he had worked during the War), Steindl linked monopolistic firm's investment planning to their levels of excess capacity. Profit expectations on new investment are a function of the extent of unused capacity, which monopolistic firms build up in anticipation of competition for market share, and which they are then reluctant to absorb via price-cutting during times of reduced demand. Another was Paolo Sylos-Labini's *Oligopoly and Technical Progress* (1962 [1956]). Sylos-Labini developed an analysis of deficient effective demand linked to oversaving and overinvestment in the oligopoly sector of the economy. He also defended Kalecki's concept of the degree of monopoly against some of its recent critics, and indicated the difficulties in Keynes's account of investment in relation to the latter's assumption of competition. A third exception was Paul Baran's *The Political Economy of Growth* (1957). Baran systematically developed an analysis of the concept of the economic surplus in the Marxian surplus-value tradition for twentieth-century developed capitalism. He distinguished the actual surplus, the potential surplus and the planned surplus, and placed important emphasis on the question of waste through unemployment, excess consumption, unproductive labour, and the irrational organization of the production process.

In the late 1960s and the early '70s, then, when low rates of growth, low rates of capacity utilization and declining productivity gains signalled the existence of serious problems of growth and accumulation in the capitalist market economies, increasing numbers of younger economists began to be attracted to the theory of monopoly capital and modern formulations of the concept of the economic surplus. In the subsequent delineation of what came to be the Monopoly Capital approach to the concept of the economic surplus, it was Baran and Sweezy's *Monopoly Capital* (1966) that, claiming the work of Kalecki and Steindl as important foundations, was especially influential in this emerging tradition, largely because it provided a single, connected argument which plausibly explained the recent direction of development of monopoly capitalism, and because it successfully linked the theory of the monopolistic firm, the theory of effective demand and the theory of the economic surplus. The central argument of the book can be summarized as follows.

In advanced capitalist economies, large monopolistic or oligopolistic firms have come to dominate most markets. These firms exercise their considerable market power by setting above-competitive prices in order to earn monopoly-type profits. The immediate consequences of this are rates of growth of output and employment less than what would occur in more competitive markets, coupled with a heightened search for additional investment opportunities brought on by the greater accumulation of profits. In terms of the concept of the surplus, in the monopoly stage of capitalism the economic surplus is concentrated both in fewer hands and also increasingly in the hands of those seeking additional investment opportunities to generate further monopoly profits. In essence, then, under monopoly capitalism there is a tendency for the surplus to rise. At the same time, however, slower rates of growth of output and employment imply slower rates of growth of demand on the part of wage and salary earners, so that profitable investment prospects in private production are increasingly difficult to find. With capitalist consumption constituting an ever-decreasing share of demand, the economy exhibits an underlying tendency toward stagnation associated with what Baran and Sweezy termed the problem of surplus absorption, the crucial manifestation of which is a continual under-utilisation of productive capacity and rising unemployment levels. In Baran and Sweezy's view, this makes monopoly capitalism a self-contradictory economic system, since with the capacity to produce always growing more rapidly than the growth of output itself, the economic problem in modern economic society paradoxically ceases to be how to make best use of scarce resources (as Neoclassical thinking has it), and rather becomes how to dispose of superabundant ones.

On this view, a fundamental aspect of modern capitalist development becomes the system's increasing dependence upon the promotion of waste and rise in unproductive expenditure. Baran and Sweezy describe three forms of unproductive expenditure that tend to counter-act the stagnationist tendencies of the system as additional modes of surplus absorption. First, with the demise of price competition attendant upon the rise of monopoly power, the sales effort, in its various manifestations as advertising, packaging, product differentia-tion, artificial obsolescence, etc., has become a crucial means of enhancing demand, while simultaneously generating an entire industry on its own closely intertwined with and involved in the very pro-duction of traditional commodities. Second, the growth of government at all levels has created a demand for idle capital and labour, and put into place an administrative apparatus that is lobbied to the advantage of the giant corporation. Third, the commitment to high levels of military spending in times of both peace and war has provided a vast source of expenditure for privately produced goods, while also creating a world economic environment receptive to big business.

The Monopoly Capital approach to the concept of the economic surplus, then, drew upon themes familiar to many in the 1970s and 80s, and as such gained in influence with economists and social theorists seeking alternatives to Neoclassicism (see, Foster and Szlajfer, 1984; Foster, 1986). Indeed, together with Cambridge Neo-Keynesianism, Neo-Ricardianism, more Classically-inspired Marxism, Post-Keynesianism and Institutionalism, Monopoly Capital theory has been an important theoretical alternative to orthodox Neoclassicism and Neoclassical Keynesianism. Yet though low rates of growth, significant under-capacity, and declining rates of productivity growth gave impetus to the Monopoly Capital framework at the end of the quarter-century-long postwar boom of the early 1970s, other subsequent developments in the capitalist market economies raised questions concerning the applicability of its analysis. Most obviously, there was the need to explain the simultaneous development of stagnation and inflation – stagflation – as it emerged in the middle 1970s, since the Monopoly Capital theory emphasis on the manifestation of surplus absorption problems in realisation crises implied that stagnation should generally not be accompanied by significant upward pressure on prices (Howard and King, 1990). On this score, Sweezy later argued that the long postwar boom had been made possible in large part by a continuous growth of public and private debt (Sweezy, 1981). Debt creation combined with downward price rigidity in the monopolistic sectors of the economy to generate a wage–price spiral that continued until producers, consumers and governments were too over-extended to borrow further, thus allowing the underlying stagnationist tendencies to re-assert themselves (Sweezy, 1982). The low rates of growth and low rates of inflation in the 1980s would argue in favor of this interpretation. The tremendous development of finance in the decade raises other questions.

Thus, in his contribution to this collection, Sweezy goes on to argue that recent developments in the financial sector of the capitalist economy indicate the need for still further reflection upon the nature of the basic capital accumulation process. In his anniversary paper, '*Monopoly Capital* After 25 Years', Sweezy argues that though the primary argument of the book still captures the essential character of an economy dominated by a small number of giant firms, an important consequence of the buyout and takeover wave of the decade has been the adoption of a greater short-term orientation on the part of big firm management. This together with the larger part played by finance over the more recent episodes of the business cycle puts the accumulation process under monopoly capital in a somewhat different perspective, in that accumulation seems increasingly to be a matter of adding to the stock of financial assets. Further development of the understanding of monopoly capitalism, Sweezy thus suggests, will require greater attention to the interaction between real and financial aspects of the capital accumulation process.

A related challenge to the Monopoly Capital theory of the economic surplus tied to the end of the postwar expansion derives from recent empirical work arguing that the capitalist market economies experienced a profit squeeze linked to a rising wage share in national income in the late 1960s and early '70s (Weisskopf, 1979). This would appear to contradict the view that the surplus tends to rise with the continued development of the monopolistic sector of the economy, while suggesting that supply-side social and class conflict rather than demand-side realisation problems were responsible for the poor performance of the capitalist economies at the end of the postwar boom. Against this, it might be thought that the observed profit squeeze somehow masked the basic, underlying surplus creation process, especially since the theory predicts a rising share of unproductive labour with the expansion of wasteful expenditure. Can it thus be shown that the surplus still tends to rise even in the presence of falling profit rates?

Originally in the Appendix to *Monopoly Capital*, Joseph D. Phillips had constructed a measure of the economic surplus in the United States that showed that the surplus rose from 46.9 percent of GNP in 1929 to 56.1 percent of GNP in 1963. Phillips focused upon three major categories of the economic surplus: property income, waste in the business process associated with the outlay on sales, and government expenditure. He also noted that output forgone on account of excess capacity and unemployment and waste associated with the penetration of the production process by the sales effort (e.g., planned obsolescence, unnecessary model changes, etc.) constituted additional categories of the surplus, but did not include estimates of these on account of difficulties associated with their calculation. His estimate of the economic surplus was thus a very conservative one. None the less, questions were later raised about whether Phillips's reliance upon the national income accounts to produce his estimates of the surplus involved double counting, since his figures were compiled from both the income and expenditures sides of the accounts (Heilbroner, 1970; Lubitz, 1971; Stanfield, 1973). Moreover, Phillips's historical series did not extend into the crucial period of the profit squeeze at issue in the debates about the post-1973 slowdown. Thus, evaluation of the Monopoly Capital approach to the concept of the economic surplus raises the question of whether Phillips's calculations can be revised to avoid double counting in such as way as to demonstrate a tendency for the surplus to rise in the period since 1963. Phillips's piece is reprinted here both to make his results more accessible and to exhibit his methodology.

Following this, Michael Dawson and John Bellamy Foster take up the task of estimating the subsequent trend of the surplus from 1963 to 1988. They address some of the questions raised by Phillips's original analysis, and succeed in avoiding double-counting by producing their estimates from the income side of the national accounts alone. They find that the gross surplus increased from 49.9 percent of GNP in 1963 to 55.0 percent in 1988, and at the same time, find that profit plus rent plus interest declined from 35 percent of the gross surplus in 1963 to 29 percent in 1988. These results indicate that the profit squeeze hypothesis is not necessarily at odds with the Monopoly Capital approach to the economic surplus. They also re-emphasise the need to define all forms of economic surplus, however they may be obscured by traditional accounting methods.

In the next paper, however, Victor Lippit challenges the Monopoly Capital approach in a number of important respects. Noting that the capitalist world has changed significantly since the writing of *Monopoly Capital*, Lippit argues that the increasing size of the service sector, where cost-reducing productivity enhancement is difficult, and increased international competition, with its constraining effect on oligopoly pricing, makes questionable the tendency of the surplus to rise. Yet, even more importantly, the very concept of the surplus employed by Baran and Sweezy is, in Lippit's view, problematic due to a variety of difficulties in the notion of socially necessary costs of production. For example, socially necessary costs of production are almost certainly underestimated in the *Monopoly Capital* framework on account of the lack of attention devoted to externalities, especially environmental damage, and this surely must reduce the potential surplus. Lippit thus reviews the categories Phillips employed for estimating the surplus preparatory to estimating his own alternative conception of the surplus. His figures, which he allows do not adequately account for environmental damage and capital stock depreciation, show the recent surplus to be much lower than the Dawson–Foster approach. In his view, however, these results do not demonstrate that the Monopoly Capital approach to the concept of the surplus should be abandoned, but rather that the concept of the surplus must be re-evaluated to account for historical changes in monopoly capitalism since the 1960s.

Any such re-evaluation, however, will almost certainly consider one of the most significant contributions of the Monopoly Capital approach to the economic surplus to be its emphasis on waste and unproductive activity in the process of economic growth and its associated distinction between the potential and actual forms of the economic surplus. As is not always appreciated by critics of Baran and Sweezy's stagnationist perspective, when waste and unproductive activity mount increasingly over time, recorded growth over an extended period neither implies that realisation problems are non-existent, nor necessarily tells us very much about the character of economic development. Part of the difficulty here, no doubt, is due to the fact that views differ over what constitutes unproductive activity, with Baran and Sweezy in the Kalecki tradition seeing waste in forms of production undertaken when income distribution precludes production for basic needs, and other contemporary thinkers following Marx in seeing the question in terms of labour devoted to circulation and supervisory activities that do not create surplus value. Indeed, those arguing from the latter perspective have concluded that reduced surplus value production attendant upon increasing unproductive activity leads to a falling economic surplus rather than a rising one. The dispute over the nature of waste and unproductive activity, therefore, goes to the very heart of the Monopoly Capital approach to the concept of the economic surplus in bringing into question one of Baran and Sweezy's principle conclusions.

Amitava Dutt takes on these difficult issues in his contribution to this collection. Stating clearly the foundational differences in the literature on these two perspectives, he defends Baran and Sweezy's conclusions regarding the tendency of the surplus to rise under increasing levels of unproductive activity by setting forth a simple model that demonstrates how increases in unproductive activity may increase the rate of accumulation. His analysis elicits the complex interrelationships involved in the accumulation process, and adds importantly to the understanding of the connection between monopolistic firms and surplus production. In particular, he shows how in an economy in which realisation problems are important, a relative increase in the size of the unproductive sector of the economy may be associated with a higher rate of growth in the productive sector, and that parametric changes implying a higher rate of unproductive activity also may imply higher rate of growth in a productive sector of the economy. The Keynes-Kalecki effective demand focus, it thus turns out, is a necessary accompaniment to any supply-side analysis of waste and unproductive activity, in that demand interaction effects counter the logic of supply-side-only models that emphasise productivity differences between demand-autonomous productive and unproductive sectors.

Tracy Mott also undertakes fundamental issues associated with the Monopoly Capital framework in his inquiry into how this approach requires an analysis of imperfect competition. Noting that New Keynesians have recently argued that imperfect competition and costly information create price rigidities that may cause unemployment, Mott distinguishes the Kalecki–Steindl approach to the concept of the surplus as one that explains mark-up inflexibility in terms of the degree of monopoly. Unemployment, and the lost output it proxies, may be explainable in a New Keynesian world modeled on departures from perfect competition, but it is better represented by an analysis which recognizes that monopoly is the rule, and in which the surplus is consequently clearly linked to price-cost mark-ups. Mott thus develops the thinking of Kalecki and Steindl as keys to understanding the modern Monopoly Capital surplus approach, emphasizing such matters as Kalecki's principle of increasing risk and Steindl's treatment of excess capacity. These themes build upon Keynes's view that stagnation in the modern macroeconomy is not due to market imperfections but rather to constraints upon consumption and investment spending. For Steindl, those constraints had their origins in a particular historical development, namely, the emergence of monopoly capital firms in mature capitalism.

This development in the Monopoly Capital approach, ultimately reflecting Marx's influence on Kalecki, would seem to indicate that Marxists generally favor the Baran and Sweezy approach. In fact, however, among the original debates over *Monopoly Capital*, perhaps the most heated were those between those fundamentalist Marxists who argued against Baran and Sweezy that Marx's analyses of nineteenth-century capitalism applied without revision to twentieth-century capitalism, and Neo-Marxist supporters of Baran and Sweezy's views, who argued that Marxian analysis must always be historically specific. At issue was Baran and Sweezy's reliance and emphasis upon the concept of the surplus rather than upon Marx's concept of surplus value. In the view of the fundamentalists, that Baran and Sweezy did not make the concept of surplus value immediate to their analysis led them to emphasise realisation crises and give prominence to the sphere of exchange or circulation over the sphere of production. This criticism, however, ignores a central assumption of *Monopoly Capital* that monopoly capital production transforms the workings of the law of value by its increasing incorporation of unproductive labour in the value of the commodity in the form of expenses of circulation, or by the increasing penetration of the production process by the sales effort. As Baran and Sweezy put it, 'The question is, what are socially necessary costs when, in Veblen's words, the distinction between workmanship and salesmanship has been blurred?' (1966, p. 133). Henryk Szlajfer (1984) has explained this in terms of the embodiment of 'formal use values', in the value of the commodity, that is, the embodiment of use values whose sole purpose is to absorb the potential economic surplus. Under monopoly capitalism, then, waste and irrationality become intrinsic to the production process, and it becomes necessary to investigate the concept of the surplus from a vantage point that goes beyond Marx's concept of surplus value with its sole foundation in socially necessary labour.

In his contribution to the volume, Ron Stanfield, one of the original participants in this debate, distinguishes between the general concept of the economic surplus and its specific historical forms, and then briefly traces the evolution of human society according to the historically changing relation between the division of labour and the economic surplus. He then turns to the concept of the surplus in monopoly capitalism, and argues that the institutionalisation of selling costs, administered salaries, etc. in the system of monopoly capital production inevitably embed new costs in the structure of output that make determination of the surplus especially difficult. Rejecting the notion that measurement of the surplus can be achieved from an evaluation of incomes, he argues that an accurate accounting of the economic surplus in the sense of a fund for social change requires looking to the output side of the economy. The surplus as a fund for social change, he emphasizes, then possesses a dual aspect as a measure of the productiveness of the division of labour under monopoly capitalism and an indicator of social repression and irrationality in monopoly capitalist class society. Placing particular emphasis on Chapter 11 of Baran and Sweezy's *Monopoly Capitalism*, 'The Irrational System', and drawing upon Veblen's thinking regarding instrumental value, Stanfield forcefully argues that evaluation of the surplus as a fund for social change and an associated critique of monopoly capitalism as a system of social stratification and alienation, requires a focus upon people's dynamic capability to understand their possibilities for improving the human life process. This radical vision, he concludes, underlies modern historical thinking about the economic surplus, and ultimately constitutes the gravamen of any deep analysis of monopoly capitalism.

Turning to recent historical issues, Leslie Fishman notes an interesting omission in the literature on the Monopoly Capital approach to the economic surplus. Though in a number of important respects the approach makes use of the concept of a planned surplus, it has been little applied to the recent socialist economies where there was an intention to make rational use of the economic surplus. Given the collapse of the system of pricing and distribution in the socialist planned economies, one must wonder whether this failure to apply to the socialist economies the Monopoly Capital approach to the concept of the surplus is merely an oversight, or whether it is rooted in more serious difficulties. Fishman takes it to be the latter, and argues that questions of allocation and efficiency are closely tied to a theory of pricing and the market mechanism whatever the economic system at issue. He rejects, however, the traditional price theory approach to these matters, and instead sets out the elements of a new microeconomic paradigm for both Western and Eastern economies whose essential focus is the link between pricing and capital accumulation decisions. In this fashion, he generalises the Monopoly Capital approach to different sorts of modern industrial economies, and extends the line of thinking that began with Kalecki and Steindl on the capital investment process.

Relatedly, Keith Cowling turns to the major development in the world economy at the end of the century, the industrial integration of Eastern and Western Europe brought about by the approach of 1992 and the opening-up of the East, and applies the Monopoly Capital firm-based understanding of surplus production and control to these events. He explains the essence of the modern corporation and its changing transnational base in terms of how production is coordinated from one centre of strategic decision-making across national boundaries, and argues that future development of trade and industrial integration will be strongly influenced by the practice of large oligopolistic, transnational firms seeking reduced labour costs through the continual relocation of production facilities. Cowling argues that leaving the market via the agency of large, monopolistic firms to achieve such integration will inevitably generate global inefficiencies, and that democratic community-based economic planning – whether local, regional, national, or supranational – is more consonant with achieving welfare optima. Indeed, the efficiency of systems of flexible specialisation over giantism and mass production – an important lesson of the last decades in both the East and West – seems only likely to continue through the reinforcement of community oversight regarding transnational strategic decision-making.

All of these papers together, then, demonstrate the continuing significance of that surplus tradition, which arose in the era of competitive capitalism with initial insights into growth, income distribution, and economic power, and which has developed with modern capitalism as the Monopoly Capital approach to the concept of the surplus. Where, however, economists and social theorists were generally receptive to thinking about the surplus in the nineteenth century, with exceptions, they have been less so in the twentieth. This collection is, as a result, all the more valuable in light of its authors' efforts to develop clearly the understanding that the surplus tradition affords. A leader in this regard was the individual to whose memory this book is dedicated: Joseph D. Phillips, an always generous friend and teacher to many, an honest and selfless researcher, and one tirelessly committed to the cause of social justice.

REFERENCES

Baran, Paul A. (1957). *The Political Economy of Growth*, New York: Monthly Review.

Baran, Paul A. and Paul M. Sweezy (1966). *Monopoly Capital: An Essay on the American Economic and Social Order*, New York: Monthly Review.

Chamberlain, E. H. (1946 [1933]). *The Theory of Monopolistic Competition*, Cambridge, MA: Harvard University Press.

Domar, Evsey (1946). 'Capital Expansion, Rate of Growth and Employment', *Econometrica*, 14, 137–47.

Foster, John Bellamy (1986). *The Theory of Monopoly Capitalism*, New York: Monthly Review.

Foster, John Bellamy and Henryk Szlajfer, eds. (1984). *The Faltering Economy*, New York: Monthly Review.

Harrod, Roy F. (1939). 'An Essay in Dynamic Theory', *Economic Journal*, 49, March, 14–33.

Heilbroner, Robert (1970). *Between Capitalism and Socialism: Essays in Political Economics*, New York: Vintage.

Howard, M.C. and J.E. King (1990). 'The "Second Slump": Marxian Theories of Crisis After 1973', *Review of Political Economy*, 2(3), 267–91.

Kalecki, Michal (1971). *Selected Essays on the Dynamics of Capitalist Economies*, Cambridge: Cambridge University Press.

Kalecki, Michal (1972). *Selected Essays on the Economic Growth of the Socialist and the Mixed Economy*, Cambridge: Cambridge University Press.

Keynes, John Maynard (1936). *The General Theory of Employment, Interest, and Money*, London: Macmillan.

Lenin, V. I. (1970 [1914]). *Imperialism – The Highest Stage of Capitalism*, Moscow: Progress.

Lubitz, Raymond (1971). 'Monopoly Capitalism and Neo-Marxism', in Daniel Bell, ed., *Capitalism Today*, New York: Basic.

Luxemburg, Rosa (1913 [1951]). *The Accumulation of Capital*, New Haven: Yale.

Marx, Karl (1967 [1893]). *Capital*, Vol. II, ed. Frederick Engels, New York: International.

Robinson, Joan (1933). *The Economics of Imperfect Competition*, London: Macmillan.

Robinson, Joan (1956). *The Accumulation of Capital*, London: Macmillan.

Smith, Adam (1937 [1776]). *An Inquiry into the Nature and Causes of the Wealth of Nations*, Edwin Cannan, ed., New York: Modern Library.

Solow, Robert (1956). 'A Contribution to the Theory of Economic Growth', *Quarterly Journal of Economics*, 70, 65–94.

Stanfield, J.R. (1973). *The Economic Surplus and Neo-Marxism*, Lexington, MA: Lexington.

Steindl, Josef (1952). *Maturity and Stagnation in American Capitalism*, Oxford: Blackwell.

Sweezy, Paul M. (1981). 'The Economic Crisis in the United States', *Monthly Review*, 33, 1–10.

Sweezy, Paul M. (1982). 'Why Stagnation?' *Monthly Review*, 34, 1-10.

Sylos-Labini, Paolo (1962 [1956]). *Oligopoly and Technical Progress*, E. Henderson, trans., Cambridge, MA: Harvard.

Szlajfer, Henryk (1984). 'Waste, Marxian Theory, and Monopoly Capital: Toward a New Synthesis', in John Bellamy Foster and Henryk Szlajfer, eds., *The Faltering Economy*, New York: Monthly Review.

Veblen, Thorstein (1904 [1935]). *The Theory of Business Enterprise*, New York: Scribners.

Weisskopf, Thomas (1979). 'Marxian Crisis Theory and the Rate of Profit in the Postwar US Economy', *Cambridge Journal of Economics*, 3, 341–78.

2. *Monopoly Capital* After 25 Years*

Paul M. Sweezy

Monopoly Capital by the late Paul Baran and myself was published 25 years ago this year, and on the whole I think it holds up pretty well when judged in the light of all the developments and changes that have taken place in this eventful quarter century. As a basis for what follows, let me sketch in the barest outline of the basic argument of the book.

The monopoly capitalist economy is dominated by a relative handful of giant corporations that had their origins in the late nineteenth and early twentieth centuries and by the end of the Second World War had attained a certain form and structure common to most of them. They had achieved financial independence of the financiers and promoters who led them through their early years of growth. In most industries they behaved as rational oligopolists, eschewing price competition and vying with rivals through cost-cutting technologies, product innovation, and advertising. The result was a tendency of profitability to rise, generating what we called a problem of surplus absorption. Following the pioneering work of Kalecki and Steindl, we argued that an economy so structured has a strong and persistent tendency to stagnation which can be counteracted only by forces that are no part of the internal logic of the economy itself and hence fall outside the scope of mainstream economics from which historical, political, and sociological considerations are carefully excluded. In contrast, well over two-thirds of *Monopoly Capital* is devoted to analysing these forces and their interaction with economic laws and tendencies narrowly interpreted. The titles of the last seven (of a total of eleven) chapters convey a sense of the extent to which the book deviates from the confines of economics as usually conceived and taught in U.S. institutions of higher learning: The Sales Effort,

16

Civilian Government, Militarism and Imperialism, On the History of Monopoly Capitalism, and The Irrational System. These chapter titles can also serve to identify, at least in a general way, the forces Baran and I then considered to be operative in opposing the system's powerful tendency to stagnation.

As I look back on this basic plan of the book and compare it with the situation in which we find ourselves today, I conclude that for the most part there is a reasonably good fit between analysis and reality. But there is one glaring discrepancy which is not even hinted at, let alone explained, in *Monopoly Capital*. This is the burgeoning in precisely these last 25 years of a vastly expanded and increasingly complex financial sector in both the U.S. and the global capitalist economies. And this development in turn has reacted back in important ways on the structure and functioning of the corporation-dominated 'real' economy.[1]

In our analysis of the giant corporation (Chapter 2), Baran and I posited a community of oligopolies each under the effective control of its management which in normal circumstances enjoys a secure tenure and is therefore able both to make long-run plans and to insure that like-minded successors will be around to carry them out. In this connection we quoted with approval a remark of Galbraith's in his 1952 book *American Capitalism* (p. 39): '[T]he present generation of Americans, if it survives, will buy its steel, copper, brass, automobiles, tires, shortening, soap, breakfast food, bacon, cigarettes, whiskey, cash registers, and caskets from one or another of firms that now supply these staples. As a moment's reflection will establish, there has not been much change in the firms supplying these products for several generations.'

This is a picture of a corporate community with a long planning horizon and a high degree of stability over time. And as of the late 1950s and early '60s when *Monopoly Capital* was written, there seemed to be no reason to expect significant changes any time soon.

It was not long, however, before a different scenario began to unfold, culminating in the merger and leveraged buy-out mania of the 1980s. Almost overnight, it seemed, huge pools of liquid capital accumulated under the leadership of resourceful and innovative financial entrepreneurs. These people had no experience and little interest in production; their objective was to make as much money as possible and to reinvest their (and their clients') winnings in making still more money. In pursuit of this end, they bought 'paper' assets (as well as real estate, art objects, etc.) with the intention – generally realised in an inflationary period such as prevailed in the post-Second World War decades – of selling them later at higher prices. But in due course this new breed of financial entrepreneurs discovered that by amassing sufficiently large quantities of liquid capital, they could buy up controlling interests in even very large corporations by means of special deals with large stockholders and attractive tender offers to the rest, the purpose not being simply to take the place of existing managements but to be in a position to loot the acquired companies in one or more of the ways made familiar (and legal) in the course of the long and tangled history of corporate finance.

Of course only a small minority of large corporations were actually subjected to buy-outs of this type, but the impact has been far more pervasive. Many, including some of the very biggest, were vulnerable to attempted takeovers, and managements that felt threatened – or even that they might be threatened – naturally took steps to protect themselves. And this often meant doing what the buy-out artists would do if they got the chance. Thus, for example, a conservatively managed company accustomed to long-term planning and the holding of large cash reserves against future opportunities or emergencies, might well consider it necessary to shorten its planning horizon and dissipate its accumulated cash in order to make itself a less-attractive takeover target. To put the point another way, the generalised threat of financial buy-out tends to force managements socialised into an earlier corporate culture to take on the coloration of speculative finance. To the extent that this occurs, it calls into question the corporate paradigm Baran and I had treated as a built-in feature of monopoly capitalism.

Nor is this the only way the financial explosion of the 1970s and 80s affected the functioning of the system. The history of capitalism has been punctuated by recurring speculative booms. As a rule, however, these occurred in the expansion phase of the business cycle, were of relatively short duration, and had no lasting structural effects on the economy. In contrast, this latest episode developed after the long post-Second World War expansion had played itself out; it has lasted some two decades now; and it has brought about a marked and seemingly permanent change in the structure of capitalist economies.

This last point is the one that needs special emphasis in the present context. The financial explosion in question has several dimensions: the number and variety of markets involved (including some, like stock futures and options, of fairly recent origin, and others like government securities and foreign exchange traditionally tied to routine commodity and fiscal transactions); the dramatic expansion of activity in these markets; the absolute and relative growth in employment in financial occupations; and the increase in the share of finance in GNP. Along all these dimensions the relative size of the financial sector has grown enormously in the last two decades.

Another and in some ways more telling indication of the growing importance of finance in the economy as a whole is provided by an analysis of investment in plant and equipment during the cyclical upswing of the 1980s. By historical standards, the recovery of the '80s was far from vigorous, and as is well known, a considerable part of it was powered by an unprecedented peacetime expansion of the military budget. What is less well known is that the composition of the private sector's contribution was quite untypical. Activity in traditional areas of strong investment in plant and equipment (manufacturing, transportation, public utilities) rose hardly at all in the recovery, while areas that encompass finance, real estate, and commerce experienced dramatic increases.[2] Not all of this of course was attributable to finance, but no knowledgeable observer of the business scene during those years would be likely to deny that the role of finance (computers, business machines, information equipment, office buildings, etc.) was both substantial and relatively much greater than in earlier cyclical recoveries.

Why did *Monopoly Capital* fail to anticipate the changes in the structure and functioning of the system that have taken place in the last 25 years? Basically, I think the answer is that its conceptualisation of the capital accumulation process is one-sided and incomplete. In the established tradition of both mainstream and Marxian economics, we treated capital accumulation as being essentially a matter of adding to the stock of existing capital goods. But in reality this is only one aspect of the process. Accumulation is also a matter of adding to the stock of financial assets. The two aspects are of course interrelated, but the nature of this interrelation is problematic to say the least. The traditional way of handling the problem has been in effect to assume it away: for example, buying stocks and bonds (two of the simpler forms of financial assets) is assumed to be merely an indirect way of buying real capital goods. This is hardly ever true, and it can be totally misleading.

This is not the place to try to point the way to a more satisfactory conceptualisation of the capital accumulation process. It is at best an extremely complicated and difficult problem, and I am frank to say that I have no clues to its solution. But I can say with some confidence that achieving a better understanding of the monopoly capitalist society of today will be possible only on the basis of a more adequate theory of capital accumulation, with special emphasis on the interaction of its real and financial aspects, than we now possess.

NOTES

*   This paper originally appeared in *Monthly Review*, December 1991.
1. In counterposing 'financial' (or 'monetary') with 'real' I am using terminology that has a long history and can be assumed to be intelligible to readers with some knowledge of the literature of economics. But there is of course no implication that any sector of an actually existing economy is more (or less) real in the everyday meaning of the word than any other.
2. See 'The Strange Recovery of 1983-84', *Monthly Review*, October 1986.

REFERENCES

Baran, P. and P. Sweezy (1966). *Monopoly Capital*, New York: Monthly Review Press.
Galbraith, John Kenneth (1952). *American Capitalism*, Boston: Houghton Mifflin.
Sweezy, P. (1986). 'The Strange Recovery of 1983-84', *Monthly Review*, October.

3. Estimating the Economic Surplus*

Joseph D. Phillips

The problem of estimating the volume of economic surplus produced by the American economy is complicated by a dearth of statistical data that can be used directly for the purpose. It has been necessary to rely primarily upon figures developed for the national income accounts of the United States Department of Commerce. Many of these data are rather crude approximations – for example, the estimates of income of unincorporated enterprises. More serious are the differences between the categories employed in the national income accounts and those implied in the concept of economic surplus. These differences have necessitated a number of rough adjustments in the available data.

The method employed in making the estimates of economic surplus has been to proceed from the more commonly recognised elements of surplus to those less commonly included, although it has not been feasible to follow this procedure throughout. Thus the initial step was to incorporate in the economic surplus the elements of property income contained in the national income accounts. Several of these required adjustments to make them approximate the concepts employed here; these are explained below.

Next, the volume of various types of what may be called wasteful expenditures incurred in the business process was estimated. From the standpoint of the individual firm many of these expenditures appear to be necessary business expenses, but from the standpoint of the economy they constitute forms of waste. They have therefore been incorporated in the economic surplus.

The third major category of surplus for which estimates were made was that absorbed by government. All government expenditure is included in economic surplus. Thus the criterion is not whether the government expenditure is in some sense necessary or useful.

The totals of these three major categories of economic surplus – property income, waste in the business process, and government expenditure – were then added together to obtain our grand totals. It should be noted, however, that these totals still do not include all elements of surplus. Some could not be estimated on a year-by-year basis because of inadequate data. One of these elements is the penetration of the productive process by the sales effort, but some data for recent years have been assembled to indicate its order of magnitude. Another element which might reasonably be incorporated in the surplus, but is omitted here, is the output forgone owing to the existence of unemployment.[1]

PROPERTY INCOME

Corporate profits were taken after corporation income taxes had been deducted and after allowance for inventory valuation adjustment. (See Table 1.[2]) The adjustment for excessive depreciation charges was made after the profit income of unincorporated enterprises had been added to corporate profits to obtain total business profits.

Income of Unincorporated Enterprises

The general problem here is whether to treat income of unincorporated enterprises as profit or as labour income or as a mixture of both. At least one study has treated it in its entirety as labour income.[3] This procedure seems unjustified for our purpose. Data obtained from tax returns and from the census show that a considerable number of unincorporated enterprises employ a number of workers and obtain sizable profits. On the other hand, it would be inappropriate to consider all income of unincorporated enterprises as profit income since no deduction is made in arriving at the total of income of unincorporated enterprises for salaries of owners, who in many cases are the sole workers in their firms.

One suggested solution to this problem is to estimate the element of labour income in this category of income by multiplying the average earnings of employees by the number of active proprietors of unincorporated enterprises, both figures being taken separately for each major industrial division. The difference between this estimate of labour income of proprietors and total income of unincorporated enterprises is then classed as property income.[4]

Another approach to the problem has been offered by Denison. He argues that the best way to approach that question [the proportion of the income of unincorporated enterprises which represents a return for labour input] may be to assume that the total return for labour, including the labour of employees, owners, and family workers, comprises the same proportion (about three-fourths) of total income originating in unincorporated firms as it does in corporations, where the problem is minimal.

Such an assumption . . . would imply in 1952 an average return to proprietors of nonfarm unincorporated business about two-thirds as high as the average compensation of paid employees in the business economy as a whole. It would also imply that in the aggregate little more than half of nonfarm proprietors' income represents a return for labour. If these ratios should seem low, it is well to remember that most nonfarm proprietors are in firms whose total net income per proprietor is much below average employee earnings, and that the bulk of total proprietors' income is accounted for by the larger firms, where property income may predominate.[5]

This solution has been adopted here. The percentage of income originating in corporations that went to employees in each year was considered the measure of the labour component in the income originating in sole proprietorships and partnerships. From the remainder, the net interest originating in sole proprietorships and partnerships was subtracted to obtain our estimates of profits of unincorporated business. (See Table 2.) And these were added to corporate profits to obtain unadjusted totals of business profits before the adjustment for excessive depreciation charges was made.

Excessive Depreciation Charges

One adjustment which needs to be made in the profits figures given in the national income accounts arises from excessive depreciation charges. The authors of *U.S. Income and Output* acknowledge this possibility:

Profits are obviously hard to measure with precision. Difficulties associated with the making of proper allowance for depreciation should be mentioned specifically. The profit ratios [profit as percent of income originating in corporations] charted here are based upon calculations employing the depreciation concepts which have been used in corporate tax returns. These are not necessarily the most appropriate for economic analysis. For instance, they reflect changes in the tax laws, such as the special amortisation provisions enacted in 1950 and the legalisation of alternative formulae which permitted accelerated depreciation under the Revenue Code of 1954. Profit ratios adjusted to eliminate the effects of these changes might be higher by one or two percentage points for 1957 [from about 20 percent to about 21 or 22 percent], and would show a somewhat different movement over the past few years. The broad pattern of downdrift since 1951 . . . would remain, however, and no change in the interpretation of it would seem to be called for.[6]

They go on to argue, however, that for some purposes depreciation charges have been inadequate:

> The fact that tax depreciation is based on original cost values introduces an additional element that requires consideration, especially in problems involving long-term comparisons.   For many objectives of economic analysis, it would be prefereable to value depreciation in terms of current replacement cost. Generally speaking, this change of method would raise depreciation and reduce profits relatively more in the postwar period than during the 1920's.[7]

This latter point is based on the argument that the cost of replacing equipment and structures in periods of inflation is greater than current depreciation charges, which are related to original cost of these assets. Eisner has challenged this argument:

> (1) Increase in prices may not be sufficient to wipe out the excess of depreciation allowances over replacement requirements caused by growth in the real volume of investment.
>
> (2) The extent of price increase necessary to cancel the effects of growth in the real volume of investment is a function of the rate of growth of investment (in monetary terms, which is a product of the real growth and the change in prices), the length of life of assets, and the period of amortisation. Illustrative examples reveal that only when prices increase somewhat faster than real investment do replacement requirements approach the magnitude of depreciation allowances.
>
> We may conclude that the phenomenon of growth places on shaky ground those who would argue that depreciation allowances are insufficient to meet replacement requirements. To the extent that replacement requirements may offer a criterion for the size of depreciation allowances a contrary hypothesis would appear appropriate. Perhaps depreciation allowances are too high and net profits, as well as net income and net investment, are understated by conventional accounting practices! And perhaps our traditional analyses of the distribution of 'income' overlook, consequently, a substantial component of the social product which accrues to business enterprises in the form of generous depreciation allowances.[8]

Eisner also points out that 'It may be quite possible, in spite of inflated prices, to replace old assets with new ones whose dollar cost per unit of productive capacity or output is less than that of the cheaper but less efficient assets being replaced'. Furthermore, he notes that the basic relevance of replacement requirements to the consideration of depreciation allowances may be questioned. 'Many accountants will insist that depreciation accounting is merely a device for allocating original cost and is entirely unrelated to replacement requirements.'[9]

Eisner has argued elsewhere that the changes made in the Internal Revenue Code of 1954 which provide explicitly for (a) the 'declining balance' method of charging depreciation, at a rate up to twice that of the straight-line method, and (b) the 'sum of the year's digits' method cannot fail to have a tremendous effect upon corporate tax payments through their effect upon the computation of corporate profits. These alternative formulas permitted accelerated depreciation.[10] He estimated roughly that by 1960 the Treasury would be losing about $3 billion a year as a result of the 1954 changes in the law, assuming that the changes in tax liabilities had no effect on the amount of gross national product. This figure implies an estimate of nearly $6 billion in excess depreciation from this source for 1960. It thus implies that, as a result of the 1954 changes alone, business profits in 1960 should be higher by nearly $6 billion than they were reported to be.

The soundness and conservatism of his predictions, Eisner contended in 1959, were confirmed by the estimates and reports of actual corporate depreciation charges made by the Treasury and Commerce Departments and by the staff of the Joint Economic Committee. Treasury Department reports indicated that total depreciation and accelerated amortisation deductions of corporations rose from $12 billion in 1953 to $17.6 billion in 1956. Estimates of the Department of Commerce showed corporate depreciation and amortisation rising from $11.8 billion in 1953 to $19.7 billion in 1957, and the staff of the Joint Economic Committee estimated a further rise to $21.3 billion by 1958. When depreciation deductions of unincorporated enterprises were added, the rise in depreciation deductions between 1953 and 1958 was estimated to entail an annual loss to the Treasury by 1958 of over $5 billion in tax revenues. This 'includes the direct effects of the rate of growth of gross capital additions, aside from the results of changes in depreciation methods', but the part of the loss 'which can be ascribed specifically to the change in depreciation methods is undoubtedly more than the $2.5 billion' which Eisner predicted for 1958 on the basis of a 4 percent assumed growth in the rate of gross capital additions.[11] Thus, by 1958 excess depreciation charges from this source had already approached $6 billion and would increase rapidly thereafter.

These estimates are indicative of the amount of excess depreciations from only one source, the 1954 changes in the Internal Revenue Code. There is some basis for inferring that there has long been a tendency for American business to exaggerate depreciation expense. In view of Fabricant's estimate that the average life span of a capital asset in the United States is about thirty years, which was supported by oral estimates which Domar obtained from the Department of Commerce, it would seem that even before the 1954 changes the Internal Revenue Code permitted depreciation at a more rapid rate than practice with respect to replacement justified.[12] For many types of equipment the Code allowed depreciation on the basis of life spans of less than thirty years.

One attempt to estimate 'real depreciation in the USA' is that of the Soviet economist M. Golanskii:

> American statistics greatly overestimate the cost of replacement for wear and tear of fixed capital. In addition to depreciation, this item [capital consumption allowances] includes in it the cost of replacement of accidental losses of fixed capital and investments, which are treated as current expenses. . . . Nor is it possible to use official depreciation data. Depreciation represents the sum of money required to renew the value of the wear and tear of fixed capital. What is meant is the fixed capital actually participating in the process of material production. But American statistics, ignoring the distinction between productive and unproductive spheres, include in depreciation of fixed capital the wear and tear on dwellings and other buildings and property which do not participate in production.
>
> Besides the fixed capital replacement fund is greatly exaggerated by overstatement of the depreciation rates. . . .
>
> Obviously, data containing such extensive distortions cannot serve as a correct indication of the depreciation of fixed assets. . . . [their use] leads to the national income being underestimated by many billions of dollars.
>
> Lack of appropriate statistics makes it impossible for us to remove from the official depreciation total the indicated elements of surplus value. However, a rough estimate of the real value of depreciation of fixed capital in the sphere of material production may be made on the basis of the depreciation data available for U.S. manufacturing industries. The share of depreciation in the value of the final product of manufacturing industry is taken by us tentatively as being equal to the share of depreciation in the final product of all spheres of material production. . . . The lowest (4 percent) percentage of depreciation in the value of final product of U.S. manufacturing industry was recorded in 1947. This percentage, which most accurately reflects the real wear and tear of fixed capital, is taken by us as an indication of the share of depreciation in the value of the final material product in the U.S. for the entire period under consideration.[13]

Golanskii arrives at the following depreciation estimates (in millions of dollars), which are here compared with Department of Commerce totals for the same years:

Year	Golanskii	Department of Commerce[14]
	$	$
1929	2,838	7,698
1947	6,532	12,150
1950	7,831	18,042
1955	10,425	28,110

It is not feasible to apply Golanskii's method of estimation to other years, since some of the steps by which he estimated final material product, particularly those relating to indirect taxes, are not fully explained. However, we have expressed his depreciation estimates as percentages of gross private investment in producers' durable equipment and nonresidential construction for the corresponding years. The percentages range between 25 and 26.8 percent. They thus correspond rather closely to Domar's estimate of 28 percent for Soviet D/G (the ratio of depreciation to gross investment).[15] If we take 26 percent of total gross private investment in producers' durable equipment and nonresidential construction from 1929 to 1963 as the basis for our estimate of depreciation, we get a total of $204,350 million in depreciation for this period of thirty-five years.

Another estimate was obtained by expressing the total of Golanskii's estimates of depreciation for 1929, 1947, 1950, and 1955 as a percentage of the corresponding total of the revised Department of Commerce estimates of depreciation for those years after deducting depreciation on owner-occupied dwellings and institutional depreciation. This amounted to 48.2 percent, which produced an estimate of $257,655 million in depreciation for the period 1929-1963 when applied to the Department of Commerce total of depreciation, adjusted as indicated above, for the same period.

The larger of these two estimates was adopted as the total of business depreciation for the period 1929-1963. This total was distributed by years in accordance with an index which reflected the distribution by years of the Department of Commerce depreciation series, adjusted to eliminate depreciation on owner-occupied dwellings and institutional depreciation and to reduce the influence of the changes in the Internal Revenue Code of figures for 1954 and subsequent years.[16]

The estimates of depreciation obtained in this manner were then subtracted from the aggregate net receipts of business firms to obtain our estimates of business profit before taxes. (See Table 1.)

Rent, Interest, and Other Property Income

Another category listed in the national income accounts which is customarily classified as property income is the rental income of persons. In recent years, as in the 1930s, more than half of this type of income, as it appears in the national income accounts, has consisted of imputed net rent from owner-occupied dwellings. It does not seem appropriate to include this element in the economic surplus, and it was therefore subtracted from the rental income of persons to obtain the adjusted rental income that was incorporated in the estimates of economic surplus.

Interest constitutes another element of property income. In our estimates net interest, rather than personal interest income, was included in the economic surplus. Personal interest income, as it appears in the national income accounts, combines net interest (which excludes government interest payments) and interest payments by government. Since all expenditures by government are later incorporated in our estimates of economic surplus, net interest paid by government is excluded from our interest component to avoid double counting.

The only other element of income which needs to be considered here is the compensation of corporate officers. A significant part of this income represents a share of profits, although it is not explicitly treated as such. In our estimates one-half of total compensation of corporate officers in each year was included in the economic surplus of the year. These estimates appear in Table 3.

WASTE IN THE BUSINESS PROCESS

It is essential that some allowance be made for the elements of economic surplus which take the form of waste in the business process, and Table 5 includes estimates for some of these. In general, the largest part of this waste is associated with the process of selling the output of business. This includes much of such expenditures as advertising, market research, expense account entertaining, the maintenance of excessive numbers of sales outlets, and the salaries and bonuses of salesmen. Closely related are outlays for such activities as public relations and lobbying, the rental and maintenance of showy office buildings, and business litigation.

Estimates of the costs of distribution have been obtained for the years beginning with 1929. To do this, we applied Barger's estimate of the value added by distribution (percent of retail value of all commodities retailed) in 1929 to retail sales for the years 1929 to 1934, his estimate for 1939 to sales for the years 1935 to 1945, and his estimate for 1948 to sales for the years 1946 to 1963.[17] Since profits, both corporate and noncorporate, and net interest from trade have already been incorporated in our estimates of surplus, a proportionate share of these has been subtracted from our estimates of value added in distribution. The part of the remaining costs of distribution considered surplus was arrived at arbitrarily by adding to surplus 35 percent of the residual costs for each year. Corporate advertising by other than trade corporations has also been included in economic surplus.

In addition to the part of economic surplus consumed in distribution, a considerable segment is used up in the costs associated with the finance, insurance, real estate, and legal services industries.[18] The profits, rent, and net interest arising in these industries have already been included in our measures of economic surplus. The largest remaining element is employee compensation. This element was also considered part of the economic surplus. No attempt was made to incorporate that part of the income of unincorporated enterprises in these industries which we treated as a labour return to their proprietors.

SURPLUS ABSORPTION BY GOVERNMENT

The estimates of absorption of surplus by government were based on total government expenditures. From these were subtracted federal grants-in-aid to state and local governments (because otherwise they would appear twice – as federal expenditures and as state and local expenditures). These estimates are set forth in Table 4.

PENETRATION OF THE PRODUCTIVE PROCESS BY THE SALES EFFORT

Only very rough estimates can be made of the amount of economic surplus used up because of the penetration of the sales effort into the productive process itself. Here we are dealing with such costs as the expenses of changing models of automobiles and other durable consumer goods when no fundamental change in quality or usefulness is involved, with costs of providing superfluous product variation and differentiation, and with similar outlays. That such phenomena constitute a significant characteristic of the American economy is acknowledged by many business executives. A survey conducted by the *Harvard Business Review* among its subscribers revealed that of 3,100 replies to a questionnaire asking whether 'planned obsolescence' was felt to be a problem, about two-thirds were in the affirmative.[19]

Testimony before the Kefauver Committee during its investigation of administered prices in the automobile industry indicated that a 'significant portion of the automobile industry's overhead costs arise from an emphasis upon style, rather than price, competition'. Theodore O. Yntema, vice president of the Ford Motor Company, estimated that Ford's normal expenditures for model changes in all automotive lines would cost $350 million a year, although in 1957 such costs ran to $440 million. These figures covered styling, engineering, and the purchase of special commercial tools, but did not include any allowance for facilities expenditures or rearrangement costs for the model changeover. Frederick Donner, of General Motors, testified that design changes for automobiles and trucks in his firm cost 'on the order of $500 million a year'. The Chrysler representative stated that they had averaged something over $200 million a year in the cost of bringing their new models to market. The three leading automobile manufacturers were thus spending together some $1 billion a year to introduce their new models.

The extent to which styling costs have risen is indicated in a chart submitted by the Ford Motor Company depicting the change in its tool amortisation, engineering, and styling costs from 1948 to 1957. These costs, after holding stable from 1948 to 1951, doubled between 1951 and 1953 and in 1957 were 6.5 times the 1948 level. The ratio of model-change costs to sales was about 2.5 times greater in 1957 than in 1948.

Another indication of the rise in styling costs appears in the amortisation costs of special commercial tools. These include the tools and dies ordered for the production of particular model lines, and they are amortised as production costs over the model run for which they are acquired. The total of this cost item for the three leading automobile manufacturers rose from about $182 million in 1950 to $762 million in 1957. Some of this rise was due to inflation, but the greater part was the result of greater complexity and more frequent changes of models. The dependence of these costs on style changes was indicated by Yntema when he testified that 72 percent of the special tooling costs of the 1955 Ford line, which he used as an example, was for body and front-end components, which are most susceptible to style obsolescence. Chassis tooling accounted for 12

Figure 1
Surplus as Percent of Gross National Product

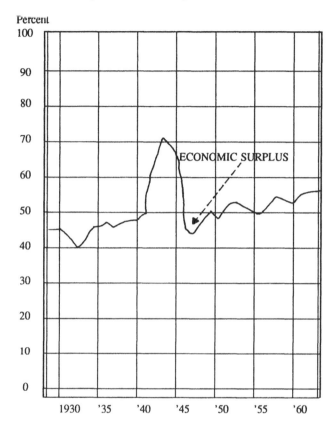

percent and engine tooling the remaining 16 percent. And of these 1955 tools only 3.5 percent, by cost, were still in use on the 1958 models.[20]

Information on the penetration of the sales effort into the productive process in other industries is more difficult to obtain. Emphasis on style changes in order to convince buyers that their older models are obsolete is characteristic of most other consumer durables industries and is reflected in frequent, sometimes annual, model changes. However, model changes in these other consumer durables are generally less expensive to design, engineer, and put into production. Since the cost of making model changes in the automobile industry amounts to something over $1 billion a year, a rough estimate of $500 million per year for model-change costs in all other consumer durables industries, which together account for about one and a half times as much consumer expenditure as automobiles, seems reasonable.

These estimates do not include any allowance for the labour, material, and other costs involved in adding the chrome, the fins, and similar frills to each unit after the model change has been made. Nor do they include any allowance for the costs arising from excessive product variation and differentiation. These costs might run two or three times as much as model-change costs. It is not unlikely that the various costs associated with the penetration of the sales effort into the production process account for 10 to 20 percent of what consumers spend on durable goods.

In the nondurable consumer goods industries the additional production costs associated with style changes are generally much smaller in relation to other costs of production or to sales than with consumer durable goods. However, the widespread product variation and differentiation found also in these industries are manifestations of the 'interpenetration effect' in the productive process. It seems reasonable to suppose that these factors account for not less than 5 percent of consumer expenditures on the products of these industries.

Thus the total of costs arising from the penetration of the sales effort into the productive process must amount to something on the order of 10 percent of consumer expenditures on commodities.

NOTES

*   This paper originally appeared as the Appendix to *Monopoly Capital.*
1.   The Conference on Economic Progress estimated the output loss for the years 1953-1960 from this source at $262 billion in 1959 dollars. *Jobs and Growth*, Washington, 1961, p.33.
2.   All tables are at the end of the text.
3.   Jesse V. Burkhead, 'Changes in the Functional Distribution of Income', *Journal of the American Statistical Association*, June 1953, pp. 192–219.
4.   Edward C. Budd, 'Treatment of Distributive Shares', in *A Critique of the United States Income and Product Accounts: Studies in Income and Wealth*, Volume 22, pp. 356–357. Budd's estimate of property income of unincorporated enterprises in 1952 amounted to 26.7 percent of the total income of such enterprises.
5.   Edward F. Denison, 'Income Types and the Size Distribution', *American Economic Review*, May 1954, p. 256.
6.   United States Department of Commerce, *U.S. Income and Output*, Washington, 1958, p.15.
7.   *Ibid.*, p. 16.
9.   *Ibid.*, p. 820.

10. Robert Eisner, 'Depreciation Under the New Tax Law', *Harvard Business Review*, January–February 1955, pp. 66–74.

11. Robert Eisner, 'Effects of Depreciation Allowances for Tax Purposes', *Tax Revision Compendium*, printed for the House Committee on Ways and Means, Washington, 1595, Volume 2, p. 794.

12. Solomon Fabricant, *Capital Consumption and Adjustment*, New York, 1938, p. 34; Evsey D. Domar, *Essays in the Theory of Economic Growth*, New York, 1957, p. 158n. Domar points out that it is possible the average life span has been declining over time because of the increasing importance of equipment as compared with structures among the depreciable assets of firms.

13. 'Methods Employed to Recalculate the National Income of the U.S.A', *Problems of Economics*, March 1960, pp. 57–63, translated from *Mirovaia Economika i Meghdunarodnye Otnocheniia*, Number 11, 1959.

14. *National Income*, 1954 ed., pp. 162-163; *Survey of Current Business*, July 1957, pp. 8–9. These were the sources used by Golanskii, which we have therefore used for comparative data, although the depreciation estimates have since been revised.

15. *Essays in the Theory of Economic Growth*, p. 160. Domar cites Norman Kaplan's estimates of Soviet investment (*Soviet Capital Formation and Industrialisation: A Rand Corporation Study* [P 277], Santa Monica, California, 1952) to show that Soviet D/G in current prices averaged between 12 and 25 percent over the period 1930–1950, but he considers the range not very meaningful because of sharp inflations. Domar therefore develops his own estimate of Soviet D/G on the basis of Kaplan's estimate of the real rate of growth of Soviet investment and his own estimate of the average life span of Soviet investment assets.

16. The latter adjustment was made by subtracting from the Department of Commerce series Eisner's estimate of the excess depreciation made possible in each of these years by the use of the 'sum of the year's digits' method in place of 'straight-line' method of depreciation. The amounts subtracted appear in Joint Committee on the Economic Report, *Federal Tax Policy for Economic Growth and Stability*, Washington, 1955, Column 6, Table 4, p. 520. Eisner later indicated that these estimates had proved to be conservative. *Tax Revision Compendium*, p. 794.

17. Harold Barger, *Distribution's Place in the American Economy Since 1869*, pp. 57–60. His percentages do not include freight charges between producer and initial distributor, but do include transportation charges between initial distributor, subsequent distributors, and consumers. The figure for 1929 was 36.6 percent for 1939, 37.3 percent, and for 1948, 37.4 percent.

18. Even in the most rationally-conducted economy there would of course be some costs arising from the need for financial settlements between enterprises and for the services of lawyers rendering legal aid to people or helping settle controversies between economic units. However, these costs would still be defrayed out of economic surplus.

19. John B. Stewart, 'Problems in Review: Planned Obsolescence', *Harvard Business Review*, September–October 1959, p. 14.

20. All the above data are from *Administered Prices: Automobiles*, Report of the Subcommittee on Antitrust and Monopoly of the Committee on the Judiciary, U.S. Senate, 85th Congress, 2nd Session (1958), pp. 121–123. For a discussion of the costs to the economy as a whole of automobile model changes, see Chapter 5 above, pp. 135–138.

Table 1

Elements of Profit Income in Economic Surplus
(Millions of Dollars)

	Corporate profits after taxes	Profit income of unincorporated enterprises	Total business profits, unadjusted (1) + (2)	Official depreciation estimates all business	Aggregate net receipts (3) + (4)	Adjusted depreciation estimates	Total business profits adjusted (5) − (6)
	(1)	(2)	(3)	(4)	(5)	(6)	(7)
	$	$	$	$	$	$	$
1929	8,731	5,449	14,180	6,627	20,807	3,556	17,251
1930	5,740	3,512	9,252	6,660	15,912	3,578	12,334
1931	1,136	1,148	2,284	6,493	8,777	3,482	5,295
1932	-2,355	-822	-3,177	5,995	-2,818	3,217	-399
1933	-2,513	-797	-3,310	5,612	-2,302	3,011	-709
1934	347	911	1,258	5,531	6,789	2,967	3,822
1935	1,967	2,129	4,096	5,593	9,689	3,004	6,685
1936	3,593	2,957	6,550	5,616	12,166	3,018	9,148
1937	4,702	3,591	8,293	5,811	14,104	3,121	10,983
1938	3,234	2,635	5,869	5,836	11,705	3,136	8,569
1939	4,248	3,181	7,429	6,004	13,433	3,225	10,208
1940	6,286	4,553	10,839	6,170	17,009	3,313	13,969
1941	6,901	7,036	13,937	6,872	20,809	3,688	17,121
1942	8,263	10,010	18,273	7,878	26,151	4,226	21,925
1943	9,707	11,608	21,315	8,485	29,800	4,557	25,243
1944	10,084	11,726	21,810	9,334	31,144	5,014	26,130
1945	7,724	10,909	18,633	9,695	28,328	5,205	23,123
1946	8,177	11,183	19,260	7,468	26,728	4,012	22,716
1947	12,343	12,696	25,039	9,314	34,353	4,999	29,354
1948	18,365	15,767	34,132	11,186	45,318	6,007	39,311
1949	17,851	13,699	31,550	13,016	44,566	6,987	37,579
1950	17,798	16,017	33,815	14,210	48,025	7,627	40,398
1951	18,507	17,682	36,189	16,208	52,397	8,702	43,695
1952	18,213	16,058	34,271	18,077	52,348	9,703	42,645
1953	17,092	14,793	31,885	20,020	51,905	10,749	41,156
1954	16,523	13,600	30,123	21,888	52,011	11,426	40,585
1955	21,299	16,251	37,550	24,290	61,840	12,022	49,818
1956	20,763	15,512	36,275	26,447	62,722	12,589	50,133
1957	20,747	14,948	35,695	28,972	64,667	13,296	51,371
1958	18,509	14,291	32,800	30,422	63,222	13,539	49,683
1959	24,004	16,882	40,686	32,131	72,817	13,922	58,895
1960	22,201	15,452	37,653	33,577	71,230	14,164	57,066
1961	21,868	15,506	37,374	34,740	72,114	14,356	57,758
1962	25,261	16,334	41,595	38,366	79,961	15,872	64,089
1963	26,277	16,652	42,929	40,009	82,938	16,380	66,558

Table 2

Estimates of Profit Income of Unincorporated Business
(Millions of Dollars)

	Income originating in unincorporated business	Percent of income originating in corporations going to employees	Labour income arising in unincorporated business $(1) \times (2)$	Income originating in unincorporated business other than labour income $(1) - (3)$	Net interest originating in unincorporated business	Profits of unincorporated business $(4) - (5)$
	(1) $	(2)	(3) $	(4) $	(5) $	(6) $
1929	23,941	74.6	17,860	6,081	632	5,449
1930	20,052	78.7	15,781	4,271	759	3,512
1931	15,912	87.9	13,987	1,925	777	1,148
1932	10,838	101.0	10,946	-108	714	-822
1933	10,564	101.6	10,733	-169	628	-797
1934	12,515	88.3	11,051	1,464	553	911
1935	16,330	83.8	13,685	2,645	516	2,129
1936	17,155	80.0	13,724	3,431	474	2,957
1937	20,175	79.9	16,120	4,055	464	3,591
1938	18,359	83.0	15,238	3,121	486	2,635
1939	19,285	80.9	15,602	3,683	502	3,181
1940	21,230	76.2	16,177	5,053	500	4,553
1941	27,632	72.7	20,088	7,544	508	7,036
1942	37,005	71.7	26,533	10,472	462	10,010
1943	43,045	72.2	31,078	11,967	359	11,608
1944	45,938	73.8	33,902	12,036	310	11,726
1945	48,629	77.0	37,444	11,185	276	10,909
1946	56,963	79.9	45,513	11,450	267	11,183
1947	57,978	77.5	44,933	13,045	349	12,696
1948	64,253	74.8	48,061	16,192	425	15,767
1949	58,863	75.9	44,677	14,186	487	13,699
1950	62,684	73.6	46,135	16,549	532	16,017
1951	70,238	73.9	51,906	18,332	650	17,682
1952	71,933	76.7	55,173	16,760	702	16,058
1953	71,859	78.4	56,337	15,522	729	14,793
1954	71,353	79.9	57,011	14,342	742	13,600
1955	74,722	77.2	57,685	17,037	786	16,251
1956	79,020	79.2	62,584	16,436	924	15,512
1957	81,091	80.2	65,035	16,056	1,108	14,948
1958	82,992	81.4	67,555	15,437	1,146	14,291
1959	86,360	79.0	68,224	18,136	1,254	16,882
1960	88,013	80.9	71,203	16,810	1,358	15,452
1961	81,228	81.3	74,168	17,060	1,554	15,506
1962	95,725	81.0	77,537	18,188	1,854	16,334
1963	99,106	81.0	80,276	18,830	2,178	16,652

Table 3

Other Forms of Property Income
(Millions of Dollars)

	Total business profits, adjusted	Rental income of persons	Net interest	Profit element in compensation of corporate officers	Total property income
	(1) $	(2) $	(3) $	(4) $	(5)
1929	17,251	2,703	6,445	1,668	$28,067
1930	12,334	2,352	5,985	1,570	22,241
1931	5,295	1,721	5,839	1,349	14,204
1932	-399	1,190	5,434	1,066	7,291
1933	-709	876	5,042	977	6,096
1934	3,822	801	4,869	1,086	10,578
1935	6,685	766	4,751	1,172	13,374
1936	9,148	792	4,741	1,356	16,037
1937	10,983	924	4,708	1,404	18,019
1938	8,569	1,200	4,636	1,295	15,700
1939	10,208	1,309	4,604	1,348	17,460
1940	13,696	1,410	4,490	1,475	21,071
1941	17,121	1,773	4,544	1,736	25,174
1942	21,925	2,490	4,291	1,845	30,551
1943	25,243	2,722	3,658	1,872	33,495
1944	26,130	2,734	3,342	1,880	34,086
1945	23,123	2,750	3,185	2,059	31,117
1946	22,716	3,580	3,113	2,571	31,980
1947	29,354	4,055	3,792	3,013	40,214
1948	39,311	4,535	4,179	3,366	51,391
1949	37,579	4,974	4,773	3,371	50,697
1950	40,398	5,250	5,469	3,803	54,920
1951	43,695	5,435	6,272	4,061	59,463
1952	42,645	5,724	7,084	4,169	59,622
1953	41,156	5,610	8,196	4,338	59,300
1954	40,585	5,563	9,145	4,503	59,796
1955	49,818	5,279	10,381	5,178	70,656
1956	50,133	5,249	11,716	5,500 *	72,598
1957	51,371	5,511	13,427	5,900 *	76,209
1958	49,683	5,221	14,827	6,200 *	75,931
1959	58,895	5,181	16,384	6,700 *	87,106
1960	57,066	5,329	18,050	7,000 *	87,445
1961	57,758	5,239	20,100	7,300 *	90,397
1962	64,089	5,232	22,084	7,800 *	99,205
1963	66,558	5,368	24,392	8,300 *	104,618

* Estimated.

Table 4

Surplus Absorption by Government
(Millions of Dollars)

	Federal government expenditures	State and local government expenditures	Total governmental expenditures, (1) + (2)	Federal grants-in-aid to state and local governments	Surplus absorbed by government (3) − (4)
	(1) $	(2) $	(3) $	(4) $	(5)
1929	2,645	7,699	10,344	117	$ 10,227
1930	2,766	8,381	11,147	125	11,022
1931	4,183	8,448	12,631	313	12,318
1932	3,188	7,553	10,741	134	10,607
1933	3,986	7,192	11,178	502	10,676
1934	6,394	8,069	14,463	1,633	12,830
1935	6,527	8,519	15,046	1,706	13,340
1936	8,501	8,105	16,606	724	15,882
1937	7,225	8,366	15,591	764	14,827
1938	8,451	8,916	17,367	778	16,589
1939	8,955	9,555	18,510	988	17,522
1940	10,089	9,235	19,324	857	18,467
1941	20,539	9,021	29,560	807	28,753
1942	56,141	8,779	64,920	888	64,032
1943	85,972	8,369	94,341	942	93,399
1944	95,585	8,434	104,019	947	103,072
1945	84,826	8,987	93,813	870	92,943
1946	37,104	11,098	48,202	1,108	47,094
1947	31,135	14,414	45,549	1,738	43,811
1948	35,414	17,567	52,981	1,986	50,995
1949	41,599	20,156	61,755	2,228	59,527
1950	41,027	22,428	63,455	2,339	61,116
1951	58,045	23,790	81,835	2,478	79,357
1952	71,613	25,447	97,060	2,635	94,425
1953	77,715	27,136	104,851	2,811	102,040
1954	69,570	30,053	99,623	2,882	96,741
1955	68,915	32,713	101,628	3,050	98,578
1956	71,844	35,715	107,559	3,257	104,302
1957	79,721	39,638	119,359	4,086	115,273
1958	87,921	44,108	132,029	5,445	126,584
1959	91,417	46,957	138,374	6,727	131,647
1960	93,064	49,984	143,048	6,301	136,747
1961	102,602	54,413	157,015	7,241	149,774
1962	110,424	57,341	167,765	8,000	159,765
1963	115,176	61,966	177,142	9,134	168,008

Table 5

Total Economic Surplus and Its Major Components
(Millions of Dollars)

	Total property income	Waste in distri- bution	Corporate advertis- ing other than by trade corpora- tions	Surplus employee compensation Finance, insur- ance and real estate	Legal services	Surplus absorbed by gov- ernment	Total surplus	Surplus as percent of GNP
	(1)	(2)	(3)	(4)	(5)	(6)	(7)	(8)
	$	$	$	$	$	$	$	$
1929	28,067	5,714	1,799	2,989	124	10,227	48,920	46.9
1930	22,241	5,050	1,277	2,808	131	11,022	42,529	46.7
1931	14,204	4,477	1,118	2,527	132	12,318	34,776	45.6
1932	7,291	3,572	797	2,145	126	10,607	24,538	41.9
1933	6,096	3,177	638	1,939	118	10,676	22,644	40.4
1934	10,578	3,473	797	2,031	116	12,830	29,825	45.9
1935	13,374	3,988	828	2,111	121	13,340	33,762	46.6
1936	16,037	4,488	932	2,313	126	15,882	39,778	48.1
1937	18,019	4,982	1,015	2,524	135	14,827	41,502	45.7
1938	15,700	4,636	933	2,460	138	16,589	40,456	47.5
1939	17,460	4,946	970	2,522	142	17,522	43,562	47.8
1940	21,071	5,288	1,023	2,599	144	18,467	48,592	48.3
1941	25,174	5,991	1,095	2,752	151	28,753	63,916	50.8
1942	30,551	6,028	1,056	2,864	150	64,032	104,681	65.8
1943	33,495	6,547	1,223	3,013	149	93,399	137,826	71.6
1944	34,086	7,423	1,335	3,166	159	103,072	149,241	70.6
1945	31,117	8,507	1,351	3,436	169	92,943	137,523	64.4
1946	31,980	11,012	1,616	4,307	184	47,095	96,193	45.7
1947	40,214	13,097	2,037	4,722	209	43,811	104,090	44.4
1948	51,391	14,458	2,295	5,295	228	50,995	124,662	48.1
1949	50,697	15,059	2,486	5,554	242	59,527	133,565	51.7
1950	54,920	16,050	2,739	6,159	265	61,116	141,249	49.6
1951	59,463	17,928	3,064	6,747	294	79,357	166,863	50.7
1952	59,622	19,049	3,454	7,344	325	94,425	184,219	53.1
1953	59,300	20,088	3,787	7,991	358	102,040	193,564	53.0
1954	59,796	20,280	4,026	8,720	386	96,741	189,949	52.3
1955	70,656	21,635	4,530	9,535	421	98,578	205,355	51.7
1956	72,598	22,391	4,918	10,393	459	104,302	215,061	51.3
1957	76,209	23,946	5,432	11,134	496	115,273	232,490	52.5
1958	75,931	24,191	5,597	11,905	542	126,584	244,750	55.1
1959	87,160	25,608	6,191	13,006	601	131,647	264,213	54.7
1960	87,445	26,636	6,578	13,948	670	136,747	272,024	54.1
1961	90,397	26,469	6,779	14,972	730	149,774	289,121	55.7
1962	99,205	28,380	7,200 *	15,835	809	159,765	311,194	56.0
1963	104,618	29,749	7,700 *	16,780	870	168,008	327,725	56.1

* Estimated.

SOURCES FOR TABLES

Table 1
(1) 1929–1955: U.S. Office of Business Economics, *U.S. Income and
    Output*, Washington, U.S. Government Printing Office, 1958, line 18
    minus line 20, Table I-8, pp. 126–127.
    156–63: *Survey of Current Business*, July 1964, line 18 minus line 20,
    Table 2, p. 8.
(2) Table 19, Col. (6).
(4) 1929–45: U.S. Office of Business Economics, *National Income, 1954
    Edition*, Washington, U.S. Government Printing Office, 1954, line 3,
    Table 4, pp. 164–165, minus line 12 and line 14, Table 39, p. 214.
    1946–55: *U.S. Income and Output*, line 5, Table V-1, p. 188, minus line
    12 and line 14, Table VII-17, p. 229.
    1955–58: *Survey of Current Business*, July 1961, line 1, Table 59, p. 29,
    plus line 1, Table 60, p. 30, minus line 12 and line 14, Table 73, p. 33.
    1959–63: *Survey of Current Business*, July 1964, line 1, Table 61, p. 32,
    plus line 1, Table 47, p. 28, minus line 12 and line 14, Table 72, p. 35.
(6) See text.

Table 2
(1) 1929–1955: *U.S. Income and Output*, line 15, Table I-12, pp. 134–135.
    1956–58: *Survey of Current Business*, July 1961, line 13, Table 9, p. 11.
    1959–63: *Survey of Current Business*, July 1964, line 13, Table 8, p. 13.
(2) 1929–55: *U.S. Income and Output*, line 4 divided by line 3, Table I-12,
·   pp. 134–135.
    1956–58: *Survey of Current Business*, July 1961, line 4 divided by line
    3, Table 9, p. 11.
    1959–63: *Survey of Current Business*, July 1964, line 4 divided by line
    3, Table 8, p. 13.
(5) 1929–55: *U.S. Income and Output*, line 24, Table I-12, pp. 134–135.
    1956–58: *Survey of Current Business*, July 1961, line 22, Table 9, p. 11.
    1959–63: *Survey of Current Business*, July 1964, line 22, Table 8, p. 13.

Table 3
(1) Table 18, Col. (7).
(2) 1929–55: *U.S. Income and Output*, Lline 17, Table I-8, pp. 126–127,
    minus line 5, Table VII-17, p. 229.
    1956–58: *Survey of Current Business*, July 1961, line 17, Table 2, p. 6,
    minus line 5, Table 73, p. 33.
    1959–63: *Survey of Current Business*, July 1964, line 17, Table 2, p. 8,
    minus line 5, Table 72, p. 35.
(3) 1929–55: *U.S. Income and Output*, line 25, Table I-8, pp. 126–127.
    1956–63: *Survey of Current Business*, July 1964, line 25, Table 2, p. 8.
(4) 1929–55: *U.S. Income and Output*, line 6, Table I-12, pp. 134–135,
    divided by 2.
    1956–63: Estimated from data in *Statistics of Income, Corporation
    Income Tax Returns*, 1955 to 1961–62.
(5) Sum of Columns (1) through (4).

Table 4
(1) 1929–45: *National Income, 1954 Edition*, line 2, Table 9, p. 172.
    1946–55: *U.S. Income and Output*, line 21, Table III-1, p. 164.
    1956–58: *Survey of Current Business*, July 1961, line 21, Table 20, p. 16.
    1959–63: *Survey of Current Business*, July 1964, line 21, Table 19, p. 18.
(2) 1929–45: *National Income, 1954 Edition*, line 18, Table 9, p. 172.
    1946–55: *U.S. Income and Output*, line 24, Table III-2, p. 165.
    1956–58: *Survey of Current Business*, July 1961, line 24, Table 21, p. 17.
    1959–63: *Survey of Current Business*, July 1964, line 24, Table 20, p. 19.
(4) 1929–45: *National Income, 1954 Edition*, line 13, Table 9, p. 172.
    1946–55: *U.S. Income and Output*, line 23, Table III-2, p. 165.
    1956–58: *Survey of Current Business*, July 1961, line 23, Table 21, p. 17.
    1959–63: *Survey of Current Business*, July 1964, line 23, Table 20, p. 19.

Table 5
(1) Table 3, Col. (5).
(2) See text.
(3) *Statistics of Income, Corporation Income Tax Returns*, annual, 1929 to 1961–62. Advertising expenditures of all active corporations minus those of wholesale and retail corporations (expenditures of the latter two groups reflected in estimates of Col. 2, this table). Fiscal year figures attributed to calendar years in which first part of fiscal year fell. Figures for 1962 and 1963 projected.
(4) 1929–45: *National Income, 1954 Edition*, line 44, Table 14, p. 168-79.
    1946–55: *U.S. Income and Output*, line 44, Table VI-1, p. 200.
    1956–58: *Survey of Current Business*, July 1961, line 41, Table 48, p. 26.
    1959–63: *Survey of Current Business*, July 1964, line 44, Table 50, p. 29.
(5) 1929–45: *National Income, 1954 Edition*, line 76, Table 14, pp. 178–79.
    1946–55: *U.S. Income and Output*, line 76, Table VI-1, p. 200.
    1956–58: *Survey of Current Business*, July 1961, line 73, Table 48, p. 26.
    1959–63: *Survey of Current Business*, July 1964, line 76, Table 50, p. 29.
(6) Table 4, Col. (5).
(7) Sum of (1) through (6).
(8) Col. (7) divided by GNP:
    1929–55: *U.S. Income and Output*, line 1, Table I-17, pp. 138–39.
    1956–58: *Survey of Current Business*, July 1961, line 1, Table 1, p. 6.
    1959–63: *Survey of Current Business*, July 1964, line 1, Table 1, p. 8.

4. The Tendency of the Surplus to Rise, 1963–1988

Michael Dawson and John Bellamy Foster

THE IRRATIONAL SOCIETY

In the increasingly universalised monopoly-capitalist economy and culture of the final decade of the twentieth century, people no longer need what they want or want what they need. Wants are artificially manufactured while the most desperate needs of innumerable individuals at the bottom of society remain unfulfilled. Although labour productivity has steadily risen, the total efficiency and rationality of society has in many ways declined. Indeed, it is almost impossible to arrive at any other conclusion if one considers the lavish office structures in cities like New York, Chicago, Atlanta and L.A., where employees use the most technologically advanced means available to 'develop' yet another brand of laundry detergent, television commercial or leveraged buyout, while not far away on the ground below people are living in slums and suffering from a lack of decent housing, food, clothing, medical care and education; or if one considers the automated assembly plants existing within the same social space as millions of unemployed, partially employed, 'discouraged' and poorly paid workers; or if one contemplates what it means to launch still another aircraft carrier the total costs of which are equal to half of the annual federal government budget for elementary and secondary education. All of these problems diminish in proportion, moreover, if one expands one's vision to encompass global conditions, comparing the situation of wealth-holders at the centre of the world-economy, where individual heads of corporations sometimes receive tens of millions of dollars in executive compensation, to the human degradation, squalor, misery and starvation that represent a commonplace reality for the majority of the world's population living in the underdeveloped countries (Dowd, 1989: 66; Baran, 1969: 92-111).

Nor can we afford to close our eyes for a single moment when faced with the ultimate dilemma of the closing years of the twentieth century: the fact that the rapacious growth pattern of the global free–market in which we live has now reached such an extent that it is rapidly threatening–on a time-scale of decades rather than centuries– the very natural environment on which life on this planet depends. 'The throwaway society that has emerged during the late twentieth century', Lester Brown, Christopher Flavin and Sandra Postel have written in the May 1990 issue of *Natural History*,

> uses so much energy, emits so much carbon and generates so much air pollution, toxic waste, and rubbish that it is strangling itself. Rooted in the concept of planned obsolescence and appeals to convenience, it will be seen by historians as an economic aberration. . . . If a throwaway culture leads inevitably to pollution and depletion of natural resources how can we build an environmentally stable future and still satisfy our material needs? Creating a sustainable life style requires vision. . . . If the world is not to fatally overtax its natural systems, we will need to achieve sustainability within the next forty years. If we have not succeeded by then, environmental deterioration and economic decline are likely to be feeding on each other, pulling us into a downward spiral of social disintegration. Our vision of the future therefore looks to the year 2030. (Brown, Flavin and Postel, 1990: 89)

The intensity with which these problems are pressing on the modern world can be traced primarily to the dominance of an economic system under advanced capitalism that derives its fundamental rationale from the insatiable drive to amass wealth. Such a system creates and recreates poverty alongside wealth. It builds waste into the very structure of production and consumption. And it requires steady increments in the size of the national economy. The richest 400 people in the United States, who saw their net worth triple between 1981 and 1988, have a combined wealth that not only greatly exceeds the federal deficit, but that also dwarfs the dollars spent on aiding the tens of millions of individuals among the nation's poor each year. From 1977-1988 the average family income of the poorest eight deciles of the population declined, while that of the richest two deciles rose. The change for the poorest income decile was −14.8 percent; for the wealthiest income decile it was (a positive) 16.5 percent. More significantly, the top 1 percent of the population in terms of income saw its average family income rise by 49.8 percent over the same period. In 1988 *Business Week* declared that the total compensation of the average CEO had risen to 93 times that of the average factory worker. Meanwhile the United States witnessed the growing eclipse of manufacturing by finance. In 1948 the net capital stock in manufacturing was almost 2⅓ times larger than finance, real estate, insurance, and business services; by the end of the Reagan administration in 1988 the net capital stock in the former was 14 percent smaller than the latter (Packard, 1989: 313-19; Phillips, 1990: 14-23, 166, 180; Magdoff and Sweezy, 1990: 1-10).

In the *Communist Manifesto*, written in 1848, Marx and Engels claimed that the wealth of the system was in the hands of one-tenth of the population, while nine-tenths of the people were deprived of any access to wealth. Whatever the accuracy of Marx and Engels' estimates in their own time, in 1983 the Joint Economic Committee of the U.S. Congress estimated that 83.2 percent of all U.S. wealth, excluding the value of homes owned, was held by the richest 10 percent of families, while the top 0.5 percent of families owned 45.4 percent. Moreover the richest 10 percent of families owned 89.3 percent of corporate stock, 90.4 percent of bonds and 93.6 percent of business assets (Marx and Engels, 1968: 30; Kloby, 1987; U.S. Congress, 1986).

These vast disparities in wealth and income are tied to an economy in which waste is elevated over basic needs. Corporate advertising in the United States is now running at a level of over $100 billion per year, about five times the size of the federal education budget. Medical costs and profits have skyrocketed over the last decade, while the availability of adequate health care has decreased. Approximately thirty-seven million Americans had no health care coverage in 1986, a rise of more than 40 percent since 1978. In 1988 U.S. cars were driven about 1¼ trillion miles, as much as all of the rest of the world's cars put together, and constituted the single most important source of greenhouse gas emissions worldwide. The annual public subsidy to the private automobile has been estimated at $300 billion. Los Angeles has given over two-thirds of its land area to the automobile. Yet, in a country that puts so much emphasis on the private mobility of its population, many simply have nowhere to go: an estimated 3 million people are homeless and many millions more throughout the country live in substandard housing (Woolhandler and Himmelstein, 1989: 54-60; Renner, 1988).

Reason would seem to dictate that to follow this same pattern of uneven development for much longer is to invite destruction for the world and the world's people. From the standpoint of human history and the ecological needs of the planet, a social formation and a civilisation must be judged by the way in which it utilises the human, natural and economic resources at its disposal. Very few researchers in our society, however, conditioned as they are by the class environment in which they live—and hence brought up to believe implicitly in the ability of the free—market to solve all of society's problems—actually go so far as to evaluate advanced capitalist social formations in such rational and comprehensive terms.

Especially neglected, since it goes to the heart of the matter, is the connection between social irrationality and the allocation of the rapidly-expanding economic surplus of monopoly capitalism. The economic surplus of any society represents the range of economic freedom at its disposal, the extent to which it is able to engage in socially discretionary spending that satisfies more than the basic needs of its producers. It measures the resources that are immediately available to alleviate suffering and improve the quality of life.

Like all meaningful social concepts the economic surplus must be understood in relation to historically specific conditions. Its definition may vary depending on the range of historical considerations at issue and the concept itself is best approached in a step by step manner in terms of successive approximations. In its simplest, most general definition the economic surplus of a society can be seen as *the difference between its output and its essential costs of production.*

From a practical standpoint, *essential costs of production* (as reflected at the aggregate level in national income statistics) can be defined in a highly privatised system such as that of the United States as consisting of the after-tax wages of most employees engaged in private production. These essential (or prime production) costs represent the disposable income of the workers and lower managers whose labour constitutes the real source of the nation's surplus product. Excluded from essential costs in this conception is the profit element in the compensation of corporate officers, the wages of government workers and the compensation of employees in legal and financial services and advertising (since these expenses are a use of society's overhead or surplus). The net economic surplus in this accounting is then equal to profits + rent + interest + taxes + the profit in corporate officer compensation + advertising costs + the costs of financial and related services + legal costs. Depreciation costs can be added to this (as is common in national income accounting) in order to arrive at the gross (as opposed to net) economic surplus.[1] Over the years the gross surplus as we have defined it here has slowly but fairly steadily risen from $302.9 billion (in current dollars) or 49.9 percent of GNP in 1963, to $2,684.3 billion or 55.0% of GNP in 1988 (see the tables at the end of this essay).

The *actual* gross surplus in this sense therefore is far in excess of actual gross savings, which totaled $642 billion in 1988. Yet it is *less* than two interesting alternative conceptions of surplus: (a) the *potential* gross surplus, or the quantity of economic surplus that would be available to society at full employment (in 1988 5.4 percent of the labour force was officially unemployed, while millions more were 'discouraged' and underemployed); and (b) *planned* gross surplus, which can be defined as the gross surplus available if both production and consumption were reorganised so as to achieve socially optimal levels, particularly through the elimination of waste built into the business process (e.g., elaborate packaging, frequent model changes, planned obsolescence, etc. that have become intermingled with the costs of production). 'To say that "capitalism has been simultaneously the most efficient and the most wasteful productive system in history",' Douglas Dowd has recently written in *The Waste of Nations*, 'is to point to the contrast between the great efficiency with which a particular modern factory produces and packages a product, such as toothpaste, and the contrived and massive inefficiency of an economic system that has people pay for toothpaste a price over 90 percent of which is owed to the marketing, not to the production, of the dentifrice'. The same criticism can of course be leveled at products throughout the economy: from soap, to automobiles, to computers (Dowd, 1989: 65-66).[2]

Such questioning of the structure of production, inherent in the very concept of planned gross surplus, requires of course that one 'step outside' present-day capitalist society in order to view it from the standpoint of a more optimal world order 'somewhere else'. Our goal in this essay (and in the calculations that follow) is not nearly so ambitious, however. We will be concerned almost entirely with actual gross surplus, and hence will confine ourselves to the type of criticism that is readily understood from within the conceptual boundaries of the present social order. None the less, it is essential to keep the concepts of potential gross surplus and planned gross surplus in mind–as further stages in a single line of argument–particularly since the shift to a more rational, democratic, humanistic and environmentally sustainable society (that is a free, socialist democracy) would necessitate a movement toward the kind of socially optimal production and consumption structure suggested by the concept of planned surplus.

'In a rich country like the United States', to quote Dowd again,

> there is no need for further growth in real gross national product. What is needed is a substantial change in the composition of production, in what is produced and in what relative quantities. To put it simply for the moment, we need fewer guns and more butter, fewer autos and more public transportation, fewer financial services and more health services. For the capitalist system it is quantitative increase rather than qualitative improvement that is

vital; for the population, it is the reverse if they are to have quantitative improvement along with better lives. (Dowd, 1989: 78)

The underdeveloped economies of the Third World, in contrast, still need massive real economic growth to meet the needs of their people. Yet, in those societies too these objectives will be most readily reached if resources can be mobilised in a rational fashion and if the waste and inequality in society can be reduced. And this requires a shift from capitalist to socialist priorities in economic organisation. In our increasingly irrational, class-exploitative, globally-hierarchical and environmentally-destructive world it is essential for all nations to politicise the allocation of the economic surplus of their societies, and thereby to treat the whole of their national income as a *national budget*, and the whole of their national wealth as *the collective product of society*.

'MONOPOLY CAPITAL' AND THE SURPLUS

The research on the economic surplus conducted here is based on the previous work of Paul Baran in *The Political Economy of Growth* (1957), Paul Baran and Paul Sweezy in *Monopoly Capital* (1966), and Joseph Phillips in 'Estimating the Economic Surplus' (a long Appendix to *Monopoly Capital* and Chapter 3 in this volume). In *Monopoly Capital* Baran and Sweezy argued that Marx's basic 'law of the tendency of the rate of profit to fall', associated with accumulation in the age of free competition, had been displaced under monopoly capitalism by a law of the tendency of the surplus to rise. In present-day capitalism a handful of giant firms typically determine the price, output and investment strategies of key industries. Under these circumstances, the critical problem is one of the absorption not the generation of surplus. Capitalist consumption fails to absorb sufficient surplus since it tends to account for a decreasing share of capitalist demand as income grows, while the surplus-absorbing capabilities of investment are hindered by the fact that it takes the form of new plant and equipment, which cannot be expanded for long periods of time independently of final, wage-based demand. In spite of the fact that there is always the possibility of new 'epoch-making innovations' emerging that could help absorb the surplus, all such innovations – resembling the steam engine, the railroad and the automobile in their overall effect – are few and far between. Hence, Baran and Sweezy conclude that the system has a powerful tendency toward stagnation (particularly within the realm of investment itself), brought on by the failure to find markets for all of the potential surplus the system is capable of producing. This failure of monopoly capitalism is partly compensated through the promotion of various countervailing factors in the form of economic waste, such as the growing sales effort (including its penetration into the production process), military spending, and the expansion of financial services. All such factors, however, are either self-limiting or can be expected to lead to a doubling-over of economic contradictions in the not-too-distant future.

In the age of excess productive capacity, waste becomes increasingly functional for the system as a whole. Monopoly capitalist society is haunted by continuing surplus absorption problems, and finds its savior in the proliferation of an increasingly irrational world of polystyrene-foam packaging, plastic wrap, fast-food chains, 'new and improved' laundry detergents, billboards, commercials, automobile model changes, junk bonds and MX missiles. Still, none of this is enough and the economy, faced with vanishing investment outlets, tends to sink into a pattern of long-term slow growth.

By the early 1970s it was clear that the subterranean tendency toward stagnation that Baran and Sweezy had pointed to as the most likely result of the evolution of the monopoly capitalist economy was materializing. The response of the capitalist class to the declining secular growth trend of the world economy in the 1970s and '80s was not, however, to create a more equitable distribution structure or to turn to rational planning of resource use. Rather, the ruling elements chose to conduct a massive restructuring program – under the ideological mantles of Reaganomics, Thatcherism, supply-side economics and monetarism – designed to redistribute income and wealth from the poor to the rich, to accelerate military spending, and to give a boost to the financial sector through deregulation and tax reforms. The result by the 1990s was an economic order that was more irrational on a global scale than ever before, and that saw a massive relative shift away from production and toward finance and speculation. Thus, the capitalist order twenty-five years after the publication of *Monopoly Capital* remains caught, as the authors of that work anticipated, within the parameters of: (a) persistent problems of surplus absorption; (b) a tendency toward the stagnation of investment (and hence of growth); and (c) the proliferation of economic waste of all kinds.[3]

The imperative of finding solutions to the desperate needs of large sections of humanity, the objective of uncovering the laws of motion of monopoly capitalism, and the increasingly urgent task of creating an ecologically sustainable development pattern if the world's natural environment is not to be destroyed irreparabl, all therefore demand a more thoroughgoing scrutiny of the nature and composition of society's economic surplus than has hitherto been undertaken.

In any attempt to take up this issue today it is useful to return to the earlier calculations of economic surplus for the United States provided by Joseph Phillips. Baran and Sweezy wrote in their book that,

> we have concentrated our efforts on the theoretical task [of identifying the economic surplus], introducing quantitative data mostly for explanatory or illustrative purposes. But it also seemed desirable to present systematic estimates of the surplus and its major components. Having a poor opinion of our own knowledge of statistical sources and skill at avoiding statistical pitfalls, we asked our friend Joseph D. Phillips, for whose knowledge and ability in these respects we have the highest regard, to prepare these estimates. After reading a draft of the relevant chapters and giving thought to the problem of sources, he concluded that the task was a feasible one and accepted our invitation. His estimates of the United States surplus and its major components for the period 1929-1963 are presented in the Appendix. . . . Though subject to qualifications and *caveats*, as Phillips makes clear, they are, we feel confident, reliable as indicators of the orders of magnitude involved.

Two findings in Phillips' estimates were particularly noteworthy, according to Baran and Sweezy. First, the magnitude of the surplus in Phillips' calculations had increased from 46.9 percent of Gross National Product in 1929 to 56.1 percent in 1963. Second, the portion of the surplus typically identified with surplus value had declined from 57.5 percent of GNP in 1929 to 31.9 percent in 1963. This means that more and more income to capital is hidden in the form of excess depreciation, corporate officer compensation, advertising, etc. (Baran and Sweezy, 1966: 10–11).

The Phillips calculations, although resting on what was in many ways a brilliant statistical exposition of the surplus, ran into a few difficulties – as might be expected of such pioneering work – related to the issue of double-counting. Nevertheless, Phillips' calculations continue to represent an indispensable starting point for research on the surplus. In what follows we have calculated the gross economic surplus for the United States for the years 1963-1988, following some of the guidelines that Phillips laid out, but departing from him in notable respects in light of important criticisms of his work.

Our own calculations for gross surplus (which cannot be compared directly with Phillips' somewhat different form of accounting) show not only that the *gross surplus* increased (as previously mentioned) from 49.9 percent of GNP in 1963 to 55.0 percent in 1988, but also that before-tax profit + rent + interest declined from 35 percent of total gross surplus in 1963 to 29 percent in 1988. It is therefore evident, as Baran and Sweezy wrote in 1966, that 'not only the forces determining the total amount of surplus need to be analyzed but also those governing its differentiation and the varying rates of growth of the components' (Baran and Sweezy, 1966: 11).

Given the popularity of supply-side explanations for the troubles of the U.S. economy that place the blame for an alleged shortage of capital on high wages, low labour productivity and high government spending, it is significant that a surplus perspective tells a different story: the tale of a social order consigned by its own logic to what the leading economist of this century, John Maynard Keynes, once called 'the fate of Midas' (Keynes, 1973: 219).

CALCULATING THE SURPLUS: 1963–1988

Updating Phillips' figures on the economic surplus is a formidable technical task. The amount of time required to locate, pore over, and double-check the relevant statistical tables is large indeed. Add to this the questionable basis of many offici.l economic calculations and the fact that the U.S. government does not set up its tables to facilitate research done from a class perspective, and the job appears even more daunting.

Moreover, Phillips' tables have been the subject of scattered criticisms – some of which are quite important. Thus, the technical process of creating an up-to-date estimate of the surplus and its components requires both a large amount of detailed, painstaking work with the available series of statistics and a sensitivity to the minor pitfalls inherent in Phillips' original tables.

Of course, as the authors of *Monopoly Capital* themselves put it in their 'Introduction' to that work, there is another important side to the problem of compiling data on the economic surplus. This is the problem which stems from the fact that, 'in a highly developed monopoly capitalist society, the surplus assumes many forms and disguises. Part of the problem is to identify the most important of these theoretically, and the rest is to extract a reasonable estimate of their magnitudes' (Baran and Sweezy, 1966: 10).

In other words, the calculation of the surplus demands not only a great deal of technical labour, but also close attention to the nature and logic of monopoly capitalism. In this regard, familiarity with and appreciation of the theory developed by Baran and Sweezy in the main body of *Monopoly Capital* is indispensable.

With these caveats in mind, we believe that the development of a reliable portrait of the course of the economic surplus between 1963 (the last year in Phillips' tables) and 1988 (the most recent year for which sufficient data are available) might serve to address important questions regarding the performance of monopoly capitalism in its latest phase of relative stagnation. Moreover, such a picture might shed light on the real social position of the vast majority of the population living under monopoly capitalism's crushing contradictions.

Phillips' Approach to Calculating the Surplus

Phillips derived his estimates of the surplus by creating and explaining a series of tables. These consisted of one main table entitled 'Total Economic Surplus and its Major Components' and four supporting tables elucidating Phillips' treatment of government spending, forms of property income not paid out of profit, and profit income for both the corporate and unincorporated sector of the U.S. economy.[4] Phillips also provided sixteen pages of verbal clarification along with specific source citations in his appendix to *Monopoly Capital*. We suggest a careful reading of this appendix as a preliminary step for those concerned with understanding how our estimates compare with Phillips'.

Beyond reading Phillips' own explanation of his calculations, it is important to be aware of the fact that this work has been criticised for falling into the trap of double counting. Phillips, Baran and Sweezy are taken to task over the double counting issue by the liberal critic Raymond Lubitz:

> If we had the data, we could calculate the 'national economic surplus' by two different methods: either as profits received (the income-surplus) or as expenditures out of profits (the output surplus). Because national income by definition equals national product, the two sums should give identical *measures* of the surplus. What we cannot do is *add* the two measures (or parts of them). . . . In effect, the authors have taken expenditures from the *product* side of the national income equation and added them on to the 'surplus' on the *income* side. (Lubitz, 1971: 169)

Phillips' approach has also engendered some confusion over the basic assumptions which underlie his calculations. One such criticism, posed by both Lubitz and by Robert Heilbroner, is that the relationship of taxes on the wages of the working class to the surplus is left unclear (Lubitz, 1971: 170; Heilbroner, 1970: 243). A second criticism of the assumptions of *Monopoly Capital* and its appendix stems from the confusion over which operative definition one ought to adopt in order to estimate the surplus. Lubitz, Heilbroner, and Ron Stanfield have all expressed doubt or perplexity regarding this point (Lubitz, 1971: 168–9; Heilbroner, 1970: 243; Stanfield, 1973: 4–5).[5]

General Reply to Phillips' Critics

The concern over the issue of double counting in Phillips' tables is important and relevant as a criticism. The figures derived by Phillips do indeed reflect some minor problems of double counting.

The difficulty lies in Phillips' inclusion of both the entirety of government expenditures and such elements as corporate profits in his estimates of the surplus. The dilemma encountered is that some portion of government expenditure does go directly into corporate profits, as when the Pentagon purchases a ballistic missile at a price which includes a hefty profit margin. By including both government expenditures and figures on corporate profits, some portion of the surplus may show up twice—once as profit income to the corporate sector and again as government spending. As one of the present authors has stated elsewhere with regards to Phillips' calculations,

> it seems undeniable that a certain portion of government expenditures are counted as well in property income. Much of this has to do with the intrinsic difficulty of ascertaining the relevant Marxian categories and quantities in national income accounts designed for quite a different purpose. In any case, there can be little doubt about the sheer magnitude of the surplus, or about its tendency to rise in relation to income as a whole. (Foster, 1986: 44)

In addition, Phillips builds a small amount of double counting into his estimates by including *before-tax* surplus employee and corporate officer compensation, while also including government expenditures, some of which obviously derives from taxes on surplus employee and corporate officer income.

Our solution to this relatively minor double counting dilemma is to: (a) follow the traditional approach to handling the national accounts by sticking to the income side of the ledger as much as possible; and (b) adjust all appropriate figures for taxes.

Despite the admitted difficulty which Phillips encountered over double counting in certain respects, other elements of the double counting charges leveled against him are themselves mistaken. For instance, Lubitz' statement that it is never valid to add elements from both sides of the national income and product accounts ledger in calculating the economic surplus is incorrect. It is possible to add, for example, the costs of corporate advertising costs – an expenditure – to an estimate of the surplus otherwise based on the income side of the ledger, so long as the income associated with such an expenditure has not already been counted. In the case of corporate advertising costs, this is clearly an element which is addable to state and private property income receipts. This is so because, while clearly constituting part of the surplus available to society, advertising overhead is nevertheless treated in the profit calculus as a cost deducted before traditional profit figures are derived and corporate income taxes are paid. Thus, keeping in mind the dynamics of the surplus and its allocation in the account books, we see that those parts of surplus charged as overhead expenses – which appear only on the expenditure side of the ledger – are in fact elements which can be added to profit revenue or derivatives thereof, without running into double counting.

The charge that Phillips was unclear about the relation of taxes on wages to the surplus merely stems from confusion on the part of Lubitz and Heilbroner themselves over the method Phillips adopted in making his estimates. Consistent with Baran and Sweezy's theory Phillips included taxes on wages in his surplus figures. He merely did so indirectly by counting them as they appear on the expenditure side as part of government spending.

The question surrounding which working definition of the surplus should form the basis for our estimates can be answered simply. Much confusion over the definition of the surplus intended by Baran and Sweezy has flowed from the fact that 'none of the critics of *Monopoly Capital* seem to have fully appreciated. . . that the method adopted in the book was one of successive approximations. . . . [T]he fully developed version of the surplus. . . was conceived as being an equivalent (or near equivalent) to total surplus value, deviating from the 'textbook version' of the latter as aggregate profits (profits + interest + rent)' (Foster, 1986: 44).[6] Thus, the whole point of the surplus concept developed by Baran and Sweezy was to refocus attention on the social accumulation fund as it actually operates in monopoly capitalist society, and this is the perspective from which surplus should be estimated. By recognising that the economic surplus is society's accumulation fund, we not only rehabilitate Marx's central concept of surplus value, returning it to its full critical vigor, but we thereby gain the ability to assess and compare alternative social orders in a rigorous and meaningful way. This is the true power and promise of the concept of the surplus elaborated in *Monopoly Capital*.

Explanation of Our Estimates of the Economic Surplus

Our estimates of the surplus and its components appear in Table 1: 'Gross Surplus and its Major Components: 1963-1988' at the end of this text. Supporting tables are also included. Table 2: 'Estimates of Profit Income of Unincorporated Business' replicates Phillips' table covering the same phenomenon. Table 3: 'Adjusted Surplus Employee Compensation' provides the basis for column 5 of Table 1. Table 4: 'Adjusted Corporate Advertising' provides the basis for column 6 of Table 1.

As mentioned above, our general approach has been to stick with figures taken from the revenue side of the national income accounts – with a few important and justifiable exceptions – so as to lessen the potential for double counting. We believe that our estimates, which are designed to err – if at all – on the conservative side, capture as much of the surplus as it is possible to capture with certainty given the nature of available data.

Adjusted corporate profits

These figures were taken straight from the national income accounts. They reflect before-tax corporate profits adjusted for the capital gains which appear as a result of inventory accounting practices.

Profits of unincorporated business

We have followed Phillips' approach to the letter in making these estimates, with the exception that we employ before-tax figures for profits.

Rental income, net interest, business contributions to social insurance

Figures are before-tax and were taken straight from the relevant national income accounts.

Surplus employee compensation

Following Phillips, we add together compensation of employees in the financial (including finance, insurance and real estate) and legal sectors of the economy. After obtaining the raw figures for employee compensation in financial and legal services, we subtract from employee compensation in each industry half of the total corporate officer compensation paid out in that sector (since this falls under the category of hidden profits in our estimates – see 'profit in corporate officer compensation' below). The resulting sum of the adjusted figures for financial and legal sector compensation is then finally adjusted for the taxes paid out of the compensation of employees in this sector of the economy. This allowance is necessitated by our inclusion of taxes on wages and salaries elsewhere in our estimates of the surplus (see below).

Advertising costs of corporations

Overheads associated with advertising is an important part of the 'sales effort' required by monopoly capital, as well as an important absorber of surplus in its own right. For this reason, we include it in our estimates. We include only that portion of advertising expenditures carried out by active corporations, since this magnitude constitutes the great bulk of business advertising and because figures on unincorporated business advertising are not readily obtainable. Although this is another element of surplus which we take from the expenditure side of the ledger (as is surplus employee compensation), this does not represent double counting, since such items as advertising expenses are charged to surplus value before profits are calculated and taxes are paid.

Our estimates for corporate advertising are compiled as follows. First, we take the figure for total corporate advertising for a given year. Then we subtract from this number a percentage of the total which accords with our estimate of the relative share of traditional forms of property income in all business income. This is done so as to allow for that portion of advertising expenditures which goes into the profit, rental, and interest income of advertising agencies and other businesses, and which is already counted in our estimates of incorporated and unincorporated business profits. Following this step, we then reduce the resulting figure further by deducting an amount designed to capture the 'profit element in corporate officer compensation' (which we count elsewhere). The amount deducted is based on the relative size of total corporate advertising expenditures vis-à-vis total business income. The figure obtained after these two adjustments have been made constitutes what might be thought of as the labour income which exists because of corporate advertising expenditures. We then adjust this final number downward so as to account for the taxes paid out of this income (again, see below).

Profit in corporate officer compensation

As Phillips pointed out, '[a] significant part of this income [the pay of corporate officers] represents a share of profits, although it is not explicitly treated as such' (Phillips, 1966: 379; 28 above). For this reason, we consider such income to be a disguised form of surplus.

In the interest of making a strictly conservative estimate of the surplus, we have elected to follow Phillips' assumption that one-half of corporate officer compensation represents a deduction from surplus value, with the other half representing 'labour income'. Nevertheless, it is important to note that this assumption appears to be wildly conservative in light of the recent startling rise in the average level of corporate officer compensation.[9]

Gross business depreciation

In his appendix to *Monopoly Capital*, Phillips went through a fairly detailed elaboration of his approach to the issue of depreciation. In this discussion, Phillips argued that untangling the well-known problem of excess depreciation allowances (the difference between what the government allows businesses to deduct from their profit figures as 'depreciation' and the actual amount of depreciation of plant and equipment) was the key to incorporating depreciation into the surplus. Thus, the trick for Phillips was to arrive at a solid estimate of the actual magnitude of excessive depreciation allowances, so that this could be incorporated into his table.

Our approach differs from Phillips' by treating the whole of depreciation allowances as part of the economic surplus. As Phillips himself recognised, the very term 'depreciation reserves' has the tendency to obscure how these funds are actually deployed by monopoly capital.[10] In reality, depreciation reserves have very little to do with what is socially necessary to replace plant and equipment within monopoly capitalist societies. As Harry Magdoff and Paul Sweezy have argued:

> In accounting theory. . . [depreciation] funds are supposed to be accumulated for the purpose of replacing plant and equipment worn out in the process of production. But in fact there is absolutely no reason to assume that funds accruing in the form of depreciation reserves will be used to duplicate the old machines and technology. Except in the case of irreparable breakdown, the need to scrap old productive capacity is rarely clear-cut. . . . [P]ure replacement rarely takes place: when depreciation reserves are used ostensibly for replacement they are, more often than not, invested in more advanced, more productive, and even enlarged capacity. Finally, there is no law that says depreciation reserves must be used to keep on manufacturing

the same products. These funds are in effect savings that are available for whatever management thinks will yield the best profits. (Magdoff and Sweezy, 1981: 193–4).

For this reason, we have incorporated the total amount of business depreciation into our estimates of the surplus, which should therefore be understood as gross (not net) surplus. Our approach in this respect conforms closely with standard national income accounting practices in which it is most common to refer to gross national product and gross savings in contrast to net national product and net savings.

Indirect business tax and nontax liabilities

This is another form of government revenue which is paid out by business as expenses charged against surplus value before the calculation of profits. As such, it belongs in our estimate of the surplus.

This category includes such items as the windfall profit tax on crude oil production and fines and fees assessed by regulatory agencies.

Estimated taxes on wages and salaries

Because taxes on wages and salaries go toward the funding of the state, they must be incorporated into our estimates.[11] This is not to deny that some part of this tax revenue will be returned to the working class in the form of what radical theorists now commonly refer to as 'the social wage'. But it does suggest that these revenues are more properly understood, in our view, as constituting part of the societally appropriated surplus rather than as 'wages' as such. In order to incorporate these amounts, we have taken the sum total of wages and salaries paid to individuals for each year in our table, deducted from this sum that share which represents disguised profit paid to corporate officers (see above), then estimated the size of the overall tax burden on this income for each year by assuming that 26 percent of this adjusted wage and salary figure was paid out in taxes of various sorts.

Our estimate of a 26 percent overall tax burden on wages and salaries is taken from the work of Joseph A. Pechman (already referred to above). Pechman's calculations reveal that if one makes the thoroughly reasonable assumption that corporations are successfully able to pass at least some of their tax burden along to consumers, then it is wise to conclude (since effective tax rates are flat or slightly regressive) that not only is the overall tax burden (including income, excise, sales, and social insurance taxes, etc.) equal to approximately 26 percent of income for all individuals, regardless of the size or source of their income, but that this figure has remained virtually constant over the period that we are concerned with here. In fact, Pechman's figures show that, assuming corporations can pass along some of their tax bills, the effective rate of federal, state, and local taxation for all income deciles was 25.9 percent in 1966, 26.7 percent in 1970, 25.5 percent in 1975, 26.3 percent in 1980, and 25.3 percent in 1985. Moreover, the variance from these averages is extremely small across all income deciles (Pechman, 1985: 1-10, 68.)[12]

Elements left out of our estimates

It is absolutely essential to recognize that the Phillips estimates, as well as our own, are conservative in several additional respects. Although Phillips did attempt to develop rough estimates for the penetration of the sales effort into the production process, which amounted to something like 10 percent of GNP, he was unable to compute year-by-year estimates and therefore left this component out of the economic surplus. Likewise, we also leave this element out. In addition, both sets of estimates leave out the further element of output lost through official unemployment. Finally, we have elected to exclude Phillips' category of 'waste in distribution' because of the extreme difficulty we would encounter in trying to replicate Phillips' method in this area, which relied heavily on one-of-a-kind sources of data.

Our final estimates of the surplus for the years 1963-1988 appear below.

CONCLUSIONS

We would like to reiterate that these figures were calculated using a different method from that of Phillips, and are not strictly comparable with his figures. As we have mentioned, we believe that Phillips did encounter difficulties with double counting. We have shifted his approach slightly, so as to avoid these minor problems.

Despite our qualifications and the inevitable shortcomings in the data, it seems desirable to draw some tentative conclusions from our estimates.

The first such conclusion is derived from the sheer size of the surplus in relation to the stagnant levels of real productive investment. Thus in 1988 gross investment was only 24 percent of gross economic surplus, or $632.8 billion out of a total gross surplus of $2,684.3 billion. Our estimates therefore strongly support the argument that we are in an age where capitalism is experiencing a disintegration of the last remaining vestiges of its own limited rationality as a social system. As Paul Sweezy stated in the October 1990 issue of *Monthly Review*, '[t]here's no way the capitalist class can now rationally manage the vast amount of surplus the economy is capable of producing' (Sweezy in Watanabe and Wakima, 1990: 14).

Second, our figures show an upward trend in the size of the surplus between 1963 and 1988. Thus the 'law of the tendency of the surplus to rise' has been found to be fairly consistent, with only minor interruption in the late 1960s and early 1970s. This suggests that the problem of surplus absorption continues to grow despite the declining secular trend-rate of growth in the system as a whole. In fact, our figures show that even in severe (supposedly 'corrective') downturns in the business cycle, the share of the surplus (in contrast to the share of profits as such) may not drop off by very much at all. For instance, the share of gross surplus in GNP dropped by only one-tenth of one point between 1981 and 1982, the breaking point at the beginning of the steepest post-war recession to date.

Third, the entire rise in surplus as a percentage of GNP over the quarter-century covered by our figures can be accounted for by the growth of the following four items: net interest, surplus employee compensation (i.e., finance, insurance, real estate and legal services), advertising costs, and the profit element in corporate officer compensation. Thus, if these four elements were subtracted from our estimates of the surplus, the general trend would be reversed, and gross surplus would fall as a percentage of GNP from 43.2 percent in 1963 to 40 percent in 1988 (rather than rising from 49.9 to 55 percent). Hence, the rise in gross economic surplus between the end of the Kennedy administration and the end of the Reagan administration can be accounted for entirely by factors reflecting the general shift away from production toward finance and marketing in the economy as a whole.

Finally, our estimates ought to give serious pause to those inclined toward supply-side explanations of the crisis of U.S. capitalism. Our figures, as we have seen, reveal that while traditionally defined profit figures have fluctuated, the rate of extraction of surplus product from the direct producers, as it is reflected at the aggregate level in surplus figures, has shown a far steadier upward trend. And what is true for the United States, in this respect, is obviously true in a much more heightened way for the capitalist world economy as a whole over the same period. It is only in this light that one can truly understand the

growing imperative for the creation of free socialist ecological demo-
cracies where society's economic surplus would be utilised rationally
to meet the needs in common of humanity as a whole.

NOTES

1. Gross economic surplus in our definition is meant to be equivalent to the
   gross social accumulation fund, or the range of freedom that society has at
   present both to maintain its existing infrastructure and to accomplish those
   tasks that go beyond the basic consumption needs of its employed population.
   Our definition of gross economic surplus is therefore meant to be equivalent
   to what, in Marx's terms, would be called gross surplus value—or total surplus
   value plus depreciation. This in turn reflects our view that most textbook
   definitions of surplus value, which typically identify it with profit, rent and
   interest and ignore such factors as surplus employee compensation, the profit
   element in corporate officer compensation, etc., are overly simplistic,
   downplaying precisely those elements of surplus product that are rising most
   rapidly in the current epoch.
2. On the concepts of potential surplus and planned surplus see Foster, 1986:
   24–50.
3. In later years Sweezy has frequently noted that the authors of *Monopoly
   Capital* failed to place sufficient emphasis on the role of finance within the
   overall accumulation dynamic of monopoly capitalism. For example, see
   Magdoff and Sweezy, 1987: 100–1. In this context, it is significant to note
   that Harry Magdoff, who joined Sweezy as co-editor of *Monthly Review* in
   1969, was placing strong emphasis on this aspect of the problem as early as
   1965, the year before *Monopoly Capital* was released. See Sweezy and
   Magdoff, 1972: 7–27.
4. Recognizing 'the differences between the categories employed in the national
   income accounts and those implied in the concept of economic surplus',
   Phillips strove to build his estimates by working from 'the more commonly
   recognized elements of surplus (i.e. profits, interest, rent) to those less
   commonly included' (i.e. forms of waste in the business process, the
   compensation of corporate officers, etc.). Joseph Phillips, 1966: 369 (21
   above).
5. Also, Edward Wolff has argued that the *Monopoly Capital* approach to
   unproductive labour is misguided. See Wolff, 1977: 87–8, 110–11. Wolff's
   argument that the kinds of unproductive labour generated by monopoly
   capitalism hurt the system by diverting surplus from 'productive capitalists'
   who would otherwise invest in more productive capacity, simply misses the
   central point of Baran and Sweezy's analysis: namely, that the main constraint
   of the system lies in the *absorption* not the *generation* of surplus.
6. Foster is here referring to clarifications issued by Sweezy himself in Sweezy,
   1980: 12. One of the central themes of Baran and Sweezy's work has always
   been the insistence that the concept of surplus value be rehabilitated in the
   context of the changes surrounding the emergence of the monopoly stage of
   capitalism, so as to provide the needed perspective for subjecting the entirety

of the social accumulation fund – and by extension, the social order of capitalism itself – to critical scrutiny.

7. Based on Joseph A. Pechman's authoritative study (Pechman, 1985), we assume that all U.S. individual taxpayers – regardless of income or wealth – have carried a roughly equal combined tax burden (including income, sales, property, excise, and other taxes) of about 26 percent of income throughout the period 1963–88.

8. Here we apply precisely the same method of estimating the labour/traditional property income split of business income connected with advertising that Phillips employed in estimating labour income's share of unincorporated business income. See Phillips, 1966: 370–2 (22–3 above), and 386: Table 19 (Table 2 above), Column 2.

9. For the last year in Phillips' table, 1963, corporate officer compensation represented slightly under 3 percent of GNP. By 1985, the share of corporate officer compensation in GNP had hit 4.25 percent, a remarkable jump given the small size of the population of corporate officers and the stagnating or declining fortunes of the vast majority of the population.

10. Phillips quotes Robert Eisner, who states that '[m]any accountants will insist that depreciation accounting is merely a device for allocating original cost and is entirely unrelated to replacement requirements' (Phillips, 1966: 374).

11. For a full explanation of how the taxation of wages and salaries constitutes part of the economic surplus, see Baran, 1957: 123–9. Here Baran points to 'the paradox that the larger the amount of surplus that the government must spend in order to maintain the desired level of income and employment, the larger it tends to make the surplus itself by seizing parts of income [taxes on wages and salaries] that otherwise would have been spent on consumption'.

12. See especially pages 1-10 and Pechman's Table 5-2, page 68. Our figure of 26 percent is the rounded average of the estimates of the overall tax burden in various years between 1965 and 1985 provided by Pechman in that portion of his Table 5-2 (Pechman, 1985: 68) which is based on the assumption that corporations are able to pass along some of their tax burden to consumers.

REFERENCES

Baran, Paul A. (1957). *The Political Economy of Growth*, New York: Monthly Review Press.

Baran, Paul A. (1966). *The Longer View*, New York: Monthly Review Press.

Baran, Paul A. and Paul M. Sweezy (1966). *Monopoly Capital*, New York: Monthly Review Press.

Brown, Lester, Christopher Flavin and Sandra Postel (1990). 'World Without End', *Natural History*, May.

Dowd, Douglas (1989). *The Waste of Nations*, Boulder, Colorado: Westview.

Foster, John Bellamy (1986). *The Theory of Monopoly Capitalism*, New York: Monthly Review Press.

Heilbroner, Robert (1970). *Between Capitalism and Socialism*, New York: Vintage.

Keynes, John Maynard (1973). *The General Theory of Employment, Interest, and Money*, Volume VII, *The Collected Works of John Maynard Keynes*, London: Macmillan.

Kloby, Jerry (1987). 'The Growing Divide', *Monthly Review*, 37(4), September.

Lubitz, Raymond (1971). 'Monopoly Capitalism and Neo-Marxism', in Daniel Bell and Irving Kristol, ed. *Capitalism Today*, New York: Basic Books.

Magdoff, Harry and Paul Sweezy (1972). *The Dynamics of U.S. Capitalism*, New York: Monthly Review Press.

Magdoff, Harry and Paul Sweezy (1981). *The Deepening Crisis of U.S. Capitalism*, New York: Monthly Review Press.

Magdoff, Harry and Paul Sweezy (1987). *Stagnation and the Financial Explosion*, New York: Monthly Review Press.

Magdoff, Harry and Paul Sweezy (1990). 'Investment for What?' *Monthly Review*, 42(2): 1-10, June.

Marx, Karl and Friedrich Engels (1968). *The Communist Manifesto*, New York: Monthly Review Press.

Packard, Vance (1989). *The Ultra Rich*, Boston: Little, Brown and Co.

Pechman, Joseph A. (1985). *Who Paid the Taxes, 1966-1985?*, Washington, D.C.: The Brookings Institution.

Phillips, Joseph D. (1966). 'Appendix: Estimating the Economic Surplus', in Paul A. Baran and Paul M. Sweezy, *Monopoly Capital*, New York: Monthly Review Press.

Phillips, Kevin (1990). *The Politics of Rich and Poor*, New York: Random House.

Renner, Michael (1988). 'Rethinking the Role of the Automobile', *Worldwatch Paper*, 84, June.

Stanfield, Ron (1973). *The Economic Surplus and Neo-Marxism*, Lexington, Mass.: Lexington Books.

Sweezy, Paul M. (1980). 'Japan in Perspective', *Monthly Review*, 31(9), February.

U.S. Congress, Joint Economic Committee (1986). *The Concentration of Wealth in the United States*, Washington, D.C.: Government Printing Office.

Watanabe, Yuzo and Yoshiaki Wakima (1990). 'Marxist Views: An Interview with Paul M. Sweezy', *Monthly Review*, 42(5): 1-15, October.

Wolff, Edward N. (1977). 'Unproductive Labour and the Rate of Surplus Value in the United States', in Paul Zarembka, ed. *Research in Political Economy*, Vol. 1. Greenwich, Conn.: JAI Press.

Woolhandler, Steffie and David Himmelstein (1989). 'The Case for a National Health Program', *Journal of General Internal Medicine*, 4:54-60, January–February.

TABLE 1: GROSS SURPLUS AND ITS MAJOR COMPONENTS, 1963-88
(columns 1-13: all figures current U.S. $billions)

Year	Adj. corp. profits	Est. Profits unic. business income	Rental income	Net interest	Surplus Employee comp.	Advert. costs of corps.	Profit Element in corp. off compens.	Gross business deprec.	Indirect business tax & nontax liability	Estimated tax on wages & salaries	Business contrib. soc. ins.	Gross surplus	Gross National Product	Gross surplus as % of GNP
1963	59.8	18.8	10.3	16.3	11.6	6.1	6.7	41.4	35.8	79.5	16.7	302.9	606.9	49.9
1964	66.2	19.9	10.5	18.2	12.8	6.7	7.1	44.0	38.6	85.3	17.5	326.8	649.8	50.3
1965	76.2	22.3	11.0	20.9	13.5	7.3	7.8	47.0	41.2	91.8	18.2	357.1	705.1	50.7
1966	81.2	23.1	11.4	24.3	14.7	8.0	8.4	50.6	42.7	101.1	22.8	388.4	772.0	50.3
1967	78.6	21.8	12.4	27.4	16.2	8.4	9.1	54.6	45.4	108.3	25.0	407.2	816.4	49.9
1968	85.4	22.1	12.4	29.8	18.3	9.1	9.8	58.7	52.3	119.3	27.6	444.8	892.7	49.8
1969	81.4	20.0	14.0	34.6	20.2	10.2	11.2	63.5	57.8	130.8	31.7	475.5	963.9	49.3
1970	69.5	16.1	14.7	41.2	22.3	10.7	12.1	67.9	62.1	139.1	34.3	490.1	1,015.5	48.3
1971	82.7	17.7	15.7	46.3	24.6	11.1	13.5	72.3	68.4	147.1	38.2	537.5	1,102.7	48.7
1972	94.9	19.5	17.3	51.0	27.5	12.4	15.3	80.1	73.5	160.7	44.6	596.8	1,212.8	49.2
1973	107.1	21.2	19.8	59.6	30.8	13.5	17.5	86.5	81.0	178.1	55.1	670.1	1,359.3	49.3
1974	99.4	15.4	21.9	75.5	34.1	14.8	19.6	94.2	86.2	194.0	62.6	717.7	1,472.8	48.7
1975	123.9	18.9	23.2	83.8	37.9	15.7	21.4	102.2	93.6	204.3	68.0	792.9	1,598.4	49.6
1976	155.3	21.3	25.5	88.8	42.7	18.0	23.7	109.8	101.3	225.5	79.0	890.9	1,782.8	50.0
1977	183.8	25.7	30.1	105.3	47.9	20.3	27.3	123.6	111.1	248.8	88.6	1,012.5	1,990.5	50.9
1978	208.2	28.7	35.5	126.3	55.0	23.5	31.5	138.7	121.2	280.0	101.9	1,150.4	2,249.7	51.1
1979	214.1	22.5	40.4	158.3	62.8	27.3	36.0	158.2	129.5	312.9	116.8	1,278.8	2,508.2	51.0
1980	194.0	10.9	47.6	200.9	72.6	31.3	40.3	180.3	147.2	342.6	127.9	1,395.6	2,732.0	51.1
1981	202.3	4.3	58.7	248.1	82.1	35.8	44.5	218.4	175.0	377.0	146.7	1,592.9	3,052.6	52.2
1982	159.2	-8.8	62.9	272.3	92.2	39.8	47.9	252.9	176.9	395.6	157.2	1,648.1	3,166.0	52.1
1983	196.7	2.6	67.4	281.0	103.6	42.9	52.2	336.1	194.1	417.6	171.0	1,826.0	3,405.7	53.6
1984	234.2	13.9	70.4	304.8	114.4	47.9	58.1	336.1	216.4	457.6	192.2	2,046.0	3,772.2	54.2
1985	222.6	12.9	75.1	319.0	127.3	53.7	63.2	387.8	231.9	491.4	204.8	2,189.7	4,014.9	54.5
1986	228.3	8.1	73.0	325.5	145.7	58.5	68.6	408.1	245.6	520.4	217.4	2,299.2	4,231.6	54.3
1987	247.8	20.1	75.2	351.7	163.6	64.5	75.0	417.3	259.6	558.3	227.8	2,460.9	4,524.3	54.4
1988	281.8	30.9	80.4	392.9	183.7	71.0	81.9	430.9	278.6	602.5	249.7	2,684.3	4,880.6	55.0

63

TABLE 2: ESTIMATED PROFIT INCOME
OF UNINCORPORATED BUSINESS
(columns 1, 3-6: all figures in current U.S. $billions)

Year	Uninc. business income	% Corp. income going to employees	Est. lab. income- uninc. business	Non-labour income- uninc. business	Net interest- uninc. business	Est. profits uninc. business
1963	97.2	78.7	76.5	20.7	1.9	18.8
1964	102.5	78.2	80.2	22.3	2.4	19.9
1965	108.7	76.9	83.6	25.1	2.8	22.3
1966	116.2	77.3	89.8	26.4	3.3	23.1
1967	118.8	78.6	93.4	25.4	3.6	21.8
1968	125.4	79.2	99.3	26.1	4.0	22.1
1969	131.8	81.1	106.9	24.9	4.9	20.0
1970	135.0	83.6	112.9	22.1	6.0	16.1
1971	143.4	82.6	118.4	25.0	7.3	17.7
1972	157.9	82.3	130.0	27.9	8.4	19.5
1973	187.5	82.8	155.3	32.2	11.0	21.2
1974	194.1	85.0	165.0	29.1	13.7	15.4
1975	205.8	83.3	171.4	34.4	15.5	18.9
1976	225.8	82.8	187.0	38.8	17.5	21.3
1977	248.9	81.7	203.4	45.5	19.8	25.7
1978	284.9	81.8	233.0	51.9	23.2	28.7
1979	316.4	83.5	264.2	52.2	29.7	22.5
1980	318.0	85.1	270.6	47.4	36.5	10.9
1981	342.2	84.7	289.8	52.4	48.1	4.3
1982	340.6	87.1	296.7	43.9	52.7	- 8.8
1983	361.2	84.5	305.2	56.0	53.4	2.6
1984	421.7	83.2	350.9	70.8	57.6	13.2
1985	459.2	83.4	383.0	76.2	63.3	12.9
1986	502.9	84.4	424.4	78.5	70.4	8.1
1987	548.2	83.8	459.4	88.8	68.7	20.1
1988	580.4	82.9	481.2	99.2	68.3	30.9

TABLE 3: ADJUSTED SURPLUS EMPLOYEE COMPENSATION
(all figures in current U.S. $billions)

Year	Total employee compensation in finance insurance & real estate	Corp. officer compensation in finance insurance & real estate	Adjusted total employee compensation in finance insurance & real estate	Total employee compensation in 'legal services' sector	Estimated corporate officer compensation in 'legal services'	Adjusted total employee compensation in 'legal services' sector	Total after-tax surplus employee compensation
1963	16.3	3.1	14.8	0.9	0.01	0.9	11.6
1964	17.6	2.7	16.3	1.0	0.002	1.0	12.8
1965	18.9	3.4	17.2	1.0	0.01	1.0	13.5
1966	20.5	3.6	18.7	1.2	0.02	1.2	14.7
1967	22.5	3.9	20.6	1.3	0.03	1.3	16.2
1968	25.5	4.4	23.3	1.4	0.03	1.4	18.3
1969	28.2	5.0	25.7	1.7	0.1	1.7	20.2
1970	30.9	5.3	28.3	2.0	0.1	2.0	22.3
1971	34.0	6.0	31.0	2.3	0.1	2.3	24.6
1972	37.8	6.7	34.5	2.8	0.2	2.7	27.5
1973	42.0	7.3	38.4	3.4	0.3	3.3	30.8
1974	46.0	7.7	42.2	4.1	0.3	3.9	34.1
1975	50.9	8.5	46.7	4.8	0.5	4.6	37.9
1976	57.0	9.2	52.4	5.6	0.5	5.3	42.7
1977	63.9	10.6	58.6	6.5	0.6	6.2	47.9
1978	73.1	11.8	67.2	7.6	1.0	7.1	55.0
1979	83.2	13.6	76.4	9.1	1.2	8.5	62.8
1980	95.2	15.0	87.7	11.0	1.3	10.4	72.6
1981	106.6	16.4	98.4	13.3	1.6	12.5	82.1
1982	118.7	18.1	109.7	16.2	2.6	14.9	92.2
1983	133.1	20.7	122.8	18.7	2.9	17.2	103.6
1984	146.2	22.2	135.1	21.3	3.6	19.5	144.4
1985	162.5	25.7	149.7	24.3	3.7	22.4	127.3
1986	185.2	28.5	171.0	28.1	4.3	25.9	145.7
1987	n.a.	n.a.	n.a.	n.a.	n.a.	n.a.	163.6
1988	n.a.	n.a.	n.a.	n.a.	n.a.	n.a.	183.7

TABLE 4: ADJUSTED CORPORATE ADVERTISING
(all figures except column 2 in current U.S. $billions)

Year	Total corp. advert.	General labour income share estimate from Table 2	Est. labour income from corp. adv.	Est. disguised profit in corp. officer comp., advertising	Estimated true labour income from corp. adv.	After-tax labour income from corp. adv.
1963	11.0	78.7	8.7	0.4	8.3	6.1
1964	12.1	78.2	9.5	0.4	9.1	6.7
1965	13.3	76.9	10.2	0.4	9.8	7.3
1966	14.5	77.3	11.2	0.4	10.8	8.0
1967	15.0	78.6	11.8	0.5	11.3	8.4
1968	16.2	79.2	12.8	0.5	12.3	9.1
1969	17.7	81.1	14.4	0.6	13.8	10.2
1970	18.1	83.6	15.1	0.6	14.5	10.7
1971	19.0	82.6	15.7	0.7	15.0	11.1
1972	21.4	82.3	17.6	0.8	16.8	12.4
1973	23.0	82.8	19.0	0.8	18.2	13.5
1974	24.6	85.0	20.9	0.9	20.0	14.8
1975	26.6	83.3	22.2	1.0	21.2	15.7
1976	30.8	82.8	25.5	1.2	24.3	18.0
1977	35.3	81.7	28.8	1.4	27.4	20.3
1978	40.8	81.8	33.4	1.6	31.8	23.5
1979	46.3	83.5	38.7	1.8	36.9	27.3
1980	52.3	85.1	44.5	2.2	42.3	31.3
1981	60.1	84.7	50.9	2.5	48.4	35.8
1982	65.0	87.1	56.6	2.8	53.8	39.8
1983	72.4	84.5	61.2	3.2	58.0	42.9
1984	82.0	83.2	68.2	3.5	64.7	47.9
1985	91.9	83.4	76.6	4.1	72.5	53.7
1986	99.0	84.4	83.6	4.5	79.1	58.5
1987	110.2	83.8	92.3	5.2	87.1	64.5
1988	122.7	82.9	101.7	5.8	95.9	71.0

SOURCES FOR TABLES

For the years 1963–82, all figures except some of those related to surplus employee compensation, corporate officer compensation and corporate advertising were taken from *The National Income and Product Accounts of the United States: 1929-1982* (hereafter *N.I.P.A.*), (Washington, D.C.: U.S. Department of Commerce, 1986).

For the years 1983–88, all figures except some of those related to surplus employee compensation, corporate officer compensation and corporate advertising were taken from the *Survey of Current Business* (hereafter *S.C.B.*), (Washington, D.C.: U.S. Department of Commerce, monthly). For the years 1983–84, the July 1987 edition of *S.C.B.* was used. For 1985–88, the July 1990 edition was used. *S.C.B.* tables are the exact equivalents of identically-numbered *N.I.P.A.* tables.

Figures on corporate officer compensation and corporate advertising for the years 1987 and 1988 were estimated based on a projection of the average of their respective annual rates of growth during the years 1980–86. All figures relating to corporate advertising and corporate officer compensation, and some figures related to surplus employee compensation are drawn from: *Statistics of Income: Corporation Income Tax Returns* (hereafter *S.O.I.*), published yearly by the U.S. Treasury Department, Internal Revenue Service, Washington, D.C..

Note: For convenience and clarity of understanding, in Table 3 a few figures for the years 1987 and 1988 are treated as if they were not available, when in fact one could find them in the *S.C.B.* volumes. We simply treat them as not available because other figures in these years for Table 3 *are* in fact unavailable, leaving us with no choice but to project the final 1987 and 1988 numbers in this table from the end results of full estimations for the years 1980–86. See below.

Specific, column-by-column sources are as follows:

Table 1:

CL 1)   1963–82: *N.I.P.A.*, line 21, Table 1.14, pp. 47–8.
        1983–84: *S.C.B.*, line 21, Table 1.14, p. 25.
        1985–88: *S.C.B.*, line 21, Table 1.14, p. 45.
CL 2)   Figures taken from Table 2, Column 6 below.
CL 3)   1963–82: *N.I.P.A.*, line 18, Table 1.14, pp. 47–8, minus line 49, Table 8.9, pp. 396–9.
        1983–84: *S.C.B.*, line 18, Table 1.14, p. 25, minus line 49, Table 8.9, p. 81.
        1985–88: *S.C.B.*, line 18, Table 1.1.4, p. 45, minus line 49, Table 8.9, p. 101.
CL 4)   1963–82: *N.I.P.A.*, line 29, Table 1.14, pp. 47–8.
        1983–84: *S.C.B.*, line 29, Table 1.14, p. 25.
        1985–88: *S.C.B.*, line 29, Table 1.14, p. 45.
CL 5)   Figures taken from Table 3, Column 7 below.
CL 6)   Figures taken from Table 4, Column 6 below.
CL 7)   1963–86: *S.O.I.*, table entitled 'Balance Sheets and Income Statements, by Major Industrial Group', line labelled 'Compensation of Officers' under 'Total Deductions' sub-heading for 'All Industries' sub-grouping, divided by 2. This figure then multiplied by .74 in order to adjust for taxes (see text above).

1987–88: Average annual growth rate from year to year calculated for years from 1980–86. Average of these growth rate figures then applied to figure for 1986, this column, in order to yield 1987 figure. Same average then applied to project a figure for 1988 based on 1987 figure.

CL 8) *N.I.P.A.*, line 3, Table 1.9, p. 32, minus line 28, Table 8.9, pp. 396–399.

1983–84: *S.C.B.*, line 3, Table 1.9, p. 23, minus line 28, Table 8.9, p. 81.

1985–88: *S.C.B.*, line 3, Table 1.9, p. 43, minus line 28, Table 8.9, p. 101.

CL 9) 1963–82: *N.I.P.A.*, line 4, Table 1.16, pp. 61–2.

1983–84: *S.C.B.*, line 4, Table 1.16, p. 27.

1985–88: *S.C.B.*, line 4, Table 1.16, p. 47.

CL 10) 1963–82: *N.I.P.A.*, line 2, Table 2.1, pp. 89–90 minus the appropriate yearly figure in Column 7 of this table, multiplied by .26.

1983–84: *S.C.B.*, line 2, Table 2.1, p. 37 minus the appropriate yearly figure in Column 7 of this table, multiplied by .26.

1985–88: *S.C.B.*, line 2, Table 2.1, p. 50 minus appropriate yearly figure in Column 7 of this table, multiplied by .26.

See the text above under 'Estimated Income Tax on Wages' for the rationale behind these figures.

CL 11) 1963–82: *N.I.P.A.*, line 4 plus line 15, Table 3.13, pp. 168–9.

1983–84: *S.C.B.*, line 4 plus line 15, Table 3.13, p. 42.

1985–88: *S.C.B.*, line 4 plus line 15, Table 3.13, p. 62

CL 12) 1963–88: Sum of columns 1 through 11.

CL 13) 1963–82: *N.I.P.A.*, line 1, Table 1.1, pp. 1–2.

1983–84: *S.C.B.*, line 1, Table 1.1, p. 20.

1985–88: *S.C.B.*, line 1, Table 1.1, p. 40.

CL 14) 1963–88: Column 12 divided by column 13.

Table 2:

CL 1) 1963–82: *N.I.P.A.*, Table 1.15, line 12, pp. 58–9.

1983–84: *S.C.B.*, Table 1.15, line 12, p. 26.

1985–88: *S.C.B.*, Table 1.15, line 12, p. 46.

CL 2) 1963–82: *N.I.P.A.*, Table 1.15, line 4 divided by line 3, pp. 58–9.

1983–84: *S.C.B.*, Table 1.15, line 4 divided by line 3, p. 26.

1985–88: *S.C.B.*, Table 1.15, line 4 divided by line 3, p. 46.

CL 3) Column 1 multiplied by Column 2.

CL 4) Column 1 minus Column 3.

CL 5) 1963–82: *N.I.P.A.*, Table 1.15, line 24, pp. 58–9.

1983–84: *S.C.B.*, Table 1.15, line 24, p. 26.

1985–88: *S.C.B.*, Table 1.15, line 24, p. 46.

CL 6) Column 4 minus Column 5.

Table 3:

CL 1)   1963–82: *N.I.P.A.*, Table 6.4B, line 52, pp. 263–4.
         1983–84: *S.C.B.*, Table 6.4B, line 52, p. 59.
         1985–86: *S.C.B.*, Table 6.4B, line 52, p. 79.
         1987–88: Because of unavailability of data in crucial columns of this
         table for these years, these figures have been left out of the table, and the
         final figures shown in Column 7 of this table were estimated by
         projecting the overall annual rate of growth in our adjusted surplus
         employee compensation totals for the years 1980–86.

CL 2)   1963–86: Figures taken from *S.O.I.*, years 1963–86, Table entitled
         'Balance Sheets and Income Statements, by Major Industrial Group', line
         headed 'Compensation of Officers' under finance, insurance, and real
         estate sub-heading. Page numbers vary from year to year.
         1987–88: See explanation, same years, Column 1 above.

CL 3)   1963–86: Column 1 minus half of Column 2.
         1987–88: See explanation, same years, Column 1 above.

CL 4)   1963–82: *N.I.P.A.*, Table 6.4B, line 69, pp. 263–4.
         1983–84: *S.C.B.*, Table 6.4B, line 69, p. 59.
         1985–86: *S.C.B.*, Table 6.4B, line 69, p. 79.
         1987–88: See explanation, same years, Column 1 above.

CL 5)   1963–86: *S.O.I.*, same table as used for figures in Column 2 above, line
         entitled 'Compensation of Officers' under 'Other or Miscellaneous
         Services' sub-heading. This figure then adjusted by multiplying it by the
         dividend yielded after dividing total business receipts in the 'legal
         services' sector by the total business receipts for the entire 'other or
         miscellaneous' services sector. Figures for both of these sectors' business
         receipts taken from yearly *S.O.I.*, Table 1, entitled 'Number of Returns,
         Receipts, Cost of Sales and Operations, Net Income, Net Worth, Total
         Assets, Distributions to Stockholders, Income Subject to Tax, Income Tax
         and Investment Credit by Industrial Group'.
         1987–88: See explanation, same years, Column 1 above.

CL 6)   Column 4 minus half of Column 5.

CL 7)   1963–88: Sum of Column 3 and Column 6, multiplied by 0.74.
         1987–88: Average annual growth rate from year to year calculated for
         years from 1980–86. Average of these growth rate figures then applied
         to figure for 1986, this column, in order to yield 1987 figure. Same
         average then applied to project a figure for 1988 based on 1987 figure.

Table 4:

CL 1)   1963–86: *S.O.I.*, Table entitled 'Balance Sheets and Income Statements,
         by Major Industrial Group', line labelled 'Advertising' under 'Total
         Deductions' sub-heading.
         1987–88: Same method of projecting figures used as in Table 3, Column
         7 above.

CL 2)   Same figure as utilised in Table 2, Column 2.

CL 3)   Column 1 multiplied by Column 2.

CL 4)   1963–88: Half of total corporate officer compensation (taken from 'All
         Industries' sub-heading in *S.O.I.* Table utilised above in Table 3,

Columns 2 and 5). This total then adjusted by multiplying it by an estimate of the share of the advertising sector in the overall corporate sector. This weighting factor derived by dividing total corporate advertising expenditures (Table 4, Column 1 above) by total corporate business income for each year in the table (*N.I.P.A./S.C.B.* Table 1.15, line 3).

CL 5)   Column 3 minus Column 4.

CL 6)   Column 5 multiplied by 0.74.

5. Reevaluating the Concept of the Surplus*

Victor D. Lippit

Monopoly Capital was published by Paul Sweezy in 1966, two years after the death of his co-author, Paul Baran. The book sought to update the radical analysis of the capitalist system by taking into consideration some of the basic changes that had taken place as the system evolved over time. Its focus is on the economy of the United States, but the authors argue that the tendencies uncovered there are characteristic of advanced capitalism generally.

When Marx published *Capital* in 1867, he sought to examine the inner logic of a system founded on private ownership, competition and the pursuit of profit. A century later, however, large oligopolistic firms dominated most industries, enjoying a measure of pricing power denied to competitive firms. This situation has changed the dynamics of the capitalist system, and Baran and Sweezy's *Monopoly Capital* represents an effort to reconsider the primary tendencies and contradictions in the system accordingly. 'Oligopoly capital' would have been a more precise title for their work, since the industrial structure to which they refer is generally characterised by a few sellers (oligopoly) rather than one seller (monopoly), but the logic of their argument is nevertheless clear.

As Sweezy states in the Introduction, *Monopoly Capital* 'is organised around and attains its essential unity from one central theme: the generation and absorption of the surplus under conditions of monopoly capitalism' (p. 8). 'The surplus' is a concept Baran had used in his earlier work, *The Political Economy of Growth* (1957), but in that work he had presented a number of different definitions of the surplus concept, none of which is precisely the same as the definition used in *Monopoly Capital*,[1] which defines the surplus as 'the difference between total output and the socially necessary costs of producing total output' (p. 76). Baran and Sweezy argue that under 'monopoly' capitalism, there is a systemic tendency for this surplus to rise, and that it is increasingly absorbed in wasteful fashion through military spending, manipulative marketing and so forth. They also assert that notwithstanding these various forms of waste, advanced capitalist society finds difficulty in absorbing the surplus, creating an underlying stagnationist tendency (pp. 245–8).

Sweezy and Baran argue that the characteristic institution of 'monopoly' capitalism is the large corporation, which pursues profit maximisation as vigorously as its competitive predecessor. The large corporation, however, has far more resources to pursue cost reduction relentlessly, and thus to raise productivity. On the other hand, oligopolistic pricing power results in lower costs being reflected in higher profits rather than being passed on to consumers in the form of lower prices. The combination of high and/or rising prices with falling costs of production results in a tendency for profits to rise as a share of GNP. In practice, a share of the profits is diverted to marketing expenditures, military expenditures (via taxation) and so forth, so the statistically reported profits do not necessarily rise. Profits plus such expenditures will tend to rise, however, and since taken together these constitute the surplus, Sweezy and Baran see the tendency of the surplus to rise as the core dynamic of contemporary capitalism. Joseph Phillips's pioneering effort to estimate the economic surplus, which appears as the Appendix to *Monopoly Capital* and Chapter 3 in this volume, seems to confirm their expectation of a rising surplus; his study covers the period from 1929 to 1963.

From the perspective of the early 1990s, the capitalist world appears far different than it did when *Monopoly Capital* was written in the early 1960s. In particular, two of the key tenets of the Sweezy–Baran thesis have been called into question by the historical experience of the intervening thirty years. First, with all their technical sophistication and financial resources, U.S. corporations have found it increasingly difficult to raise (labour) productivity, especially in the increasingly important tertiary (service) sector of the economy. Thus, whereas American labour productivity grew at an average rate of 3.9 percent per year from 1950 to 1970, the growth rate fell to 1.2 percent in the 1980–88 period (Baumol and Blinder 1991, 360). Second, the pricing flexibility generated by oligopolistic market structures has been severely undermined by the sharp increase in international competition. In the U.S., such major industries as automobiles, steel and so forth have suffered from severe declines in profitability in the face of increasing competition from firms based abroad, while the consumer electronics industry has been all but wiped out by such competition.

Either of these factors alone would suffice to undermine the theoretical basis of the 'tendency of the surplus to rise'. Taken together, they make it most unlikely that any such tendency can be shown to exist. At a still more basic level, the very definition of the surplus that Baran and Sweezy present is problematic. Nevertheless, the concept of the surplus affords insights into the functioning of the capitalist social formation that cannot be gained from conventional national income accounting, especially when the concept is presented in conjunction with an analysis of class structure. For this reason I would like to review the shortcomings of the Sweezy–Baran approach as the basis for formulating an alternative conception of the surplus. This alternative conception will be followed by an assessment of U.S. capitalism from the perspective it affords.

THE CONCEPT OF THE SURPLUS IN MONOPOLY CAPITAL

The definition of the surplus presented by Sweezy and Baran, 'the difference between total output and the socially necessary costs of producing total output', presents a number of problems that may not be evident at first sight. These result from the terms in the definition itself, and from the various purposes that the concept of the surplus is meant to serve. Total output is somewhat ambiguous, but any net measure of national income or output, such as net national product (NNP) can be used to represent it. The socially necessary costs of production raise rather more problems.

As a first approximation, we can equate necessary costs of production with opportunity costs, which is what the various factors of production would sell for in competitive markets (reflecting the best alternative use of those factors). But a core thesis of *Monopoly Capital* presumes that competitive markets are no longer prevalent. Any effort to estimate such costs would therefore have to be indirect and tentative. Ultimately, Sweezy and Baran treat, with certain exceptions, all nonmanagerial labour costs in the private sector as 'necessary' costs. Further, they include certain entire categories of expenditure, such as marketing and advertising, as 'unnecessary' and therefore as part of the surplus. A number of difficulties arise if we consider the implications of their approach.

In the first place, if economies of scale are present, a high level of marketing expenditure may be necessary to bring production costs down to a minimum. Consider the following example. In the absence of marketing expenditure (including advertising), three hundred toothpaste companies might produce toothpaste at an average cost of one dollar per tube. In the presence of marketing expenditure, three toothpaste companies might, benefiting from economies of scale, produce toothpaste at an average cost of ten cents per tube. Even if the marketing expenditure amounts to fifty cents per tube, average costs of production plus marketing will be much lower when marketing expenditure brings about a more concentrated market structure.

Now of course it can be argued that in a centrally-planned economy, a 'rationally-ordered' economy, a concentrated production structure could yield the ten-cents-per-tube economies of scale without the need for the wasteful marketing expenditure. But that requires an entire additional argument, and the advocate of such a position would be hard-pressed to sound coherent to anyone who has paid attention to the widespread collapse of the centrally-planned economies during the last quarter-century. For central planning has been widely attempted, and nowhere has it yielded the superior living standards that the elimination of marketing waste should apparently make possible. In effect, the production cost in the planned economy has been two dollars per tube.[2]

In addition to making economies of scale in production possible, a high level of marketing expenditures may also yield significant economies of scale in distribution. Finally, advertising expenditures (which constitute a large part of marketing costs) may also subsidise the production of unrelated goods and services. Thus, for example, shows that are free on network television because of the advertising revenues they generate would be available otherwise only on a pay-per-view or other fee basis, or newspapers and magazines would be much more costly were advertising to be eliminated. Elimination of the advertising revenue would thus raise costs elsewhere or result in a fall in the output of goods and services. These considerations suggest that however much we may recoil at the pervasiveness of commercial culture in the United States, we should not underestimate the difficulties associated with writing off entire categories of expenditure as 'unproductive'.

Above and beyond these problems, further difficulties are associated with the inclusion of the term 'socially' with 'necessary costs of production'. This inclusion suggests that externalitie – that is, the social benefits or costs that have no impact on the parties to a transaction – must be taken into account. On a conceptual level, it is entirely appropriate to include such costs, but Sweezy and Baran nowhere explore the issues that their inclusion must raise.

The inclusion of externalities is especially important with respect to environmental costs. The operation of automobiles, for example, results in a range of environmental social costs from ozone depletion to the greenhouse effect and smog. In principle, when each car is produced the discounted value of these costs should be included among the social costs of production. The only socially necessary costs that Baran and Sweezy recognise, however, are (nonmanagerial) labour costs, so their treatment of the surplus becomes internally inconsistent. Of course even if they were to recognise environmental costs of this kind, the necessary calculations could only be made with numerous arbitrary assumptions. This reinforces the conclusion that the very definition of the surplus provided by Sweezy and Baran is both conceptually problematic and incapable of providing clear guidelines for empirical estimation.

The problems posed by Sweezy and Baran's definition of the surplus are magnified by their classifying all of government spending as part of the surplus. In effect they are saying that no part of government spending represents socially necessary costs of production. Such a claim appears defensible where military expenditure or the building of monuments is at issue, but it is equally clear that ordinary production activities could not be sustained without a wide range of public services ranging from education and transportation to the repair of streets. These certainly represent socially necessary albeit indirect costs of production.

Sweezy and Baran divide surplus absorption into three categories: (a) capitalists' consumption, (b) investment, and (c) waste. The treatment of capitalists' consumption as a separate category is another aspect of their treatment that warrants further consideration. The clear-cut nineteenth-century image of the capitalist as captain of industry is no longer realistic at the end of the twentieth century. If capitalists are defined in terms of corporate ownership, then other problems are raised.

First, senior managers are usually classified as capitalists as well, which may be reasonable but which makes the category more ambiguous. More problematic, employees own some 12 percent of the stock of the largest 1000 corporations in the United States, and mutual funds and pension plans together own more than 40 percent of all U.S. equities, a percentage which is rapidly increasing. At the same time, the *average* eye-doctor in the United States earns more than $200,000 and the *average* major league baseball player close to $1,000,000. What these facts suggest is that in thinking about the surplus, it may be much more reasonable to treat all luxury consumption as part of the surplus rather than to sweep all consumption that is based on property into this category, regardless of its magnitude. It is not really clear, after all, why the consumption of a retired couple of modest means, dependent for their living expenses on bond interest (or a pension financed by bond interest), should be treated as part of the surplus.

A further conceptual problem in *Monopoly Capital*'s treatment of the surplus lies in its failure to distinguish clearly between surplus as an 'income' concept and surplus as an 'output' concept. Inevitably, this failure is accompanied by corresponding confusion in the estimation of the surplus in the Appendix. The concept of the surplus can be treated most appropriately as parallel to the income–expenditure equality in national income accounting. By definition, national income must equal national expenditure, but mixing components of the two categories can only result in confusion. In similar fashion, we can think of the surplus in terms of income concepts or in terms of output–expenditure concepts, but not as a mixture of the two. In *Monopoly Capital*, however, income and output–expenditure categories are mixed in both the body of the text and in the Appendix. Thus in Table 22 in the Appendix, 'Total Economic Surplus and Its Major Components' (p. 389), most of the entries are based on income, but 'surplus absorbed by government' is in the expenditure category.

ESTIMATING THE SURPLUS IN MONOPOLY CAPITAL

Joseph Phillips' estimate of the surplus in the Appendix to *Monopoly Capital* (pp. 369–91) follows the conceptual framework elaborated in the body of the text, and thus reflects its strengths and weaknesses. Phillips defines the surplus as the sum of (a) total property income; (b) waste in distribution; (c) nontrade corporate advertising; surplus employee compensation in (d) finance, insurance and real estate, and (e) legal services; and (f) government expenditure. He presents estimates for each of these components of the surplus, for total surplus, and for surplus as a percentage of GNP for each year from 1929 through 1963 (p. 389). According to the figures he presents, surplus rises from 46.9 percent of GNP in 1929 to 56.1 percent in 1963. As I have indicated earlier, the underlying conception of the surplus in *Monopoly Capital* is the difference between national product and the socially necessary costs of production. An examination of the six categories into which it is divided will add to the earlier discussion concerning difficulties raised by *Monopoly Capital*'s treatment.

The first category, total property income, reflects the roots of Sweezy and Baran in Marxian theory; this is the modern variant of capitalists' (profit) income.[3] As a first approximation, it is indeed appropriate to treat such unearned income–consisting of profit, rent and interest – as a socially unnecessary cost of production. There are several points that must be made in this regard, however. First, insofar as profit represents a return to innovation and entrepreneurship, profit may be a necessary cost of production. Second, the class conception underlying the treatment of property income bears decreasing relevance to modern capitalist society.

In the first place, recipients of interest income do not simply constitute a rentier capitalist class. Many retired people, for example, depend on interest for a sizable share of their income – and of their essential consumption requirements. Even more important, pension plans have come to own a substantial share of corporate equity in the U.S. Thus, for example, the California Public Employees' Retirement System alone has $58 billion under management of which 36 percent is in equities, and new funds flowing in at the rate of $12 million per day; it estimates that by the end of the decade it will have $200 billion under management (*Fortune*, 29 July 1991: 132). Indirect worker ownership is further swelled in the U.S. by the existence of employee ownership of corporations, in whole or in part, through employee stock ownership plans (ESOPs); when holdings in company pension plans, savings plans and ESOPs are included, employees own an estimated 12 percent of the equity in the 1000 largest U.S. companies with employee ownership exceeding 4 percent (*Business Week*, 15 July 1991: 108). Thus a significant share of profits (and of property income as a whole) is used to finance the essential consumption requirements of retired workers. In no sense is this income 'surplus' in the sense of constituting a portion of society's discretionary income. The living costs of childhood and old age, as well as those of currently active members of the labour force, are properly part of socially necessary costs. In contemporary capitalist society, a portion of these costs appears under the guise of 'property income', but must nevertheless be excluded from the surplus.

'Waste in distribution' is Phillips's second surplus category. The discussion in the main body of the text, in addition to decrying the waste associated with advertising and other promotional activities, pays considerable attention to the waste associated with product design and model changes geared to increasing sales rather than to embodying any new or improved technology. Sweezy and Baran acknowledge that although the surplus can be estimated readily when the waste takes the form of advertising and so forth, it cannot be readily estimated when it is integrated in the production process in the form of (unneeded) model or design changes.

To deal with the resulting ambiguities, Phillips estimates waste in distribution by subtracting profits from value added in distribution (since profits are already included in the first surplus category) and then arbitrarily including 35 percent of the residual costs of distribution in the surplus. On the one hand, this clearly omits the 'wasteful' design and model change expenses that Sweezy and Baran make prominent. On the other, it is not really clear what the 35 percent is meant to measure.

Presumably distribution costs represent the retail sales price less the cost of goods produced at factories; this would include transportation costs, the commissions and salaries of salespeople, promotional expenditures and so forth. Transportation costs, however, are clearly necessary and should not be considered part of the surplus. With regard to sales and marketing expenditures, on the other hand, while it is clear that some portion of them can be considered wasteful, it is by no means clear how the 35 percent figure is arrived at or how it can be justified. Few of us, for example, would voluntarily wait an extra half-hour at supermarket check-out lines to eliminate the waste associated with 'unnecessary' employees in retailing. By contrast, enormous wastage of food through spoilage and long lines associated with most retail purchases in Soviet-type economies show the problems that can be presented by neglect of the critical role of distribution.

In sum, an understandable distaste for commercial civilisation should not blind us to the necessary functions performed in distribution. And finally, as I have already indicated, marketing expenditures may well contribute to economies of scale, and this effect may be substantial. All of these considerations taken together suggest that not only the 35 percent figure for 'waste in distribution' but indeed the entire category is arrived at arbitrarily.

The third surplus category, nontrade corporate advertising, clearly represents an implicit critique of the manipulative commercialism of contemporary society. Nevertheless, as indicated in the earlier discussion, a variety of problems is presented by efforts to include this category in the surplus. The prices of newspapers, magazines and television programs would be much higher without the support provided by advertising expenditure. The smaller markets for unbranded merchandise would reduce the scale of production and might well raise production costs in numerous industries. At the end of this process, it is not clear just how much social savings would be provided by the elimination of nontrade corporate advertising.

The fourth and fifth categories similarly represent some rather cavalier assumptions about what is socially necessary. These categories sweep into the surplus value added via employee compensation in (d) finance, insurance and real estate, and (e) legal services. Again we find the prejudice that tends to exclude service activities from the sphere of the productive. Some people do sell their homes by themselves, others pay the typical 6 percent commission to real estate agents. Presumably they do so because they find the service provided to be of value. Similarly, people do benefit from being able to use the services of insurance agents, make deposits at banks, and so forth. To suggest that people in these industries provide socially unnecessary services appears quite arbitrary.

There is an important qualification to this criticism, however. To the extent that the U.S. has become an excessively litigious society, or where financial services include high-priced advice to corporate raiders or management defenders, a strong case can be made for including such payments in the surplus. The point here is that no effort has been made to make this argument or to estimate the relative importance of these activities. By including the output of all these service activities in the surplus, *Monopoly Capital* implies that there would be no need, for example, of financial service employees in a rationally-ordered society. And that conclusion is simply inadmissible.

The sixth and final category in Phillips's estimate of the surplus is government expenditure. All government expenditure is treated as part of the surplus, a procedure which fails to make sense whether the surplus is treated as output less socially necessary costs of production (as in *Monopoly Capital*), or as output less essential consumption (as in the alternative definition suggested below).

Some part of government expenditure does represent surplus absorption; military expenditure provides the clearest example. On the other hand, it is equally evident that part of government expenditure reflects socially necessary costs of production. Expenditure on law and order, for example, provides an institutional framework and security that are essential for a large part of economic activity. Security can be provided by a police force or private security guards. The socialisation of security expenses (their provision by society rather than privately) does not render them optional or less necessary. Similarly, expenditure on education (at least through high school) provides employees with skills essential to functioning in the labour force. The fact that the expenditure is public does not make it any the less essential for the successful functioning of enterprises, whether they are in the private sector or the public sector. Any treatment of the surplus that indiscriminately includes all of government spending, therefore, cannot be justified.

In *Monopoly Capital*, one of the fundamental theses presented concerns an alleged tendency for the surplus to rise (chapter 3). In the Introduction, Sweezy takes note (p. 11) of Phillips' finding that the surplus rose from 46.9 percent of the GNP in 1929 to 56.1 percent in 1963 as supportive of this thesis. *However, the rise in the surplus as calculated by Phillips is accounted for entirely by the rise in government expenditure. In fact, all his table shows is that government expenditure rose as a share of GNP.* From 1929 to 1963, government expenditure rose from $10.2 billion to $168.0 billion, increasing from 9.8 percent to 28.8 percent of GNP (p. 389). The other surplus categories taken together *declined* from 37.1 percent of GNP in 1929 to 27.3 percent in 1963. It is thus only the unacceptable inclusion of all government spending in the surplus that accounts for the statistical support the Appendix provides for the key Baran–Sweezy hypothesis concerning the tendency of the surplus to rise.

A final note concerning the estimates of the surplus provided in *Monopoly Capital* has to do with the omission of a critical category that must be subtracted from national income in calculating the size of the surplus. Only private costs are included in costs; environmental (and other) externalities are excluded. But surely, net output can be meaningfully calculated only when such negative externalities are taken into account. A chemical firm that poisons local rivers must have the costs of its poisoning deducted from its net private output in calculating its net social product, and this procedure is implied by Sweezy and Baran's reference to *socially* necessary costs (p. 76) in calculating the surplus. But nowhere do they follow up on this and the Appendix, following their lead, also omits any calculation of environmental costs. This is not surprising in a book written in the early 1960s, but it represents a serious omission nevertheless. Moreover, as environmental costs tend to rise disproportionately with the growth of population and real GNP, it is certain that they have risen over time, exerting downward pressure on the share of surplus in GNP.

AN ALTERNATIVE CONCEPTION OF THE SURPLUS

It is not difficult to imagine why the concept of the surplus is not present in conventional national income accounting. The conventional accounts have been developed to serve and enhance the modern capitalist system in ways that range from clarifying industry sales prospects to prompting government interventions to ensure the stability of the system. The concept of the surplus, by contrast, is potentially subversive of the system and its chief beneficiaries.

The surplus can be thought of as society's discretionary income, or as that portion of national output that is not needed to provide the population's basic consumption requirements. The elite groups or classes in society are, by definition, those which receive and dispose of the surplus. They do so, of course, in ways that reflect their own interest, but their actions simultaneously shape the character and determine the direction of the entire society. Clarifying the concept of the surplus, measuring it and estimating it call to attention both its unequal appropriation and the frequently deleterious consequences of its disposal by society's elite.

The reasons for considering the nature of the surplus and estimating its size, moreover, may go beyond the demands of social criticism. If, as I argue here, the surplus can be thought of most appropriately as society's 'discretionary' income, then the flexibility or potential scope for action of any given society facing a period of crisis will be circumscribed by the size of its surplus. Further, if the surplus is shrinking over time, as I will argue below is indeed the case in the U.S. and the other advanced industrial countries, then rapid action to deal with crises becomes all the more compelling. Before addressing this issue, however, I would like to clarify the concept of the surplus with which I am working.

On the output–expenditure side of the ledger, the surplus can be thought of most usefully as the difference between national income and the essential consumption requirements of the entire population. That is,

$$Surplus = Y - C_{ess} \qquad (1)$$

The essential consumption requirements do not measure a physical subsistence minimum, but are determined by the prevailing social norms in each country. They include essential public consumption as well as essential private consumption. Thus, for example, if a sixth-grade education is considered basic in one country, then the cost of providing it is part of the country's essential consumption and does not constitute part of the surplus.

It is evident that the concept of 'essential consumption' introduces an element of ambiguity, but it should be kept in mind that that is also true of the conventional national income accounting concepts that we nevertheless find useful. For example, gross national product (GNP) excludes housework, do-it-yourself projects and indeed all productive activities that are not associated with markets, materially understating a nation's production of goods and services, while net national product (NNP) introduces substantial elements of overstatement by failing to take into account the depletion of natural resources, environmental destruction, and so forth. Despite these shortcomings, however, the national income accounts provide valuable information concerning the functioning of national economies. In like fashion, the concept of the surplus, despite the inevitable ambiguities associated with it, can help to provide insights into the functioning of national economies that are otherwise not readily gained.

Like the 'national product' of national income accounting, the surplus can be estimated in 'gross' or 'net' terms; the Appendix to *Monopoly Capital* uses a 'gross' concept, estimating the surplus as a percentage of gross national product. Since we are concerned with using the surplus as a measure of society's 'discretionary' income, however, the net concept would appear to be more useful. This means that in addition to meeting the basic consumption requirements of the population, it is presumed that society must replace the capital stock used up in the production process before the remaining output can be thought of as subject to 'discretionary' allocation.

The term 'discretionary', it shou'd be stressed, is not meant to imply that the surplus is subject to some conscious decision-making process. To the contrary, its appropriation and allocation are embedded in the institutions and class structure of each society. Rather, the surplus is discretionary purely in the sense that it represents resources above and beyond what society requires to reproduce its capital stock and maintain its population at a basic level of decency (according to its own internal standards). In view of these considerations, net investment, whether public or private, must be considered part of the surplus, while depreciation had best be excluded from it. In the equations that follow, however, Y (national income) can be treated as GNP or NNP (and I as gross or net investment accordingly). It will be useful to retain such flexibility at this stage of the analysis so that comparisons can later be made to the estimates of the surplus that appear in *Monopoly Capital*.

In the light of this discussion, the surplus can be presented more explicitly than in equation (1) as

$$\text{Surplus} = Y - C_{ess} - G_{ess} \tag{2}$$

and since

$$Y = C_{noness} + C_{ess} + I_p + I_g + G_{noness} + G_{ess} + (X - IM), \qquad (3)$$

then

$$\text{Surplus} = C_{noness} + I_p + I_g + G_{noness} + (X - IM), \qquad (4)$$

where C_{ess} represents private essential consumption, G_{ess} public essential consumption, C_{noness} private nonessential (luxury) consumption, I_p private net investment, I_g public net investment, G_{noness} public nonessential consumption (such as military expenditure), and $(X - IM)$ exports minus imports (net exports). I will not focus on the net exports concept here, but its formal inclusion in the surplus reflects the fact that part of the surplus can be reflected in an increase in assets held abroad (whether financial or real).

On the income side, the surplus is represented by adding together those sources of income that are not needed to finance essential consumption. As an *initial approximation*, the property share of national income – profits + rent + interest – can be regarded as representing the surplus. This must be adjusted, however, to take into account the various ways in which the nonproperty share fails to measure precisely (the financing of) essential consumption.

First of all, the recipients of property income, like other members of the population, also have essential consumption requirements. That part of the property income that is needed to provide those requirements must be excluded from the surplus.

Second, not all labour (nonproperty) income finances essential consumption. The *average* income of physicians in the U.S. is approximately $150,000 per year, and many professional athletes earn in excess of $1 million. Clearly, the labour income in excess of the amount needed to purchase essential consumption requirements is considerable and must be added to the property share of national income when calculating the surplus.

Finally, some people lack the income to provide even the basic essential consumption requirements. Twenty percent of the children in the United States, for example, grow up in poverty. The income needed to bring that portion of the population up to the essential consumption standard can be called 'the labour income deficit', and it must be subtracted from the property share of national income when calculating the surplus. Thus, from the income side, the surplus can be represented as

Surplus = profit + rent + interest − the essential comsumption of unearned income recipients + that part of labour income which supports nonessential consumption − the labour income deficit.   (5)

Equation (5) calculates the surplus before taking into account the role of the government. To make it parallel to equation (4), government must be included. To do so, we must first specify that all of the income categories noted in equation (5) are post-tax. Next we must add to the other surplus categories that portion of government income that is not used to finance essential public services. This enables us to specify the surplus from the income side in a way that is consistent with equation (4):

Surplus = profit + rent + interest − the essential consumption of unearned income recipients + that part of labour income which supports nonessential consumption − the labour income deficit + that part of government income which is not used for essential public services   (6)

As I have noted, all of the private income categories in equation (6) are after-tax. The most important categories of government income that must be specified as part of the surplus include the income used for (net) public investment, the income used for military spending, and the income drawn off through corrupt activities. This third category is extremely significant in many third-world dictatorships, but is not very important in the advanced industrial economies, where government revenues used to finance military expenditure and (net) public investment constitute the dominant factors in the government's share of the surplus.

Equations (1) and (4) represent alternative ways of looking at the surplus from the output–expenditure perspective of national income accounting; compared to equation (1), equation (4) explicitly takes into account the role of government and international trade. Equation (5) represents the surplus in terms of income categories, while equation (6) modifies (5) to take the public sector into account. Equation (4) can also be thought of as expressing the various ways in which the surplus can be absorbed. No one of these approaches is more valid than the others; they merely provide different perspectives. In calculating the surplus, however, it is important to avoid the conceptual confusion and double-counting that mixing income and expenditure categories can cause.

The conception of the surplus presented here can be thought of as representing society's 'discretionary' income. There is an implicit suggestion that the basic claim on any society's national product is providing for the essential consumption requirements of the entire population. Output above and beyond this represents the surplus. It can be absorbed in a wide variety of ways ranging from luxury consumption and military expenditure to investment.   The dominant classes in any society are composed of those who receive and dispose of the surplus. The character of the society is reflected in and shaped by their use of the surplus.

A PRELIMINARY ESTIMATE OF THE U.S. SURPLUS

Since the national income accounts in the United States are not compiled with a view to facilitating estimates of the surplus, any estimates we can make will of necessity be quite rough, and will require making use of materials gathered for other purposes. Thus, for example, the U.S. Bureau of the Census and the Conference Board have produced jointly a book entitled *A Marketers' Guide to Discretionary Income*, with editions published in 1983 and 1989. As the title indicates, this book is meant to help marketers identify those parts of the population with enough income to buy luxury goods. The way in which discretionary income is specified may not provide precisely what we are looking for, but it is close enough to facilitate an initial rough estimate.

As equation (4) indicates,

$$\text{Surplus} = C_{noness} + I_p + I_g + G_{noness} + (X - IM).$$

An estimate of the surplus in the U.S. can be based on estimates of each of the components indicated. C_{noness} (nonessential consumption) can be estimated according to the data presented in *A Marketers' Guide to Discretionary Income* (U.S. Bureau of the Census, 1983 and 1989).   The 1983 edition provides data for 1980 while the 1989 edition provides data for 1986; the 1986 data cited here are from *The Statistical Abstract of the United States 1990* (U.S. Bureau of the Census, 1990), p. 448, which cites the 1989 edition as its source.

According to the *Marketers' Guide* (1980),

The term 'discretionary income' is widely used to denote the money available for luxuries and the good life after all necessary expenditures. . .

[Discretionary income] is defined as the amount of money that would permit a family to maintain a standard of living higher than the average of that of similar families. . . Households with spendable income exceeding the average of their group by 30% or more were considered to have discretionary income. (p. 7)

In 1980, slightly over 25 million or about 31 percent of U.S. households were in the discretionary income class, with the proportion dropping to 28.9 percent in 1986. The proportion of after-tax household income regarded as discretionary, however, rose from 14.4 percent in 1980 to 14.7 percent in 1986. As an approximation, I will treat 14.7 percent of 1986 consumption or $411.2 billion as representing the nonessential (luxury) consumption component of the surplus (figures for consumption and the other national income categories that follow are from the *Statistical Abstract 1990*, pp. 275, 425 and 428). Since about 5 percent of disposable income goes into saving in the U.S., and since those households with discretionary income undoubtedly account for a disproportionate share of national saving, an argument could be made for adjusting the C_{noness} figure down by about 10 percent. I have not done so, however, since a number of offsetting considerations exist.

First, the income data come from tax returns, and it has been easier to hide property income, which is not susceptible to withholding taxes, than wage and salary income, which is. Moreover, depreciation charges for houses and other structures have tended to sharply overstate their actual depreciation, arbitrarily understating the income of real-estate holders. Various tax shelters, moreover, of greater use to high-income recipients than to low income recipients, also provide ways of disguising income.[4] Finally, the 30-percent-above-average criterion for discretionary income is of course arbitrary; why not 25 percent, for example? When these various considerations are taken into account, it seems best to retain the $411.2 billion figure for C_{noness}.

Gross private investment (I_p) in 1986 was $659.4 billion, while government investment (I_g) was $104.1 billion. Government investment includes state and local investment, but excludes military investment, which is part of government spending on national defense (G_{noness}). National defense spending amounted to $277.8 billion in 1986. Net exports (X − IM) in 1986 were −$97.4 billion. Subtracting this amount from the other components of the surplus raises some questions. For example, an increase in imports of Mercedes Benz and other luxury automobiles reduces net exports and therefore the surplus. At first glance this does not appear to be reasonable. Nevertheless, if we think of the surplus in terms of domestic production, then the borrowing from abroad that a deficit in the trade balance implies represents a use of the foreign surplus rather than the domestic one.

To return to equation (4), and presenting estimates of the 1986 U.S. surplus components in billions of dollars:

$$\text{Surplus} = C_{noness} + I_p + I_g + G_{noness} + (X - IM) \qquad (4)$$
$$\text{Surplus} = 411.2 + 659.4 + 104.1 + 277.8 - 97.4$$
$$\text{Surplus} = \$1,355.1 \text{ billion}$$

Since GNP was $4,231.6 billion in 1986, (gross) surplus as a share of GNP was 1,355.1 divided by 4,231.6 or 32.0 percent. However, as I have argued above, the net surplus is a more appropriate concept. Since 1986 depreciation was $460.1 billion and NNP $3,771.5 billion, the net investment was $199.3 billion and the net surplus was $895.0 billion, constituting 23.7 percent of NNP.

CONCLUSION

The estimates presented here suggest that (net) surplus amounted to 23.7 percent of the U.S. net national product in 1986. Like the estimates presented in *Monopoly Capital*, these estimates are based on government data collected for other purposes and perforce are extremely rough. They do not take into account environmental destruction, moreover, and thus like the estimates in *Monopoly Capital* tend to overstate the surplus in this regard. At the same time, there are elements of probable understatement. The calculation of depreciation, for example, which is needed to estimate net investment, is based on government accounting rules that often bear little relation to the actual useful life of productive assets. My guess is that depreciation is too high, especially in the case of structures, systematically lowering the value of the surplus. At the same time, I have included only government investment and military spending as part of the government's absorption of surplus, and a case could be made for including some additional portion of government spending.

In spite of these qualifications, however, a major difference emerges between my estimate of the surplus and that presented in *Monopoly Capital*, between the 23.7 percent of NNP (or 32.0 percent of GNP) I estimate for 1986, and the 56.1 percent of GNP *Monopoly Capital* estimates for 1963, a figure it was claimed tended to rise on a secular basis – and which therefore would presumably have been larger by 1986. The difference is based both on conception and method, and the approach I have presented here suggests a quite different understanding of the dynamics and contradictions of advanced capitalism than that presented in *Monopoly Capital.*

The work of Sweezy and Baran grows out of both the tradition of Marxian scholarship that emphasises the productivity and waste of advanced capitalist society, and the progressive cultural critique that emerged in the U.S. in the 1950s decrying commercialism and economic irrationality, a critique reflected in works like John Kenneth Galbraith's *The Affluent Society* (1958) and Paul Goodman's *Growing Up Absurd* (1960). Sweezy and Baran counterpose the vast and growing productive capacity of advanced capitalism on the one hand to its destructiveness and inability to meet human needs on the other, a juxtaposition that is given specific form in their theory of the tendency of the surplus to rise. The rising surplus reflects for them the fact that the growing productive capacity of advanced capitalism is matched by growing wastefulness in the absorption of the goods and services it generates.

Their vision is a powerful one, but I believe it simplifies far too much. Wastefulness and irrationality are certainly present, but the capitalist world system toward the close of the twentieth century must also be understood in terms of expanding population and world economic production raising sharply environmental and other costs generated by increasingly dense and complex human interaction. Most of these costs appear in the form of externalities, so that they are systematically understated by vast amounts in the national accounts of both advanced capitalist societies and the state 'socialist' ones of the Soviet type. The failure to take these costs into account makes the surplus appear to be far larger than in fact it is.

Nevertheless, a substantial surplus is being generated in the economies of the advanced capitalist countries, and the manner of its absorption does contribute to shaping their destiny. I have argued that a more useful conception of the surplus can be specified as the difference between net output and essential consumption (with net output being smaller than it appears on the surface due to the rising externalities noted). Those who control the use of the surplus in the advanced capitalist countries are no longer the nineteenth-century-type captains of industry (although the late twentieth century has created its own variant of a few of these in the form of people like William Gates of Microsoft and Sam Walton of Wal-Mart). They are primarily financial deal-makers on the one hand, and those with special talents and skills on the other, people who are successful in their rent-seeking endeavors. This latter group includes those entertainers, professional athletes, lawyers, doctors and other professionals who are able to raise their earnings far above what competitive markets would yield.

Like their nineteenth-century counterparts, the contemporary recipients of the surplus perceive their interest in terms of low taxation and high luxury spending. Unlike them, they have devoted a much larger share of national income to national defense, itself a reflection of the growing inter-connectedness of the world. Outside of national defense, however, the other problems evoked by changed world conditions have not evoked a substantial response. World overpopulation, social deterioration and environmental destruction, which of course are related phenomena, are sharply raising the social costs of productive activity. Unless a means can be found to divert a significant share of the surplus to addressing these problems, they may well grow beyond the capacity of the surplus to finance solutions. Sweezy and Baran were correct in seeing the use of the surplus in advanced capitalism as supporting waste and self-indulgence. They were incorrect in seeing it as growing. And they failed to perceive the emerging crisis of social and environmental deterioration that a shrinking surplus must be used to address while it is still large enough to do so. Unless the surplus is redirected in large measure to this end, the capacity of advanced industrial society to reproduce itself will be sorely tested in the century to come.

NOTES

* I am indebted to Professors A. R. Khan and Robert Pollin, colleagues of mine in the Economics Department at the University of California, Riverside, for their constructive criticisms of an earlier draft of this essay.

1. In his Foreword to the 1962 printing, Baran presents still another conception of the surplus, one which is quite distinct from the others. For a discussion of the various conceptions of the surplus presented by Baran in *The Political Economy of Growth*, see Lippit (1985).

2. The systemic problems of Soviet-type economies have been well documented in the literature. Problems range from the lack of criteria for efficient resource allocation to the establishment of incentives for work effort and innovation. See, for example, Alec Nove (1986).

3. Sweezy suggests (Introduction to *Monopoly Capital*, p. 11) that total property income – profit + rent + interest – can also be thought of as the national income accounting expression of Marxian theory's 'surplus value'. Marx's theory, however, assumed, in addition to competitive product markets, competitive labour markets with an endemic oversupply of labour that would force wages down to subsistence levels (the levels needed to maintain and reproduce the labour force). Marx's surplus value, therefore, the difference between the total product of labour and the (subsistence) wages it receives,

has no precise counterpart in the national income accounts of 'monopoly' capitalism.
4.   Such tax shelters include mortgage interest deductions for vacation homes, business travel, entertainment expenses, and so forth.

REFERENCES

Baran, Paul (1957). *The Political Economy of Growth*, New York: Monthly Review Press.

Baran, Paul and Paul Sweezy (1966). *Monopoly Capital*, New York: Monthly Review Press.

Baumol, William and Alan Blinder (1991). *Macroeconomics*, Orlando: Harcourt, Brace, Jovanovich.

Business Week, 15 July 1991.

Fortune, 29 July 1991.

Galbraith, John K. (1958). *The Affluent Society*, Boston: Houghton Mifflin.

Goodman, Paul (1960). *Growing Up Absurd*, New York: Random House.

Lippit, Victor D. (1985). 'The Concept of the Surplus in Economic Development', *Review of Radical Political Economics*, 17 (1 & 2), 1–19.

Marx, Karl (1967). *Capital*, vol. 1. New York: International Publishers.

Nove, Alec (1986). *The Soviet Economic System*, 3rd ed. Boston: Allen & Unwin.

U.S. Dept. of Commerce, Bureau of the Census (1990). *Statistical Abstract of the United States: 1990*, Washington, D.C.: U.S. Government Printing Office.

U.S. Dept. of Commerce, Bureau of the Census, and The Conference Board (1983 and 1989). *A Marketer's Guide to Discretionary Income*. Washington, D.C.: U.S. Government Printing Office.

6. Stagnation, Growth, and Unproductive Activity

*Amitava Krishna Dutt**

INTRODUCTION

Baran and Sweezy (1966) examined the behaviour of an advanced capitalist economy in the stage of monopoly capitalism, in which the economy is dominated by large, oligopolistic firms which, rather than taking prices from markets, set them. At the prices they set, these firms may not be able to sell all the output that they can produce; consequently, they will cut production and not realise their entire surplus value. According to Baran and Sweezy, firms in this situation try to increase their sales through increased unproductive activity (such as advertising), and the government also increases unproductive activity, primarily by spending on national defense. This activity may have the effect of increasing output by increasing demand (as a result of sales promotion) directly through particular forms of unproductive activity, and indirectly, by increasing employment, wage payments, and hence aggregate demand. It follows from this analysis that increased unproductive activity has a positive effect on the economy.

In what appears to be sharp contradiction to Baran and Sweezy's analysis, several analysts of advanced capitalist economies have tried to explain stagnation in terms of the growth of unproductive activities and sectors. The definition of such sectors is not always uniform in these discussions – with some focusing on services (Baumol, 1967) and non-market (Bacon and Eltis, 1976) sectors as the problem sectors[1] – but a number of analysts (Wolff, 1987, Moseley, 1988) seem to have used the same Marxian notion of unproductive activities used by Baran and Sweezy. This notion draws on Marx's (1977) distinction between productive and unproductive labour: productive labour is used in production proper and the creation of value, while unproductive labour is involved in circulation and supervisory activities which are necessary for the sale of commodities or the maintenance or transfer of their ownership.[2] Wolff (1987) develops a growth model of an economy with an unproductive sector and shows how this sector, because it experiences no productivity growth, increasingly draws away resources from the technologically-progressive productive sector, slowing down the rate of growth of the economy. Moseley (1988) argues that because unproductive labour does not experience productivity growth and productive labour does, production increasingly requires a relatively larger amount of unproductive labour, which reduces the surplus available for capital accumulation.

This paper attempts to resolve this contradiction between the recent analysis which emphasises the stagnating effects of the growth of unproductive activity, and the growth-inducing effects of such activity discussed by Baran and Sweezy. The next section briefly examines the recent contributions and discusses how they ignore important issues stressed in the Baran–Sweezy vision of the economy. It will be argued, in particular, that the recent contributions employ different notions of surplus than that emphasised by Baran and Sweezy. The subsequent section develops a simple model of unproductive activity along Baran–Sweezy lines to show that a relative increase in unproductive activity may increase the rate of accumulation. The penultimate section considers some modifications of the model to show that this positive effect may in fact be reversed in certain situations.

RECENT ANALYSES OF THE ROLE OF UNPRODUCTIVE ACTIVITY

Wolff (1987) argues that the slowdown in growth in the U.S. in recent years has been caused by a relative expansion of unproductive activity in the Marxian sense described earlier. Not only has he marshalled a large amount of empirical data to show the connection between stagnation and the growth of unproductive activity in the U.S. economy, but he has also developed a formal growth model to explain the nature of the causal mechanism. We use this model as a point of entry into our discussion.

In this model Wolff divides the economy into two sectors, one in which activity is productive and the other in which it is unproductive. Each sector uses labour, capital (which is produced by the productive sector) and intermediate inputs purchased from the other sector.[3] In the unproductive sector labour (which is by definition entirely unproductive) and capital bear a fixed ratio to the output of the productive sector, and unproductive labour in the productive sector also bears a fixed ratio with productive sector output. The output of the productive sector is produced with a Cobb-Douglas production function using productive labour and capital as inputs (which implies that unproductive labour and inputs purchased from the unproductive sector have no impact on output), and there is a given rate of disembodied, neutral, technical progress over time. Output of the productive sector used as intermediate input into the unproductive sector and unproductive inputs purchased by the productive sector are fixed proportions of total output of the productive sector. Final product, which includes final output only of the productive sector, is either consumed or invested, each of these being a constant proportion of final product (which is consistent with the assumption of a constant saving rate out of final income). The rate of growth of the labour force is fixed exogenously.

At a point in time total labour supply is allocated between the two sectors as productive and unproductive labour according to the assumptions stated above, and so is the available supply of capital. Over time the stock of capital increases due to investment, and labour supply and the productivity in the productive sector grow at the exogenously fixed rates. Wolff shows that over time the rate of growth of labour productivity falls, and ratio of unproductive labour to total labour increases. As time approaches infinity, the overall rate of productivity growth approaches zero, the rates of growth of productive output and capital approach the rate of growth of labour supply, and the ratio of unproductive to total labour approaches one. Finally, Wolff shows that in comparison to a similar model (making the same assumptions and with the same parameters and Cobb-Douglas production function), but one which does not contain an unproductive sector and unproductive labour, the limiting values of output growth, capital accumulation and labour productivity growth are all lower in his model.

As Wolff himself notes, the basic assumption of his model is that unproductive inputs are absorbed in productive output at a constant ratio. Since productivity (of productive labour and capital) in the productive sector is growing over time, but unproductive inputs enter into production with fixed proportions, unproductive employment as a percentage of total employment rises over time. The same also happens to capital, which is increasingly absorbed by the unproductive sector. This growing importance of the technologically stagnant unproductive activity reduces the growth of output of the productive sector over time in an economy in which labour and capital are fully employed.

Three crucial features of Wolff's model, which are important for understanding its differences with Baran and Sweezy's analysis, may be noted.

First, Wolff assumes that productive inputs (labour and capital in the productive sector) experience a given rate of technological change, but this is not the case with unproductive inputs and labour which are always required in a fixed proportion to productive output. This follows Baumol's (1967) distinction between the technologically-stagnant services sector and the technologically-progressive industrial sector, and exactly as in Baumol's model, provides a reason both for a relative expansion of unproductive activity and for its stagnating role in the growth process.[4] Both Wolff (1988) and Moseley (1988) argue that given the nature of unproductive activity (that is, it is intensive in labour services), it cannot be technologically progressive like productive activity. Baran and Sweezy, on the other hand, do not distinguish between the technological progressiveness of the different kinds of activity,[5] and instead focus on the fact that due to the rise in monopoly power and the consequent rise in importance of sales problems, firms would increase their use of unproductive inputs, for instance, to increase sales efforts.

Second, Wolff assumes that labour is always fully employed in the economy, and that the real wage varies to clear the labour market as in Solow's neoclassical growth model. This implies that his vision of the functioning of the economy is very different from the Marxian vision which takes the economic surplus to given by the state of class struggle. In the Marxian vision, given the existence of a reserve army of the unemployed, the distribution of income between workers and capitalists is given by class struggle.[6] Workers consume all their income, and capitalists receive the surplus, out of which saving and hence accumulation takes place. In this vision the surplus determines the rate of accumulation (with saving perhaps a constant fraction of the surplus), while in Wolff's model saving is assumed to be a constant fraction of total income, so that the surplus, and hence income distribution, are irrelevant in determining the rate of accumulation. In Wolff's model unproductive activity causes stagnation by absorbing a rising amount of fully-employed labour, whereas in a Marxian approach one would need to focus on the surplus and the capital accumulation process.

Moseley (1988) has recently adopted such a Marxian surplus approach in explaining stagnation due to the growth of unproductive activity: because unproductive labour does not experience technological progress and productive labour does, the economy requires an increasingly higher amount of unproductive labour per unit of productive labour, which under certain conditions implies that a larger proportion of the surplus (defined as output minus payments to productive inputs) must be paid to unproductive labour, thereby slowing down the rate of accumulation.[7] This approach, which places the surplus at centre stage, is closer to the Baran–Sweezy approach than Wolff's neoclassical approach assuming fully employed labour.

Third, both Wolff and Moseley assume that all saving is automatically invested, which implies that firms are able to sell all they produce and that they face no realisation problems. This is in sharp contradiction to the approach of Baran and Sweezy, which assumes that firms cannot sell all they can produce, so that they cannot realise their *potential* surplus. It is because of such realisation problems that firms with monopoly power, as well as the government, increasingly resort to unproductive activities. For Baran and Sweezy the *actual* surplus, which is affected by the firms' sales constraints, is what is relevant for the rate of accumulation, whereas Moseley, by not distinguishing between the potential and actual surpluses, does not give any role whatsoever to the problem of realisation.[8]

Wolff, among the more recent writers, does realise that his analysis is very different from that of Baran and Sweezy regarding this last point. He writes:

> Whereas the emphasis of their argument is on the *realisation* of surplus value, the one presented here is on the *disposition* of surplus value. In particular, an increase in unproductive activity must reduce, ceteris paribus, the amount of surplus product available for capital formation. So, even if unproductive expenditures should stimulate production by closing the effective demand "gap", their effect on capital accumulation is, at best, indeterminate and most likely, negative. . . . In general, unproductive activity reduces the resources available for capital accumulation and therefore exerts a deleterious effect on productivity and overall growth. The approach here emphasises the supply-side consequences of unproductive activity, whereas the Baran and Sweezy approach emphasises the demand-side effects.
>
> Another way of contrasting. . . [Wolff's approach] with that of Baran and Sweezy is that. . . [Wolff's] looks at the *dynamic* implications of unproductive expenditure, whereas theirs looks at its static implications. Their approach also reflects the Keynesian bias of considering the short-term effects of inadequate demand on the *current level* of output. [Wolff]. . . is more concerned with the long-run implications of the effect of unproductive activity on capital formation and thus the *growth* of output. (Wolff, 1987: 22-3, italics in original)

He continues:

> [Baran and Sweezy's] conception grows out of a Keynesian-type effective demand model that is essentially *static* in character. From a dynamic perspective, unproductive activity must be considered irrational from a social viewpoint since it diverts resources away from capital formation. (Wolff, 1987: 173, italics in original)

Wolff's position, based on the distinctions between demand and supply factors, short-term and long-term factors, and static and dynamic analysis, however, may be argued to be untenable. Regarding the role of demand and supply-side factors, the only way to satisfactorily resolve the issue is to develop an analysis which incorporates both sides. In Wolff's model, there is no demand side at all, even though firms are assumed to spend on advertising and other unproductive activities which actually presuppose that demand problems exist. Regarding the role of short run versus long run, unless one develops a specific theory to show that demand problems disappear in the long run (defined in a suitable way), Wolff's argument is a *non sequitur*. Several models have been built extending Keynes–Kalecki-type analysis where effective demand plays a role in affecting growth rather than just the level of output, with Robinson (1956) playing a pioneering role in these developments. The Baran–Sweezy argument can also not be called a static one. The failure of firms to realise their potential surplus in their analysis implies that they obtain low rates of profit, and experience low rates of capacity utilisation, and both of these tendencies can depress their rate of accumulation. This would depress the rate of growth of output, a 'dynamic' variable, in addition to the level of output in the short run. We may conclude that the contradiction between Baran and Sweezy's analysis and the more recent contributions cannot be resolved by appealing to distinctions like those mentioned by Wolff.

A BARAN–SWEEZY MODEL WITH UNPRODUCTIVE ACTIVITY

In this section we develop a model of an economy with an unproductive sector along the lines of Wolff which is closer to Baran and Sweezy's view of the advanced capitalist economy. The model draws on the work of Kalecki (1971) and Steindl (1952), who were in fact cited by Baran and Sweezy in providing some of the theoretical underpinnings of their own work.[9]

The Model

We assume, following Wolff, that there are two sectors in the economy, one productive and the other unproductive, denoted by p and u, respectively. Productive output is used for consumption and for investment in the two sectors (and for simplicity we ignore its intermediate use in either sector), while unproductive output is used in the p-sector, not as a factor of production in the usual sense, but to facilitate sales: we could think of it as advertising products. Each sector uses capital and labour in production, and labour is by definition unproductive in the u-sector, and partly productive and partly unproductive in the p-sector.

The economy is oligopolistic, and producers set prices by marking up their prime costs by given markup rates which depends on the degree of monopoly power – *à la* Kalecki (1971) – in each sector. Firms hold excess capital, require direct labour (which is productive labour in the p-sector) in production in a fixed proportion to production, and treat overhead labour (which is unproductive labour in the p-sector) as having no necessary relation to the level of output. Expenses on the output of the u-sector are also treated as overhead (there is no necessary relation between output and unproductive inputs) by p-sector firms, and such inputs are ignored in the u-sector (or netted out). It follows from all this that the price in each sector is given by

$$P_i = b_i W(1+z_i) \qquad (1)$$

for $i = p, u$, where P_i is the price of the output, b_i the unit direct labour requirement, and z_i the markup, all for sector i, and W the money wage which is assumed to be given, for simplicity. Also for simplicity we assume fixed coefficients technology regarding direct labour, so that b_i are fixed.

Firms also make decisions regarding the use of unproductive labour, the use of the product of the unproductive sector (only in the productive sector) and the level of investment. Each sector uses overhead labour as a fixed proportion, c_i, of its capital stock, and the productive sector demands the output of the unproductive sector which is a given proportion, Θ, of the stock of capital of that sector. These ratios depend on a variety of factors, including the degree of monopoly in the economy (which affects the amount of sales effort), the development of technology in a broad sense (to cover communications and media technology), and the nature of work organisation (if we include supervisors as unproductive labour). Finally, following Steindl (1952), we assume that the rate of investment of firms depends on the degree of capacity utilisation; for simplicity we assume this dependence to be linear, so that investment is given by

$$I_i/K_i = \alpha_i + \beta_i(X_i/K_i) \tag{2}$$

for $i = p, u$, where I_i is the level of investment, K_i the stock of capital and X_i the level of output, for sector i. Both coefficients in the functions are assumed to be positive. The intercept terms reflects business psychology and technological factors which necessitate the introduction of new machines to allow firms to compete successfully with their rivals, and β_i measures how firms respond to increases in the rate of capacity utilisation by increasing the rate of investment.[10]

Workers, who earn wage income, consume all of it, and are in unlimited supply, while capitalists – who receive the entire profit income – save a fraction s of it; s is taken to be given for now. This, and our earlier assumptions, imply that total demand the output of the each sector is given by

$$D_p = (b_pX_p+b_uX_u+c_pK_p+c_uK_u)(W/P_p)+(1-s)[(z_pb_pX_p+z_ub_uX_u \\ -c_pK_p-c_uK_u)(W/P_p)-\Theta K_p(P_u/P_p)]+I_p+I_u \tag{3}$$

$$D_u = \Theta K_p \tag{4}$$

where D_i is the demand for the output of sector i in physical units.

We examine the behaviour of this economy in the short run and the long run.

The Short Run

In the short run K_p and K_u are given, and production in each sector adjusts to meet the demand for its product. We formalise this adjustment with the simple equations

$$dX_i/dt = \Sigma_i[D_i - X_i] \tag{5}$$

for $i = p,u$, where t denotes time, and where $\Sigma_i>0$ are speed of adjustment constants.

Equation (5) can be written, upon substitution from equations (1) through (4), as

$$dX_p/dt = \Sigma_p\{-[s(z_p/(1+z_p))-\beta_p]X_p+[((1+z_u)b_u/\mu_p)-(sz_ub_u/\mu_p)+\beta_u]X_u \\ + [(c_pK_p+c_uK_u)/\mu_p] + \alpha_pK_p+\alpha_uK_u - (1-s)[(1+z_u)b_u/\mu_p]\Theta K_p\} \tag{6}$$

$$dX_u/dt = \Sigma_u[\Theta K_p - X_u] \tag{7}$$

where $\mu_i = (1+z_i)b_i$.

For short-run equilibrium we require stationary values of X_i for given values of the parameters in the short run. For the u- sector this requires

$$X_u = \Theta K_p \tag{8}$$

For the p sector it requires, taking equation (8) into account,

$$X_p = \frac{[((sb_u/\mu_p)+\beta_u)\Theta+\alpha_p+(sc_p/\mu_p)]K_p+[\alpha_u+(sc_u/\mu_p)]K_u}{[s(z_p/(1+z_p))-\beta_p]} \tag{9}$$

The (local) stability of short-run equilibrium requires

$$s(z_p/(1+z_p)) - \beta_p > 0$$

which is the usual macroeconomic condition that the responsiveness of saving to the level of activity exceeds that of investment. Note that this condition guarantees a positive solution to X_u in equation (9). We further assume that the solution values of X_i in equations (8) and (9) obey the technical constraints to guarantee the existence of excess capacity, or that $K_i/X_i \geq a_i$ where a_i is the technologically required capital–output ratio.

The Long Run

In the long run, when K_i are no longer fixed, assuming that there is no depreciation of capital, we get

$$dK_i/dt = I_i \tag{10}$$

for $i = p, u$. To examine the movement of the economy in the long run we define $k = K_u/K_p$, which implies that (with overhats denoting time-rates of growth)

$$\hat{k} = \hat{K}_u - \hat{K}_p \tag{11}$$

We examine the growth rates of K_u and K_p to examine that of k. From equations (8) and (2) and (10) for i=u we get

$$\hat{K}_u = \alpha_u + \beta_u\Theta/k \tag{12}$$

From equations (9) and (2) and (10) for i=p we get

$$\hat{K}_p = \alpha_p + \beta_p \{ [(sb_u/\mu_p) + \beta_u]\Theta + \alpha_p + (sc_p/\mu_p) + [\alpha_u + (sc_u/\mu_p)]k \} / [s(z_p/(1+z_p)) - \beta_p]$$

(13)

Figure 1 shows the curves corresponding to equations (12) and (13) as the g^u and g^p curves respectively, showing the growth rates of K_u and K_p respectively, with k as the independent variable. The g^u curve is seen to be downward-sloping, while the g^p curve to be upward-rising. By equation (11), the g^k curve, showing the growth rate of k, is seen to be given by the vertical difference between the g^u and g^p curves.

We therefore find that we can write equation (11) as

$$\hat{k} = F(k)$$

(14)

where the derivative, $F'<0$. The long run equilibrium value of k is k_e, where $k_e = F^{-1}(0)$. Since $F'<0$, this long run equilibrium is seen to be stable. Thus, starting from any $k = K_u/K_p$, the economy is seen to attain its long-run equilibrium at k_e.

Implications of the Model

We comment on two properties of the model.

First, we see that for given values of the parameters of the model, there is no inverse relation between the growth rate of the productive sector (measured by g^p) and the relative size of the unproductive sector (measured by k) on the dynamic growth path of the economy.[11] Quite to the contrary, if the economy starts from k below (above) k_e, k will rise (fall) over time, and g^p will rise (fall); this implies that the growth rate of the productive sector and the relative size of the unproductive sector will actually be *positively* related over time, *ceteris paribus*. This relationship can be explained as follows. Our assumptions make the rate of growth of the productive sector independent of the *scale* of the economy (that is, the absolute size of the stocks of capital in the two sectors as long as their ratio is constant). A higher level of capital stock in the unproductive sector, for a given level of capital in the productive sector, however, results in a higher relative rate of accumulation and growth in the unproductive sector. This increases the demand for the output of the productive sector as an investment good, and also increases the demand for the productive good as a consumption good because of the increased spending by unproductive labour employed in the unproductive sector. This expansion in demand (which is magnified by the standard multiplier effect) increases the rate of accumulation in the productive sector through the accelerator effects on investment.

Second, we examine the implications of parametric shifts. We confine here our attention to shifts in c_i and Θ, parameters which directly capture the importance of unproductive activity. Equation (13) shows that an increase in c_p or c_u, measuring the use of unproductive labour in the p and u sectors as a ratio of stocks of capital increase g^p for given k, implying an upward shift in the g^p curve of Figure 1. Equation (12) shows that the g^u curve is unaffected. The consequence of these changes is a short-run (for given k) increase in g^p, and then a reduction in g^p (as the economy moves down the g^p curve) to a new long-run equilibrium with a higher g^p than the initial long-run equilibrium, and a lower k_c. The effect of an increase in Θ is more difficult to analyse, since equations (12) and (13) show that *both* curves move upward. The effect on g^p is clearly positive – both in the short and the long runs. The effect on k_c, however, is indeterminate in general. The positive effect on the growth rate of an increase in unproductive activity is due to the fact that an increase in such activity transfers income from profits to wages, out of which there is a higher propensity to consume, therefore raising aggregate demand, capacity utilisation, and growth.

We have here assumed that an increase in unproductive activity does not change the rate of saving by capitalists. If we instead assume that an increase in c_p and Θ results in an increase in *total* consumption demand, and this is reflected by a reduction in s,[12] we get

$$s = s(\Theta, c_p) \qquad (15)$$

where both partial derivatives are negative. It is easy to see from equation (13) that an increase in Θ or c_p, by reducing s, will further shift the g^p curve upwards, further increasing the rate of growth of the economy. Thus the results of the previous paragraph are strengthened if we take this effect into account. Having noted this, we henceforth assume that s is exogenously fixed.

These effects on the growth rate can be examined in terms of the effects on different notions of surplus. To do so, let us rewrite the short-run equilibrium conditions from equation (6) and (7), with $dX_i/dt = 0$, as

$$s[r_p K_p + r_u K_u] = g^p K_p + g^u K_u \qquad (16)$$

where r_i are rates of profit in the two sectors, given by

$$r_p = [z_p/(1+z_p)](X_p/K_p)-(c_p/\mu_p)-(\mu_u/\mu_p)\Theta \qquad (17)$$

and

$$r_u = [(z_u b_u/\mu_p)\Theta/k]-(c_u/\mu_p). \qquad (18)$$

Equation (16) is simply the aggregate saving–investment equality condition for the economy. The effects on investment, and hence capital accumulation, can thus be examined by focusing on the effects on saving, or the surplus.[13]

To simplify the discussion, consider the case of one sector in which output is produced with productive and unproductive labour, and there is no unproductive sector. In this case the actual surplus, or saving, is given by

$$S_A = srK = s\{[z/(1+z)](X/K)-(c/\mu)\}K \qquad (19)$$

where subscripts have been dropped since there is only one, productive, sector. This actual surplus, which is equal to investment, however, is different from potential surplus which would determine the rate at which the economy could potentially invest. If we assume that workers are earning 'subsistence' wages, and that profit earners have negligible (zero) consumption needs, and ignore output lost 'because of the irrational and wasteful organisation of the existing productive apparatus' other than that due to the existence of unproductive activity (Baran, 1957: 24), the difference between actual and potential surplus arises only because of (a) capitalist consumption, (b) the existence of unproductive labour and output and (c) the deficiency of demand. The potential surplus is thus given by

$$S_P = [z/(1+z)]aK \qquad (20)$$

which sets s=1 (so that capitalists do not consume), c=0 (so that there is no unproductive labour) and X/K=a (so that there is no deficiency in demand resulting in excess capacity with X/K<a) in (19), where a is the maximum technologically-feasible output–capital ratio. Alternative concepts of potential surplus, intermediate between S_A and S_P, are

$$S_{P1} = \{[z/(1+z)]a - (c/\mu)\}K \qquad (21)$$

and

$$S_{P2} = s\{[z/(1+z)]a - (c/\mu)\}K \qquad (22)$$

where the former takes into account the loss in potential surplus due to the existence of unproductive labour, and the latter also takes into account the loss due to capitalist consumption.

A rise in the use of unproductive labour in this simple model implies a rise in c. This clearly has no effect on S_P, since this is defined by ignoring unproductive labour, but it does affect S_A, S_{P1} and S_{P2}. From (21) and (22) we see that the two latter surpluses indeed fall. However, these surpluses are irrelevant for the actual rate of growth of the economy, since they are defined for the hypothetical situation in which there is no demand problem in the economy. In reality, $X/K < a$, due to demand deficiency. A rise in c tends to reduce the actual surplus by reducing the second term in (19), but in Baran and Sweezy's analysis the rise in labour demand also redistributes income from profit-recipients to workers, raises demand and hence capacity utilisation, both directly and through the induced increase in investment. Since in this one-sector case

$$X/K = \alpha + (sc/\mu)/\{s[z/(1+z)] - \beta\} \qquad (23)$$

the rise in c increases X/K, and since the saving–investment equality implies

$$S_A = [\alpha + \beta(X/K)]K$$

S_A increases with c.[14] It thus follows that the surplus-reducing effect of the rise in c is more than offset by the surplus-increasing effect. It is only by ignoring the surplus-increasing effect, that is, by ignoring the problem of demand deficiency, and using surplus concepts S_{P1} and S_{P2}, that the inverse relation between c and accumulation can be obtained in our model.

The two-sector extension of this analysis only needs to take into account the fact, as shown in equation (16), that accumulation in the productive sector is equal to the surplus in the productive sector plus the surplus in the unproductive sector less accumulation in the unproductive sector. Since this extension is straightforward, and does not provide further insight into the relation between unproductive labour and different concepts of surplus, we eschew its detailed examination.

MODIFICATIONS OF THE MODEL

The previous section has shown that in an economy in which realisation problems are important, a relative increase in the size of the unproductive sector is associated with a higher rate of growth of the productive sector, and parametric changes implying a higher rate of unproductive activity also imply a higher rate of productive sector growth. This section examines three simple modifications of the model to show that these results do not always hold.

Differences Between Direct and Overhead Workers

In the first modification we allow for the possibility that direct and overhead workers may belong to different classes, so that they may have different characteristics. We assume, in particular, that overhead workers receive a higher wage, mW (where $m>1$), which is a multiple of the wage of direct workers, and that they are therefore rich enough to save, so that they save a fraction s_w of their income. But since they are poorer than profit-recipients we assume that $s_c>s_w$, where s_c is the saving rate of capitalists. For simplicity, we consider the one-sector case, following Nichols and Norton (1990).[15]

Our assumptions imply that aggregate demand is given by

$$D = [bX+(1-s_w)mcK+(1-s_c)(X-bX-mcK)]W/P + I \qquad (24)$$

We also depart from our earlier analysis and take into account the fact that the rate of profit, in addition to the rate of capacity utilisation, may have an effect on the desired rate of investment,[16] so that we replace (2) by

$$I/K = \alpha + \beta(X/K) + \tau r \qquad (25)$$

where τ is a positive parameter, and

$$r = [z/(1+z)](X/K) - mc/(1+z)b \qquad (26)$$

Using (1) (dropping subscripts), and (24) through (26), we can show that in equilibrium, when $X = D$,[17]

$$X/K = [\alpha+(s_c-s_w-\tau)mc]/b[(s_c-\tau)z-\beta(1+z)]. \qquad (27)$$

The equilibrium rate of accumulation is given by

$$g = \alpha + \{\beta+\tau[z/(1+z)]\}(X/K) - \tau mc/(1+z)b \qquad (28)$$

where X/K is given in (27).

To examine the consequences of a rise in unproductive activity we differentiate g with respect to c in equation (28), using (27), to get

$$dg/dc = [m/(1+z)b][s_c\beta-s_w(\beta+\tau Z)]/[(s_c-\tau)Z-\beta] \qquad (29)$$

where $Z = z/(1+z)$. Since the sign of $s_c\beta-s_w(\beta+\tau Z)$ is indeterminate, we cannot definitely sign dg/dc, so that an increase in unproductive activity may reduce the growth rate of the economy in this model.

In the one-sector version of the model of the previous section we had $m=1$ (productive and unproductive workers received the same wage), $s_w=0$ (unproductive workers do not save), and $\tau=0$ (the rate of profit does not affect investment independently of the rate of capacity utilisation), so that $dg/dc>0$. In the present case, if $s_w=0$ *or* if $\tau=0$ (as long as $s_c>s_w$) we still get $dg/dc>0$. If $s_w>0$ *and* $\tau>0$ and is sufficiently large, we may get $dg/dc<0$. What happens in this case is that the rise in the use of unproductive labour reduces profits sufficiently – despite the rise in capacity utilisation (equation (27) shows that $d(X/K)/dc>0$) – to reduce the desired investment of firms.

The Case of Full Capacity Utilisation

In the second modification we assume that demand is high enough in the economy to take the productive sector to full capacity utilisation. For simplicity, we continue assuming that the economy is a one-sector one.[18]

If capacity is fully utilised, so that $X/K = a$, variations in capacity utilisation cannot bring the demand and supply of goods to equality as it did in the model of the third section. Here we consider two alternative mechanisms of macroeconomic adjustment.[19]

In one case, excess demand (or supply) causes a rise (or fall) in the price level, given the money wage, and this, by shifting the distribution of income between classes with different saving propensities, results in macroeconomic equilibrium. Assuming that desired investment is given by equation (25), and $X/K = a$, the macroeconomic balance equation can be written as

$$sr = \alpha + \beta a + \tau r$$

which implies that the equilibrium rate of profit is

$$r = (\alpha+\text{ß}a)/(s-\tau) \tag{30}$$

The rate of profit, from its definition, and with $X/K = a$, is

$$r = a - (ba+c)W/P \tag{31}$$

so that the equilibrium real wage is given by

$$W/P = [a/(ab+c)]-[(\alpha+\text{ß}a)/(s-\tau)(ab+c)]. \tag{32}$$

From (32) it follows that a rise in c in this case reduces the equilibrium real wage; this occurs because the rise in the employment of unproductive labour increases the demand for goods and increases the price level given the money wage. But from (30) it follows that the rate of profit is fixed by the investment and saving parameters and the output–capital ratio, so that the rate of profit and hence the rate of accumulation (since $g = sr$), do not change when c increases: in equation (31) the rise in c is exactly compensated by the fall in W/P.[20] It follows, then, that with full capacity utilisation, there may not be a rise in the rate of capital accumulation when there is a rise in the use of unproductive labour.

Second, we consider the case in which no adjustments in the real wage are possible because the real wage is at its minimum level determined by subsistence. Here, assuming the existence of excess demand in the economy, we assume that actual investment is determined by saving, and that investment plans cannot be realised. For this case, the macroeconomic balance equation can be written as

$$s[a - (ab+c)V] = g_a \tag{33}$$

where V is the exogenously given subsistence real wage, and g_a is the actual rate of accumulation of capital. Here, an increase in c, by reducing the rate of profit for a given real wage, reduces the savings of the economy, and hence rate of accumulation.[21] In this case there is no deficiency in demand, so that in the terminology of the previous section, the actual surplus, S_A, is the same as potential surplus S_{P2}, so that a rise in the use of unproductive labour causes a fall in the rate of accumulation.[22]

Technological Change

In the previous section we assumed that the productive sector produced a final good which was consumed and invested, while the output unproductive sector was an intermediate good and did not add to final output. In our final modification, we introduce another distinction between productive and unproductive sectors: not only do we continue to assume that the unproductive sector does not contribute directly to final production, but we assume that a relative expansion of unproductive activity slows down the rate of technological change in the economy because learning in the productive sector, but not in the unproductive sector, generates technological progress.[23]   In economies where full employment prevails, an increase in the relative size of the unproductive sector would then imply lower rates of growth. However, for economies in which growth is constrained by demand, higher productivity does not necessarily imply higher growth, since it is possible for such changes to reduce employment, and thereby reduce aggregate demand, output, and growth rates.[24]   It would thus appear that shifts toward unproductive sectors could actually *increase* the rate of growth.

However, it should be remembered that technological change does not merely imply changes in input–output coefficients. Perhaps of far greater significance are product innovations – both new machines and new consumer goods. Indeed, Baran and Sweezy (1966) distinguished between epochal innovations and other innovations to highlight the demand-creating effects of the former. Such changes would increase the rate of growth of the economy by increasing the rate of investment and the level of aggregate demand in general, and thereby increase the rate of growth.[25]

A simple formalisation of the effects of this type of technological change can be developed as a modification of the model of the previous section. That model had growth constrained by demand, so that technical change has a beneficial effect by increasing the level of (say) investment demand, rather than by changing input–output coefficients.

Define the two sectors in the same way as in the previous section so as to use the same model. In addition, assume that technological change, which affects only the investment parameter α_p of the productive sector, depends on the relative size of the productive sector, since that sector is the one in which new technology is generated. Assume, as a simple formalisation, that

$$\alpha_p = \alpha(k) \tag{34}$$

where $\alpha' < 0$.[26] With this assumption, equation (13) implies that the g^p curve may become downward-sloping. The condition for this to happen is

$$-\alpha' > \beta_p \{\alpha_u + sc_u/\mu_p\}/\{s[z_p/(1+z_p)]-2\beta_p\} \qquad (35)$$

When this is satisfied, so that g_p has a negative slope, if we start from $k<k_e$ (the long-run equilibrium value of k), k will increase over time (with the size of the unproductive sector growing relatively) and the productive sector will experience declining growth, as illustrated in Fig. 2(a). Note that equation (34) is not enough to guarantee this result; the technological effect, measured by $-\alpha'$ must be strong enough to satisfy (35). In this case, the rise in the relative size of the unproductive sector continues to have the demand-creating role discussed in the third section, but there is also a reduction in the rate of technological change, which reduces investment incentives sufficiently to reduce demand overall. Note also that if the effect is very strong, g^p may be more strongly downward-sloping than the g^u curve. This would make the long-run equilibrium, if it exists, unstable: the economy could then possibly have indefinitely increasing k and decreasing g_p. This possibility is illustrated in Figure 2(b).

CONCLUSION

This paper has tried to reconcile Baran and Sweezy's discussion of the expansionary role of unproductive activity with recent explanations of stagnation – such as Wolff's – in terms of the growth of unproductive activity. It has argued that the recent discussions have departed from Baran and Sweezy's analysis in several ways, most importantly by ignoring the problem of demand deficiency. It has also developed a theoretical model following Wolff, but incorporating the characteristics of advanced capitalist economies emphasised by Baran and Sweezy, and considered several variants of the model.

The analysis has shown that a rise in unproductive activity in advanced capitalist economies in which demand problems are important may well have an expansionary effect, as argued by Baran and Sweezy. However, this is not a necessary outcome: if there are important class differences between productive and unproductive workers, if the economy is at (or more generally, close to) full capacity utilisation, or if productive sectors are the technologically progressive ones, it is possible that a relative expansion in unproductive activity may imply stagnation.

NOTES

* I am grateful to Fred Moseley and Bruce Norton for comments and discussions.
1. See Dutt (1990b) for a brief survey of this literature.
2. Marx also defined the two in another way, with productive labour involved in commodity production (that is, production for sale) and unproductive labour not so employed, but we shall confine our attention to the definition given in the text.
3. It is assumed, for simplicity, that no sector uses its own output as an intermediate good.
4. Baumol's and Wolff's model have some apparent differences: while in Baumol's model both sectors produce final products, one being a good and the other a service, for Wolff's model the unproductive sector is only an intermediate good; and while in Baumol's model there is no capital and its accumulation, Wolff allows for capital accumulation. But there are important similarities: both models assume that resources are fully employed, both assume that there is technological change only in the productive sectors, and both assume a constant ratio between the output of the two sectors.
5. As we shall see later, technological change in a Baran–Sweezy framework has a very different effect than it does in Wolff's.
6. See Marglin (1984) and Dutt (1990a) for a fuller analysis.
7. See Dutt (1991) for a formal model along these lines.
8. The actual and potential surpluses can also be different due to other reasons; see below.
9. This model follows the one-sector models of Dutt (1984, 1990a), modifying them to incorporate an unproductive sector and unproductive labour.
10. We could also allow the rate of investment to depend positively on the rate of profit in the sector, but that would result in only minor modifications of the analysis of this section, and is hence eschewed for simplicity (see Dutt, 1984, 1990a). The effect, however, will be introduced in the next section, where it will play a more important role.
11. Similar conclusions can be arrived at if we measure growth rate and relative size in terms of production rather than capital stock.
12. Since advertising also takes place for producer goods, it could also increase α_p, with the same general effect as that analysed here. There is no reason why increases in these parameters must necessarily reduce s and raise α_p, since increased advertising could simply shift demand between firms and not affect total demand.
13. Baran and Sweezy (1966) and Baran (1957) had several different notions of surplus, which are critically discussed by Lippit (1985). Here we focus only on notions which are relevant for our analysis.
14. Since there is no capital allocation problem for the one-sector case, these results hold for the short run when K is fixed, and for the long run, when K is variable.
15. The extension to the two-sector case complicates the algebra considerably, without changing the qualitative nature of the analysis.
16. See Dutt (1984, 1990a).

17.   We assume that the stability condition, which requires the denominator of (27) to be positive, is satisfied, and also that the parameters are such as to ensure positive output and rate of profit.

18.   Once again, the two-sector extension complicates the algebra without changing the main conclusion of this subsection.

19.   The two cases considered here correspond to the neo-Keynesian and neo-Marxian cases discussed by Marglin (1984) and Dutt (1990a).

20.   If the rise in c causes a fall in s, as discussed in the third section, there would be a rise in r, and a rise in g=sr.

21.   For the two-sector version, we have

$$s[a_p-(b_pa_p+c_p+\Theta b_u+c_uk)V] = g_a^P+g_a^uk$$

If we assume that investment in both sectors is rationed according to the rule

$$g_a^P = \sigma sr, \quad g_a^u = (1-\sigma)sr,$$

at long-run equilibrium we would get

$$k = (1-\sigma)/\sigma.$$

Thus, for this version too, a rise in c decreases g_a^P.

22.   The two cases just discussed may be combined, with adjustment falling partly on the real wage and partly on actual investment. For a model along these lines, which incorporates inflationary dynamics into the analysis, see Marglin (1984) and Dutt (1990a). In this model a rise in c would partly reduce V, but there would be a fall in the rate of profit, since the real wage would not fall as far as it could in the first case discussed in this section.

23.   The productive sector is thus the engine-of-growth sector. See Dutt (1990b) for a brief discussion and references.

24.   See Dutt (1986, 1990a, chap. 5).

25.   See Dutt (1986).

26.   This is meant as no more than a simple, illustrative formalisation, rather than a definitive model. A more appropriate formalisation ought at least to involve a ratio of unproductive to productive labour, which is not proportional to the ratio of capital stocks.

REFERENCES

Bacon, R. and W. Eltis (1976). *Britain's Economic Problem: Too Few Producers*, London: Macmillan.

Baran, P. (1957). *The Political Economy of Growth*, New York: Monthly Review Press.

Baran, P. and P. Sweezy (1966). *Monopoly Capital*, New York: Monthly Review Press.

Baumol, W. J. (1967). 'Macroeconomics of Unbalanced Growth: The Anatomy of Urban Crisis', *American Economic Review*.

Dutt, A. K. (1984). 'Stagnation, Income Distribution and Monopoly Power', *Cambridge Journal of Economics*, 8(1), March, 25–40.

Dutt, A. K. (1986). 'Growth, Distribution and Technological Change', *Metroeconomica*, 38(2), June, 113–34.

Dutt, A. K. (1990a). *Growth, Distribution and Uneven Development*, Cambridge: Cambridge University Press.

Dutt, A. K. (1990b). 'Unproductive Sectors and Stagnation: A Theoretical Analysis', University of Notre Dame unpublished.

Dutt, A. K. (1991). 'Unproductive Activity and Stagnation: A Neo-Marxian Model', University of Notre Dame unpublished.

Hunt, E. K. (1979). 'The Categories of Productive and Unproductive Labour in Marxist Economic Theory', *Science and Society*, 43(3), Fall, 303–25.

Kalecki, M. 1971). *Selected Essays in the Dynamics of the Capitalist Economy*, Cambridge: Cambridge University Press.

Lippit, V. D. (1985). 'The Concept of the Surplus in Economic Development', *Review of Radical Political Economics*, 17(1/2), 1–19.

Marglin, S. A. (1984). *Growth, Distribution and Prices*, Cambridge, Mass.: Harvard University Press.

Marx, K. (1977). *Capital*, volume 1, 1867, New York: Random House.

Moseley, F. (1988). 'The Increase of Unproductive Labour in the Postwar US Economy', *Review of Radical Political Economy*, 20(2&3), 100–6.

Nichols, N. and Norton, B. (1990). 'The Effects of a Managerial Class on the Stability of a Capitalist Economy', Wellesley College.

Robinson, J. (1962). *Essays in the Theory of Growth*, London: Macmillan.

Steindl, J. (1952). *Maturity and Stagnation in American Capitalism*, Oxford: Basil Blackwell.

Wolff, E. N. (1987). *Growth, Accumulation and Unproductive Activity*, Cambridge: Cambridge University Press.

Figure 1
Long - Run Dynamics

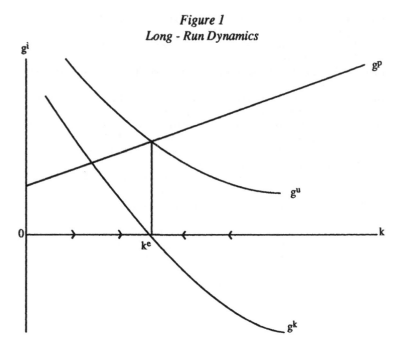

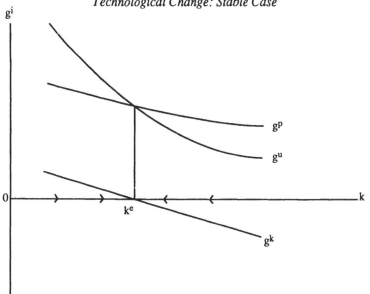

Figure 2(a)
Technological Change: Stable Case

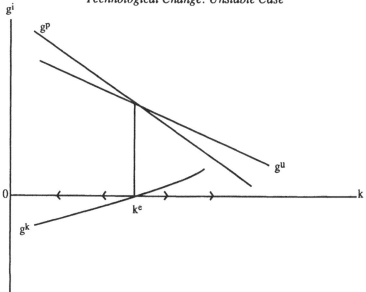

Figure 2(b)
Technological Change: Unstable Case

7. In What Sense Does Monopoly Capital Require Monopoly? An Essay on the Contribution Kalecki and Steindl

Tracy Mott

On one occasion I talked with Kalecki about the crisis of capitalism. We both, as well as most socialists, took it for granted that capitalism was threatened by a crisis of existence, and we regarded the stagnation of the 1930s as a symptom of such a major crisis. But Kalecki found the reasons, given by Marx, as to why such a crisis should develop, unconvincing; at the same time, he did not have an explanation of his own. 'I still do not know', he said, 'why there should be a crisis of capitalism'. He added: 'Could it have anything to do with monopoly?'

Josef Steindl[1]

The theory of monopoly capital, Paul Baran and Paul Sweezy (1966) tell us, is the attempt to rework Marxian economics for the stage of capitalist development in which oligopoly has replaced a more competitive form of capitalism. For Baran and Sweezy this suggests primarily the analysis of the twin phenomena of the tendency for the potential economic surplus to rise and of the problem of absorption of the surplus. The first phenomenon might be loosely classified as a microeconomic matter and the second as macroeconomic in nature. Baran and Sweezy (1966: 53–6) note that within 'bourgeois', or mainstream, economics there has been little attempt to link up the development of theories of 'imperfect' competition with the theory of effective demand problems launched by John Maynard Keynes. The major concern to make such a link, they say, is found in the (non-mainstream) work of Michał Kalecki and Josef Steindl.[2]

114

IMPERFECT COMPETITION AND 'NEW KEYNESIAN' ECONOMICS

Kalecki's and Steindl's recognition of a link between the question of monopoly, or oligopoly,[3] and the issue of effective demand failures, wherein all of the surplus is not 'realised' and unemployment of labour and capital results, has been taken up recently, however, by some mainstream economists. A growing body of economists, grouping their work under the heading of 'New Keynesian' economics, are appealing to market 'imperfections' as a way to explain the existence of effective demand problems.[4]

The main thrust of this work is to generate non-market-clearing outcomes due to the failure of some prices to adjust properly even under rational behavior on the part of all economic agents. Thus it differs from older versions of Keynesian economics which were accused of assuming wage or price rigidities without an adequate explanation underlying such behavior. Imperfections in competition are not sufficient by themselves to generate the failure of markets to clear, and they are not the only way to generate such failures, but their use for such a function is widespread enough for us to examine what might be called a Neoclassical version of monopoly capital.

The role of monopoly in such a framework is to establish a sufficient degree of rigidity of the mark-up of price over cost. This can be done by assuming that firms in imperfectly competitive industries set prices by a simple rule of thumb mark-up or by optimising given their price elasticity of demand. In either case shifts in aggregate demand are not likely to alter the mark-up very much, if at all. In fact, with perfect money wage and price flexibility nothing real should change. The higher is the 'degree of monopoly', the lower is the level of output and employment, but this does not cause 'involuntary' unemployment, since it merely lowers the real wage, moving employment down along the labour supply curve.

Combining imperfect competition with price-changing, or 'menu' costs, however, will retard the ability of the economy to respond to a demand shock by merely changing nominal magnitudes and so will rather cause movements in output and employment. When firms have some power over setting prices and changing prices is costly, it can be shown that the gain to each firm of price adjustment to a shock may not outweigh the cost, while the loss to the economy in terms of output and employment is significant.[5]

The role of monopoly here is not sufficient, but it is necessary. Keynesians also of course have generated nominal rigidities causing unemployment in the labour market by means of devices such as long-term explicit or implicit contracts, though there is some agreement at present that imperfect competition plus costly information leading to price rigidities may be more important than labour market rigidities in explaining unemployment. Gregory Mankiw (1987) notes that many of the money wage rigidity arguments are hard to reconcile with rational behavior, that if money wages relate to a long-term contract, they may then not affect the short-term employment decision, and that real wages are not actually observed to be at their highest in business cycle downturns.

THE ROLE OF IMPERFECT COMPETITION IN KALECKI'S ECONOMICS

How does the New Keynesian use of monopoly in explaining fluctuations in output and employment compare to that of Kalecki and Steindl? The reader will probably have noted some similarities with Kalecki, who also wanted to establish the rigidity of the price–cost mark-up. The role of rigid mark-ups in Kalecki's explanation of output and employment fluctuations, however, is not to help justify the existence of price rigidity. Rather, it functions to relate the distribution of income between profits and wages and the propensities to save out of each category to the level of effective demand. Since a fall in the overall level of mark-ups will transfer income from profits to wages, if the propensity to save out of profit income is greater than the propensity to save out of wage income, a fall in investment spending will not be offset by a rise in consumption spending if mark-ups do not decrease.[6]

The New Keynesians, however, do not discuss differential propensities to save. Their models are cast in terms of the representative household or firm, either of which receives its proportionate share of attributable income of whatever type. The main concern in these models is, as discussed above, to generate sufficient price inflexibility to prevent market-clearing which would continuously restore the full employment level of output.

That price flexibility will clear markets and maintain full employment is often taken these days without question. This was not the case immediately following the publication of Keynes' *General Theory of Employment, Interest, and Money*. There Keynes (1964 [1936], ch. 19) discusses the possible effects of money wage flexibility and allows, with a high degree of skepticism, for the possibility of an employment-increasing fall in interest rates due to an increased real quantity of money as falling money wages cause falling prices.

Kalecki (1944) was perhaps the first to argue against the efficacy of A.C. Pigou's (1943) argument that falling prices generate a wealth effect in a world with debt fixed in nominal terms.[7] Kalecki's critique was based on his perception that only what we today call 'outside money' represents net wealth and that this forms a rather small quantity to depend on for Pigou's effect. Additionally, as James Tobin (1980) has pointed out, if the propensity to spend of debtors is higher than that of creditors, not to mention bankruptcies' reducing the value of creditors' holdings,[8] it is hard to imagine that the road to full employment runs on price deflation's increasing the real value of assets denominated in money.[9]

Kalecki's effective demand story then is not dependent upon price inflexibility which prevents sufficient spending out of wealth but rather upon mark-up inflexibility which prevents sufficient spending out of wage income when investment decreases. What does this strictly have to do with monopoly? To get an expansion in aggregate demand when investment declines, in effect the degree of monopoly must decrease. This then is a matter of *changes in* rather than *the level of* the degree of monopoly. Since in the case of 'perfect' competition the degree of monopoly cannot decrease, we cannot rely on proper mark-up flexibility to increase demand there, either.[10]

Thus, though 'imperfect' competition is surely the general case and perfect competition a limiting and even mythological case, imperfect competition is not a necessary case for the effective demand results of Kalecki or Keynes or Baran and Sweezy. Keynes certainly saw this, for he deliberately assumed perfect competition, probably to ensure that his theory of unemployment could not be interpreted simply as the result of output restrictions that were already known to follow from imperfect competition.

THE MEANING OF PERFECT VS. IMPERFECT COMPETITION

Before proceeding further, it might be appropriate to say more about the usage of the terms 'perfect' and 'imperfect' competition. For Neoclassical economics and for Kalecki perfect competition refers to a situation of zero profits. Thus 'monopoly' is necessary for Kalecki's model of the capitalist economy in that it is necessary to generate positive profits. Many Marxian and neo-Ricardian economists, however, maintain that 'competitive' capitalism refers to a situation of positive profits with *equal* rates of profit across industries, while 'monopoly' capitalism refers to a situation of *unequal* profit rates, unequal due to the 'imperfections' in competition arising from the emergence of oligopoly.[11]

Thus far we have established that monopoly capital does not require monopoly to generate problems in the realisation of the potential surplus and attendant redundancy of labour and capital due to effective demand failures. It may require monopoly to generate any potential surplus at all, if one defines perfect competition to mean zero profits. Certainly the idea of profits as the goal of capital accumulation and spending out of profits as an important determinant of aggregate demand is hardly consistent with a world in which zero profits are the norm.[12]

STEINDL'S THEORY OF THE COMPETITIVE PROCESS

A deeper connection between the existence of monopoly and concern over surplus absorption, however, which also I think clears up some of the confusion about the question of differing types of competition, is found in Steindl's (1976 [1952]) *Maturity and Stagnation in American Capitalism*. This represents Steindl's work on the relation of monopoly to the crisis of capitalism, as Kalecki had suggested before he left the Oxford Institute of Statistics, where both he and Steindl were working, in 1944.

The book seeks to explain the long-run forces underlying the Great Depression of the 1930s. Steindl (1976 [1952]: xii) contends that 'the growth rate of private wealth had declined for a long time before it stagnated in the 1930s'. To show what caused this, he works on Kalecki's edifice, adding some essential modifications concerning the theory of oligopoly and its effects on investment that complete the open parts of Kalecki's system with respect to the idea of the degree of monopoly and the question of the flexibility of price–cost mark-ups.

Steindl reconstructs Alfred Marshall's explanation of differences in profit margins among firms in an industry as *differential rent*, as in David Ricardo. In industries where entry is easy and there are size differences among the firms, the small producers are the 'infra-marginal' firms earning zero, or 'normal', profits, while bigger firms will be earning excess profits, or 'rent', according to their cost advantages over the small firms. Competition proceeds through cost reduction by means of innovations and scale economies. This entails reinvestment out of profits in order to innovate and grow at the same rate or better than one's rivals. Certainly some of the investment is financed by new issues of debt and equity, but the ability to borrow and to issue new shares is also a function of the firm's profits, in accordance with Kalecki's (1937) 'principle of increasing risk', which argues that illiquidity concerns limit the amount of borrowing a unit of capital can undertake.[13]

The competitive process also entails the deliberate holding of excess capacity. Steindl contrasts his argument for excess capacity with the theories of imperfect competition, which hold that excess capacity is due to excessive profit margins. His theory maintains just the opposite: excessive profit margins are due to holding excess capacity. Firms want to be built up ahead of demand to ensure their ability to keep up with their competitors.

Both price-cutting when costs fall and expenditures on selling costs, where this is feasible, are open to firms as a way to fight for growth and market share. Price competition, however, as a method of growth is only useful where it is possible to drive out marginal producers by pricing below their costs. Otherwise a cut in price is likely to be followed by rivals, as in the 'kinked demand curve' story, and so will not bring a bigger market share and more profits with which to reinvest. Where industries reach a stage such that even the smallest firms hold considerable capital and earn more than marginal profits, cost differentials across firms are probably not large enough to allow price competition to serve as a useful strategy.

What will happen, though, if excess capacity should become greater than the deliberately desired amount? This will certainly weaken the inducement to invest in more capacity, but there are different further repercussions in 'competitive' vs. 'mature', or oligopolistic, industries described above. In a 'competitive' industry, which we described as one with several small producers who are operating on the margin and so can be driven out easily, we might expect a reduction in prices and thus in mark-ups as the utilisation of capacity starts to decline below the desired level. This will drive some smaller firms out of business, utilisation for the remaining firms will rise, and investment and the competitive process will resume.

In a 'mature' industry, however, where there is a significant minimum size required for existence and thus even the highest cost firm has a small enough cost differential relative to the others, it is not so much in anyone's interest to reduce mark-ups. Instead of maintaining demand and therefore utilisation, a strategy of price-cutting will not attract enough new demand to any firm to help. The overall profit margin of price over cost will shrink due to a fall in utilisation and thus a rise in overhead, but the mark-up of price over direct cost will probably be maintained. The mark-up has become inflexible, or inelastic, downwards.

Steindl (1976 [1952]: 137) identifies this as an historical process as follows:

> Under what circumstances will this type of inelasticity appear? As has been explained, the squeezing of profit margins happens through the competition of entrepreneurs, which is essentially a process of squeezing out the weakest competitors. It is obvious that this mechanism works relatively well in a system where there are plenty of small producers, and plenty of competitors anyway. Thus, no difficulties of this type should appear in early capitalism, and even in fully developed capitalism for quite a time. In a mature capitalism, however, where large-scale production becomes the only possible form in many industries, and where, moreover, the number of competitors is reduced to a very few in a great number of cases, the profit margin becomes inelastic in the downward direction.

The relation of monopoly to downward rigidity in the mark-up and thus to the tendency for the potential surplus to rise and the relation of monopoly to weakness and instability in investment spending and thus to the problem of absorption of the surplus are demonstrated by Steindl to be a matter of the logic of the historical process of capitalist development. As Karl Marx (1967 [1894]: 250) puts it, 'The *real barrier* of capitalist production is *capital itself*'.

Mark-ups become downwardly inflexible because firms with large amounts of fixed capital will be able to fight too strongly in a price war to make it worth anyone's while to engage in such a strategy. This means that undesired excess capacity won't be eliminated by firms' lowering prices to sell more. This in turn slows down investment in new capacity. This fall in investment spending is not offset by a rise in consumption demand because mark-ups won't fall. And nothing in this story is inconsistent with the kind of rational behavior that the New Keynesians want to have for 'microfoundations' of macroeconomics. Finally, Steindl provides us with the proper meaning of the distinction between competitive and monopoly capitalism.

Steindl's work represents an advance upon, or better a completion of, Kalecki's pricing theory. Kalecki realised the weakness of seeking to determine the level of mark-ups on the basis of firms' profit maximization under less than perfect price elasticity of demand, but he never got beyond discussing the static determinants of the 'degree of monopoly' facing a firm or industry.[14]

LOGICAL-HISTORICAL PROCESSES VS. 'IMPERFECTIONS'

This of course does not exhaust the contribution of Kalecki and Steindl to the theory of monopoly capital. The main point this essay seeks to make, though, is that the thrust of Kalecki's and Steindl's concern for monopoly is not to establish some 'imperfections' that prevent market-clearing. Effective demand failures, as Keynes well realised, can be explained within a framework of 'perfect' competition, however mythological such a framework is for the theory of a capitalist economy. Conversely, the New Keynesians cannot generate equilibrium unemployment from models with 'imperfect' competition without also adding at least one other 'imperfection'.

The purpose of Steindl's analysis of the process of competition and the emergence of monopoly is to relate that emergence to the slow-down and instability in investment plaguing the 'mature' capitalist economies of the twentieth century. The rigidity in mark-ups that occurs in mature industries is not a matter of 'imperfect' as opposed to 'perfect' competition but of the emergence of small as opposed to large cost differentials across firms as the process of competition proceeds.

Starting from Neoclassical conceptions of economic rationality and coordination, as the New Keynesians do, makes it hard to avoid locating effective demand failures in imperfections in the neo-Walrasian system. The New Keynesians deserve credit, I believe, for discovering logical contradictions in the neoclassical argument for continuous full employment purely on the basis of Neoclassical reasoning. What they fail to do, however, is to penetrate to the conclusion that the logic of the economic system as a whole overrides individual rationality so much so that studying the logic of the development of the system is what is required.

MODIFICATIONS AND EXTENSIONS OF KALECKI'S AND STEINDL'S THEORIES

Nina Shapiro (1988) has critiqued a key assumption of *Maturity and Stagnation*, that firms invest only in their own industries. She argues that the development of new products is consistent with the type of competitive process that Steindl himself describes. Upon reconsideration Steindl (1976: xi-xii; 1990 [1979], ch. 9) has indicated that he now concedes that he was mistaken to dismiss the development of

inno:ations.[15] He attributes this error to his impression of a great
length of time normally required between a scientific discovery and
its exploitation by business. He says that he did not realise that those
ideas which are sufficiently developed to be attractive to business are
scarce enough to attract a great deal of investment. He also was
afraid that using innovations to generate an exogenous trend would
inaccurately fail to leave room for the importance of the endogenous
trend following from his theory of maturity.

Steindl (1990 [1981], ch. 10) has since written on the relation
between exogenous innovations and endogenous forces, concluding
that though innovations can stimulate economic activity, eventually the
endogenous forces will overtake them. Thus, as in, for example
Kalecki (1969 [1952]), a continuing stream of innovations can serve
as exogenous 'shocks' which will ensure a positive trend to a model
economy, while there are endogenous effective demand limitations
dampening the effect of the shocks. This, as is well known, can
produce a marriage of trend and cycle which looks very much like the
behavior of actual economies.[16] It also fits with Baran and Sweezy's
(1966) discussion of the importance of 'epoch-making' innovations.

Another potential problem for the Kaleckian and Steindlian
underpinnings of the theory of monopoly capital arises from the
empirical failure of the average mark-up to rise in the post-World War
II U.S. economy. That is, the mark-up, measured by the ratio of price
to unit labour costs, has not shown any significant tendency to rise
and actually has been slightly lower in the 1970s and 1980s compared
to the 1960s. Similar behavior for other industrialised countries is
noted by Malcolm Sawyer (1989). Sawyer suggests that increasing
international competition may explain this. Steindl (1990 [1989])
notes that Sawyer's measure may be affected by changes in the utilisation of capacity but believes that profit margins at a given degree of
utilisation have still declined and agrees that increasing international
competition may explain this. In Steindl (1990 [1981], ch. 10) he
mentions a factor also emphasised by Kalecki (1971 [1954], ch. 5),
the ability of organised labour to cut into the mark-up. This may have
kept the mark-up from rising as increases in labour productivity
lowered costs, while increasing international competition ate into the
mark-up after 1969.[17]

Steindl's basic theory of the emergence of maturity, however, is
only modified by considering the development of new products and
the power of trade unions. Increasing international competition is but
another example of Steindl's framework and only alters it to the extent
that political economic factors (e.g., protectionism) may more easily
play a bigger role there than in a purely domestic case. An excellent

example of the process of competition as described by Steindl, I believe, is seen in the behavior of the U.S. airline industry after the deregulation of the mid-1970s. Initially the high profits available to the previously cartelised industry attracted a bunch of startups and led the already-existing firms to penetrate each other's regional markets and to cut prices on well-traveled routes in the attempt to drive out rivals. Eventually, however, the smaller firms, which could least afford to bear the massive losses being rung up by the intense price competition, went out of business or became absorbed in mergers. Today the number of likely nation-wide survivors is widely predicted to be three – American, Delta, and United – and fares are expected to rise once the now- or near-bankrupts finally give up.

Baran and Sweezy's problem of absorption of the surplus has also been modified somewhat by the greater internationalisation of domestic economies but even more so by political economic factors. Kalecki (1971 [1943], ch. 12) predicted this in his famous article, 'Political Aspects of Full Employment', which gave us the first usage of the term 'political business cycle'. Kalecki (1972 [1956]; 1972 [1964]; 1972 [1967]) and Steindl (1976 [1952]: ix-xvii; 1990 [1982] [1979] [1989] [1982] [1985] [1983] [1985], chs. 8–9, 1317) discuss some of the political factors involved in the postwar revival and subsequent stagnation of the industrialised economies. Their explanations of the revival are similar to Baran and Sweezy's – tax-financed government spending, mainly on military and related expenditures, as governments learned to use 'Keynesian' demand-creating fiscal policy tools and found what they considered to be suitable subjects for such expenditures. The subsequent stagnation they attribute also to the usual suspects – increased international interpenetration of economies, rising inflation, hostility towards minority and imported workers, energy shortages, etc. – all of which give support to advocates of demand-restricting policies, since they are taken to reward the performance of economies which can restrain wage increases.

The critique of monopoly capital from within Marxian economics by those arguing for a return to the orthodox 'falling tendency of the rate of profit' argument or those favoring a 'profit squeeze' theory of business cycles have interpreted the macroeconomic history of the post-World War II period differently, in a way that supports each of their own respective views. They see in the fall in the mark-up and profit share refutations of the 'demand-side' or 'Keynesian' views of the monopoly capital school and backing for Marxian 'supply-side' types of arguments.[18]

If we add, however, financial factors and the political economy of the conflict between interest recipients and everyone else to the story, we have more support in favor of using and modifying Kalecki's and Steindl's theories to interpret this era. Cycle downturns and stagnant recoveries since World War II have, I believe, been largely precipitated and maintained by financial stringency to fight inflation and balance of payments concerns, which particularly bother interest recipients and are taken to be hurtful to all. Anti-inflation policy of this type, however, of course decreases profit and wage income. This is compounded by the build-up of debt as firms and households attempt to maintain themselves in the face of profit and wage stagnation, which in turn makes these entities more sensitive to credit restrictions at the same time that they are more dependent on borrowing.

This gives us a view also very similar to that of Hyman Minsky (e.g., 1986) and moves us away from a strict reliance upon investment accelerator or capital stock adjustment business cycle theories and so the emergence of excess capacity as an explanation for (rather than a consequence of) every cycle downturn. I locate the parentage of this finance capital perspective in Kalecki's (1937) 'principle of increasing risk', presented above. The competitive process and so investment decisions are thus affected by the availability of finance in a way quite in tune with the monopoly capital framework. As argued above, investment spending is financed primarily, though not exclusively, by internally-generated funds. Upon reaching the stage of maturity, there become agglomerations of finance seeking investment outlets. The accompanying slowdown in investment, however, reduces profits. Renewed expansion requires increasing debt loads. The rise in interest rates by which interest recipients and/or central banks protect themselves from inflation increases the burden and riskiness of debt charges. This in turn slows down investment spending, which reduces aggregate demand and profits, decreasing investment further, and so on, analogously to downturns caused by the emergence of excess capacity. In an era in which governments know how to affect aggregate demand with policy, recessions are more often attributable to policy. The particular version which Kalecki's 'political cycle' has taken, I believe, has become this story of now fighting recession with fiscal and monetary policy, now fighting inflation and/or a balance of payments deficit largely with monetary tightness.[19]

CONCLUSIONS

The importance of monopoly to the theory of monopoly capital has much more to do with the emergence of chronic macroeconomic stagnation than it does with any effect on microeconomic allocation. As a 'microfoundation' for macroeconomics, monopoly does not work so much as an 'imperfection' within the neo-Walrasian conception of market-clearing but rather as a restraint on adequate consumption and investment spending. As demonstrated by Steindl, building on the foundations established by Kalecki, the competitive process in any industry logically develops towards a stage of 'maturity', in which price-cutting to increase demand and capacity utilisation no longer is a sensible business practice. This in turn both slows down further investment spending and prevents decreases in mark-ups which would increase consumption spending.

The twin problems of monopoly capital identified by Baran and Sweezy – the tendency for the potential surplus to rise and the problem of absorption of the surplus – are explained by Steindl's theory of the emergence of maturity. Modifications which need to be made to this theory involving such matters as the development of new products, wage pressure on mark-ups, political cycles, and increasing internationalisation of capital represent re-examinations following upon the logic of the theory itself. What it explains then becomes not simple secular stagnation but a broader process of uneven development, also bringing in political factors and the interaction between politics and economics in a world of nation-states within an increasingly international economy. Seeking to understand what new developments this conjuncture will itself entail gives us much future work to do.

NOTES

1. This quote is from Steindl (1990 [1984]: 246).
2. Baran and Sweezy (1996: 56) also note that Kalecki discovered Keynesian effective demand failures independently of Keynes and add that 'anyone familiar with the work of Kalecki and Steindl will readily recognize that the authors of the present work owe a great deal to them'.
3. Baran and Sweezy (1966: 6, n.3) write, 'Throughout this book, except where the context clearly indicates otherwise, we use the term "monopoly" to include not only the case of a single seller of a commodity for which there are no substitutes, but also the much more common case of "oligopoly," i.e., a few sellers dominating the markets for products which are more or less satisfactory substitutes for one another'. I will follow their usage in this paper as well.
4. See, e.g., Olivier Blanchard and Stanley Fischer (1989, chs. 8–9) or Robert Gordon (1990) and the references contained therein.
5. See, e.g., Julio Rotemberg (1987) or Blanchard and Kiyotaki (1987).

6. See Kalecki (1971 [1954], ch. 8).
7. See also Irving Fisher (1933), who in effect argued against Pigou in advance.
8. See also Frank Hahn (1969 [1965]) for a critique of Don Patinkin's (1965 [1956]) work on this question.
9. There is some New Keynesian work, e.g., Bradford DeLong and Lawrence Summers (1986), Bruce Greenwald and Joseph Stiglitz (1988a, 1988b), and Ben Bernanke and Mark Gertler (1989) which recognises that wealth effects due to price flexibility may work in the wrong direction.
10. If firms were to drop prices *below* costs, or if the real wage were to increase due to productivity increases, aggregate demand would increase, but neither of these possibilities could be taken to be systematic responses to decreases in effective demand.
11. See Donald Harris (1988: 159–61) for a discussion of this point of view. Amitava Krishna Dutt (1990) argues that the fundamental distinction between the 'classical theory of competition' and monopoly capitalism is not whether or not profit rates across industries are equalised but, rather, whether or not profit rates are equalised, prices are *determined* by monopoly power. He points out that this in turn implies that competition in the Classical sense of movements in capital in response to profit rate differentials could intensify following a rise in monopoly power as James Clifton (1977) and others have claimed, but a different theory of price determination would still be required. The most serious problem with the Classical theory of competition, I believe, is that pointed out by David Levine (1980), namely, that the Classical theory does not treat the role of the firm in the competitive process adequately.
12. See, however, Keynes's (1971 [1930]) *Treatise on Money*, wherein changes in profits relative to zero are taken as signals to expand or contract output, and spending out of such 'windfalls' is also taken into account.
13. See also Kalecki (1971 [1954], ch. 9) and Tracy Mott (1982). Some of the New Keynesians (e.g., Greenwald, Stiglitz, and Weiss, 1984) have made the same argument based on considerations of asymmetric information and moral hazard.
14. There is a considerable literature devoted to Kalecki's pricing theory, involving questions such as its influence, its development over time, its problems, and whether or not Kalecki's notion of the 'degree of monopoly' is a tautology. Peter Kriesler (1987) seems to have written the definitive work on this.
15. Kalecki (e.g., 1969 [1952]) had always acknowledged the importance of innovations, seeing them as vitally important for the existence of long-run growth in a capitalist economy.
16. Today there is some feeling that damped linear models relying on exogenous shocks to maintain persistence should be replaced by nonlinear models which can maintain persistence endogenously. In response to such an argument by Richard Goodwin (1989), Steindl (1989) has commented that the exogenous innovations are there and have to be taken into account in any event. Since they are asymmetric, they can be used with a linear model to get something that should look a lot like actual cycles.
17. Keith Cowling (1982, ch. 6) argues that increasing internationalisation of trade need not decrease mark-ups. Whether it does or not, he says, should depend upon whether or not there are significant asymmetries in competition present. That is, do new rivals see benefits coming from price competition or not? He cites the case of new Japanese penetration as one in which asymmetries leading to price-undercutting by the Japanese firms are often perceived, since the Japanese are protected from retaliation in their home market. This view fits of course with Steindl's analysis.

Cowling goes on to say that freer trade may well be looked upon by companies as a way to increase profits through wage-cutting, since international mobility of capital and distribution allows firms to seek out the lowest wage cost production site without regard for product demand in that particular country. This of course will tend to increase mark-ups. It also supports Kalecki's and Steindl's views regarding when we should see political backing for 'stagnation policy' to keep wages down, to be discussed later in this paper.

18. See, for example, Paul Mattick (1969); David Yaffe (1973); Andrew Glyn and Bob Sutcliffe (1972); and Samuel Bowles, David Gordon, and Thomas Weisskopf (1983). John Bellamy Foster's (1986) *The Theory of Monopoly Capitalism* provides a discussion from the monopoly capital point of view, of this and other debates among rival schools of modern Marxian thought.

19. The association between monopoly and finance capital goes back to Rudolf Hilferding (1981 [1910]). Steindl (1976 [1952]) gives credit to changes in the cost of finance for determining the timing of the onset of the Great Depression and to the debt–equity ratio as a determinant of investment spending in general. Amit Bhaduri and Steindl (1985) suggest that the doctrine of monetarism may be a means of support for the 'rentier' (interest-receiving) class. Some of my own ideas on these issues can be found in Mott (1985–6, 1989) and Mott and Grainger Caudle (1991).

REFERENCES

Baran, Paul and Paul Sweezy (1966). *Monopoly Capital*, New York: Monthly Review Press.

Bernanke, Ben and Mark Gertler (1989). 'Agency Costs, Net Worth, and Business Fluctuations', *American Economic Review* 79: 14–31.

Bhaduri, Amit and Josef Steindl (1985). 'The Rise of Monetarism as a Social Doctrine', in Philip Arestis and Thanos Skouras, eds., *Post Keynesian Economic Theory*, Brighton Sussex: Wheatsheaf Books.

Blanchard, Olivier and Stanley Fischer (1989). *Lectures on Macroeconomics*, Cambridge, Mass: MIT Press.

Blanchard, Olivier and Nobu Kiyotaki (1987). 'Monopolistic Competition and the Effects of Aggregate Demand', *American Economic Review* 77: 647–66.

Bowles, Samuel; David Gordon, and Thomas Weisskopf (1983). *Beyond the Wasteland*, New York: Anchor Press.

Clifton, James (1977). 'Competition and the Evolution of the Capitalist Mode of Production', *Cambridge Journal of Economics* 1: 137–51.

Cowling, Keith (1982). *Monopoly Capitalism*, New York, John Wiley.

DeLong, Bradford and Lawrence Summers (1986). 'Is Increased Price Flexibility Stabilizing?' *American Economic Review*, 76: 1031–44.

Dutt, Amitava Krishna (1990). 'Competition, Monopoly Power, and the Prices of Production', in Philip Arestis and Yiannis Kitromilides, *Theory and Policy in Political Economy*, Hants, Aldershot: Edward Elgar Publishing, pp. 157–98.

Fisher, Irving (1933). 'The Debt-Deflation Theory of Great Depressions', *Econometrica* 1: 337–57.

Foster, John Bellamy (1986). *The Theory of Monopoly Capitalism*, New York: Monthly Review Press.

Glyn, Andrew and Bob Sutcliffe (1972). *Capitalism and Crisis*, New York: Pantheon.

Goodwin, Richard (1989). 'Kalecki's Economic Dynamics: A Personal View', in Mario Sebastiani, ed., *Kalecki's Relevance Today*, New York: St Martin's Press, pp. 249–51.

Gordon, Robert (1990). 'What Is New-Keynesian Economics?', *Journal of Economic Literature*, 28: 1115–71.

Greenwald, Bruce and Joseph Stiglitz (1988a). 'Imperfect Information, Finance Constraints, and Business Fluctuations', in Meir Kohn and Sho-Chieh Tsiang, eds., *Finance Constraints, Expectations, and Macroeconomics*, Oxford: Clarendon Press, pp. 103–40.

Greenwald, Bruce and Joseph Stiglitz (1988b). 'Money, Imperfect Information, and Economic Fluctuations', in Kohn and Tsiang, *op. cit.*, pp. 141–65.

Greenwald, Bruce, Joseph Stiglitz, and Andrew Weiss (1984). 'Informational Imperfections in the Capital Market and Macroeconomic Fluctuations', *American Economic Review Papers and Proceedings*, 74: 194–9.

Hahn, Frank (1969 [1965]). 'On Some Problems of Proving the Existence of Equilibrium in a Monetary Economy', in Robert Clower, ed., *Monetary Theory*, Harmondsworth, Middx: Penguin, pp. 191–201.

Harris, Donald (1988). 'On the Classical Theory of Competition', *Cambridge Journal of Economics*, 12: 139–67.

Hilferding, Rudolf (1981 [1910]). *Finance Capital*, ed. Tom Bottomore, London: Routledge and Kegan Paul.

Kalecki, Michał (1937). 'The Principle of Increasing Risk', *Economica*, 4 (new series) 440–7.

Kalecki, Michał (1944). 'Prof. Pigou on 'The Classical Stationary State'. A Comment', *Economic Journal*, 54: 131–2.

Kalecki, Michał (1969 [1952]). *Theory of Economic Dynamics*, New York: Augustus M. Kelley.

Kalecki, Michał (1971 [1943]). 'Political Aspects of Full Employment', in *Selected Essays on the Dynamics of the Capitalist Economy 1933–1970*, Cambridge: Cambridge University Press, pp. 138–45.

Kalecki, Michał (1971 [1954]a). 'Costs and Prices', in *Selected Essays, op cit.* pp. 43–61.

Kalecki, Michał (1971 [1954]b). 'Determination of National Income and Consumption', in *Selected Essays, op cit.* pp. 93–104.

Kalecki, Michał (1971 [1954]c). 'Entrepreneurial Capital and Investment', in *Selected Essays, op cit.* pp. 105–9.

Kalecki, Michał (1972 [1956]). 'The Economic Situation in the United States as Compared with the Pre-War Period', in *The Last Phase in the Transformation of Capitalism*, New York: Monthly Review Press, pp. 85–97.

Kalecki, Michał (1972 [1964]). 'The Fascism of Our Times', in *The Last Phase in the Transformation of Capitalism, op cit.* pp. 99–105.

Kalecki, Michał (1972 [1967]). 'Vietnam and U.S. Big Business', in *The Last Phase in the Transformation of Capitalism, op cit.* pp. 107–14.

Keynes, John Maynard (1964 [1936]). *The General Theory of Employment, Interest, and Money*, New York: Harcourt Brace Jovanovich.

Keynes, John Maynard (1971 [1930]). *A Treatise on Money*, London: Macmillan.

Kriesler, Peter (1987). *Kalecki's Microanalysis*, Cambridge: Cambridge University Press.

Levine, David (1980). 'Aspects of the Classical Theory of Markets', *Australian Economic Papers*, 19: 1–15.

Mankiw, Gregory (1987). 'The New Keynesian Microfoundations: Comment', *NBER Macroeconomics Annual 1987*, pp. 105–10.

Marx, Karl (1967 [1894]). *Capital*, vol. III, ed. Frederick Engels, New York: International Publishers.

Mattick, Paul (1969). *Marx and Keynes*, Boston: Porter Sargent.

Minsky, Hyman (1986). *Stabilizing an Unstable Economy*, New Haven: Yale University Press.

Mott, Tracy (1982). 'Kalecki's Principle of Increasing Risk: The Role of Finance in the Post-Keynesian Theory of Investment Fluctuations', Ph.D. dissertation, Stanford University.

Mott, Tracy (1985–6). 'Kalecki's Principle of Increasing Risk and the Relation Among Mark-up Pricing, Investment Fluctuations, and Liquidity Preference', *Economic Forum*, 15: 65–76.

Mott, Tracy (1989). 'The Structure of Class Conflict in a Kaleckian–Keynesian Model', Jerome Levy Economics Institute Working Paper No. 21.

Mott, Tracy and Grainger Caudle (1991). 'A Kaleckian Approach to a Synthesis of Ricardo and Keynes', mimeo.

Patinkin, Don (1965 [1956]). *Money, Interest, and Prices*, New York: Harper and Row.

Pigou, A.C. (1943). 'The Classical Stationary State', *Economic Journal*, 53: 343–51.

Rotemberg, Julio (1987). 'The New Keynesian Microfoundations', *NBER Macroeconomics Annual 1987*, pp. 69–104.

Sawyer, Malcolm (1989). 'Kalecki's Economics and Explanations of the Economic Crisis', in Sebastiani, *op. cit.*, pp. 275–308.

Shapiro, Nina (1988). 'Market Structure and Economic Growth: Steindl's Contribution', *Social Concept*, 4: 72–83.

Steindl, Josef (1989). 'Reflections on Kalecki's Dynamics', in Sebastiani, *op. cit.*, pp. 309–13.

Steindl, Josef (1976 [1952]). *Maturity and Stagnation in American Capitalism*, New York: Monthly Review Press.

Steindl, Josef (1990 [1979]). 'Stagnation Theory and Stagnation Policy', in *Economic Papers 1941–88*, New York: St Martin's Press, pp. 107–26.

Steindl, Josef (1990 [1981]). 'Ideas and Concepts of Long Run Growth', in *Economic Papers, op cit.*, pp. 127–38.

Steindl, Josef (1990 [1982]). 'Technology and Economy: The Case of Falling Productivity Growth in the 1970s', in *Economic Papers, op cit.*, pp. 94–103.

Steindl, Josef (1990 [1983]). 'The Control of the Economy', in *Economic Papers, op cit.*, pp. 216–29.

Steindl, Josef (1990 [1984]). 'Reflections on the Present State of Economics', in *Economic Papers, op cit.*, pp. 241–52.

Steindl, Josef (1990 [1985]a). 'Saving and Debt', in *Economic Papers, op cit.*, pp. 208–15.

Steindl, Josef (1990 [1985]). 'Structural Problems in the Crisis', in *Economic Papers, op cit.*, pp. 230–38.

Steindl, Josef (1990 [1989]). 'From Stagnation in the 30s to Slow Growth in the 70s', in *Economic Papers, op cit.*, pp. 166–79.

Tobin, James (1980). 'Real Balance Effects Reconsidered', in *Asset Accumulation and Economic Activity*, Chicago: University of Chicago Press, pp. 1–19.

Yaffe, David (1973). 'The Marxian Theory of Crisis, Capital, and the State', *Economy and Society*, 2: 186–232.

8. The Fund for Social Change

James Ronald Stanfield

> But in order to have plunder, there must be something to be plundered. . .
> Moreover, the manner of plunder depends itself on the manner of production.
>
> Karl Marx

The economic surplus is a vitally important concept for radical social analysis, without which it is virtually impossible to analyse critically issues about the structure of social output and the relationships of domination and exploitation that are intertwined with that structure. The absence of a workable surplus concept also severely delimits the critical vision with respect to designed social change because the surplus is quite literally the fund for social change.

In this chapter, I review the essential Marxian concept of economic surplus and relate it to the seminal work of Baran, Sweezy, and Phillips in conceptualising and measuring the surplus in a manner appropriate to the era of monopoly or late capitalism (1966). In doing so, a key connection is that between the economic surplus and surplus labour. I shall focus on this connection and the role it plays in Marxist theory and, in my view, radical economics in general.

The economic surplus results from collective social labour that results in output beyond that required for maintaining the status quo. This need not become a mechanistic distinction between the needed status quo and the non-needed expanded output. Harry Pearson's critique of such views of the surplus should not be neglected (1971). No doubt human culture simultaneously generates needs along with the new output. Still, the concept of potential output beyond that needed to reproduce society is vital to critical thought. The idea of a fund for social change asks for conscious understanding of our ability to expand output and the relation of this ability to qualitative social change. The concepts of economic surplus and surplus labour are vital because they bring this question to light in a fundamentally radical way: *we* produce, what do *we* want to produce in relation to what *we* want to become?

The concepts focus attention on exploitation since some labour beyond necessity because others do not labour or do so in activities that do not contribute to generic social reproduction. This necessarily links the concepts to the well-known institutionalist concept of instrumental value. Another possibility is that some labour at tasks that society would deem necessary but are paid in excess of what is necessary to have these tasks performed. This links the concepts to the economic theory of necessary supply price and is the key to the modification of surplus analysis proposed by Baran and Sweezy. The economic surplus concept in conjunction with surplus labour not only indicates that a fund for social change exists but also that the status quo of monopoly capitalism is fundamentally bankrupt and thus in need of fundamental social change (Baran and Sweezy, 1966, ch. 11).

DEFINITION OF ECONOMIC SURPLUS

The economic surplus is roughly the difference between what a society can produce and what it must produce to reproduce itself. Short of reproduction, a society experiences decline in its productive capacity, population, or standard of living. Above reproduction, a society experiences increase in its capacity, population, or living standard.

More technically, the surplus is the difference between potential output and essential consumption. Potential output is actual output plus any 'shortfall' due to unemployment of labour and excess capacity of the capital stock. Essential consumption is the sum of essential personal consumption, capital consumption, and necessary state expenditures for such things as roads, education, and public health.

The principle that underlies essential consumption is social reproduction. That is, essential consumption includes all personal, capital, and social consumption which is necessary to reproduce society and its productive capacity at the previous period's level. In each case, consumption which increases capacity is investment rather than consumption. Therefore, maintenance of old highways or the previous level of health and education would be consumption, construction of new highways or improvement in health and education would be investment. Likewise, essential consumption for the previous population level would be consumption, but additional essential consumption as a result of population increase would be investment.

The *form* of the surplus is defined as the way in which it is utilised. This may be non-essential consumption for the population, waste, 'shortfall', ceremonial public works, etc. The form of the surplus is clearly a matter of power: who controls the surplus. Particular stress has been placed, justifiably, on the surplus value form of the surplus in competitive capitalist society. None the less, it is important to treat surplus value as but one specific historical form of the surplus. Surplus value is relevant to societies organised upon the law of value whereas the economic surplus concept is relevant to all but the most primitive of human societies. The more general concept thus applies to pre-capitalist and post-capitalist societies as well as to the monopoly capitalist phase of capitalism. The application of the surplus value concept to this latter phase of capitalism is at least problematic in the quantification of the surplus since the lever of competition no longer operates as forcefully on relative prices. Even qualitatively, it is arguable that the focus on surplus value obscures much of the reality of late capitalism. This implies no reduction in emphasis upon surplus labour nor the necessity for radical analysis to emphasise the relation between status and surplus labour. A change in the form not the importance of surplus labour is the issue.

SURPLUS LABOUR AND SOCIAL EVOLUTION

The principle of surplus labour is fundamental to Marx's holistic social theory and the Marxian view of the rise and evolution of class society to and through capitalism toward a classless, new (communist) society. Surplus labour, first, is important in defining the human species. Marx noted a qualitative difference between humanity and other species in the fact that human beings work beyond instinct and necessity to develop skills and knowledge – broadly art and science – and therefore work not simply by the criteria of function but also in accordance with the standards of aesthetics and the inherent pleasure of activity contained in work. This invests human work with a universalising, developmental tendency that is, in scope at least, unique among the species of nature.

The division of labour, so well identified by Adam Smith as a powerful moving force in human history, is founded upon surplus labour. The surplus, the division of labour, and the accretion and innovative use of tools are as three moments of the unified process of production which is the core of social evolution. The generation of a surplus allows the support of labour specialists which in turn allows the development of more specialised tools. Increasing specialisation and intensified tool use in turn generate a larger surplus which allows again greater specialisation and tool development.

This process also then generates social stratification. The generation of an economic surplus and division of labour permit the formation of social strata classified according to economic function. The amalgamation of these strata into broad groups is the seat of class society. The form of the surplus is therefore an effective way to approach class society.

The rudimentary degrees of division of labour in human history appear to be more or less the result of natural evolution in that they do not require explanation in terms of human or cultural evolution. The earliest human division of labour was that between the sexes and this differentiation is common in other natural species. However, human cultural evolution extends this differentiation qualitatively. The sexual division of labour for rank or invidious comparison described by Thorstein Veblen (1953) in *The Theory of the Leisure Class* is far removed from the functional division of labour associated with bearing children.

Another division of labour which occurred early in human history was leadership. This too was likely based initially upon superiority of function and implied no necessary superiority of status. Those able to take charge probably did so spontaneously. In lowly productive, subsistence economies there was little room for leadership to develop into rulership. The ablest may have received some deference but they probably received no special access to economic goods nor certainly exemption from producing these goods. They may have had privileged access to the group's women. This is evident in nonhuman animal species and can be reasonably argued to enhance survival in the earliest human environments. So long as leadership is derivative from functional superiority in meeting the challenge of survival this tendency of natural evolution remains.

As in the case of sexual differentiation, the leadership function evolved to the point that it owed little of its character save its primordial origin to its natural history past. In natural evolution the fittest may lead but rulers do not lead by virtue of the ritual of their rule. The distinction between those who coordinate the work process because they are leaders and those who do so as rulers is very important. It is the root of Marx's concept of alienation, i.e., the control of the work process by an alien power (Marx, 1967: I. 332; Stanfield, 1979a).

The further evolution of the division of labour into occupational division of function also illustrates the principle of surplus labour. The carpenter extends his craft of furniture construction not only beyond the bare level of functional serviceability, but also and especially beyond the requirements of his own family. He relies upon those in other occupations to reciprocate so that he need not interrupt his carpentry to fashion his own household utensils or grow his own food. This occupational division of labour is far more advanced than the primitive differentiation we have been discussing. It probably evolved from the incipient sexual division of labour, itself evolved so that it fell to the women to carry on the routine tasks of householding such as pottery, tanning, cooking, grinding, and even farming. This left to the men those tasks culturally identified as exploit, adventure, and romance.

As leadership flows into rulership, the social division of labour becomes more pronounced and associated with social stratification. The principle of surplus labour becomes ever more clearly manifest to the extent that society becomes divided into two general classes. The ruling class generally occupies a position of privilege, so much so that its status usually exempts, indeed precludes, its members from engaging in productive labour in the provisioning process. The class of immediate producers thus labour to provision not only themselves but also their social superiors and to enable the social change that is shaped by the interests of the ruling class and the conflict among the classes. This need not preclude the social change from being progressive in some generic human sense – indeed, such unintended consequences are central to the Marxian concept of history.

Marx emphasised the division of society into two overarching classes, be they slave and slave-owner, serf and lord, or proletariat and bourgeois. He considered their economic relationship to be the fundamental determinant of the social order. Reference is, of course, to Marx's famous dictum that the form of surplus labour, i.e., how the surplus is extracted, is the key determinant of the character of a social system (Marx, 1967: I. 217 and 235; and III. 791).

Given that rank and status are associated with ruling, it early on became customary in human society to practice ceremony and ritual testifying to the exalted status of the rulers. This not only provides the ruling class with something to do, it also continually recreates the requisite awe among those ruled so that the current order of things retains its consonance with prevailing ideas of legitimacy, function, and equity.

The evidential basis of the ruling class's exalted stature consists primarily of the surplus labour of others. There is thus what might be called a status thirst for surplus labour in stratified human societies. The powerful and privileged are such precisely because they control the surplus labour of others. The powerful compete with one another to collect and display the surplus labour of others. This process can take many forms, i.e., the form of surplus labour and the sentiments and methods surrounding its collection and use vary.

Early ruling elites evidenced their exaltation by their women and later by their slaves. Having this origin, the concept of property within the group has different roots than the intergroup principle of territoriality since the latter refers to the territory or natural workshop of the community and not the privileged access and status within the community. The two separate principles merge historically and modern private property represents a fusion of surplus labour and territoriality, although the distinction between intergroup (later national) territory and intragroup social structure has not disappeared, as continuing conflicts between us/them and mine/yours attests.

From its origin in women and then slaves, the intragroup principle of private property develops intermediate forms. The access of the ruling class to the surplus labour of the ruled class becomes ever less direct in this process of evolution; but it remains no less the fundamental principle of social organisation in a class society for all its intermediation into less-apparent formations.

Marx delineated in this evolution several general modes of production or processes by which the ruled class is exploited of their surplus labour by the ruling class. In primitive communism he found very little surplus labour and division of labour and therefore very little leeway for the status thirst of a ruling class for the surplus labour of the ruled class. In slave society he found direct ownership of the ruled class to be the representative mode of extracting surplus labour and somewhat more division of labour and status thirst. In feudal society, rank and status are substantially more mature and the serf–landlord relation yields far more status thirst. The court and retainers of the lord were supremely evidential of his worth and represented the surplus labour of his serfs. In capitalist society surplus labour takes the form of surplus value and the status thirst has been rid of almost all bounds of directly personal use and customary reciprocal obligation.

Precapitalist societies were comprised of relatively stationary economic systems in that the aggregate surplus labour of the producing class was roughly matched by the surplus consumption of the ruling class and its attachers. In capitalist society this is decidedly not the case. Here the aggregate of surplus labour exceeds the surplus consumption of the non-productive classes. This difference is the basis of capitalism's unique economic growth and accumulation, from which Marx deduces the passionate possibilities that capitalist society presents. Surplus labour allows class society to arise but it imposes upon class society internal contradictions which carry it forward to the passionate possibilities of classless, communist society. Marx's insight thus sets for contemporary radical economists the definite task of 'demystifying Modern Economics [thereby] helping. . .people everywhere to discover a world of passionate possibilities' (Hunt and Schwartz, 1972: 33; see also Stanfield, 1982). With this task in mind, we can turn our attention to surplus labour and capitalism.

SURPLUS LABOUR AND COMPETITIVE CAPITALISM

Surplus labour in competitive capitalist society takes the form of surplus value, i.e., that portion of total value imparted to the commodity by the activity of workers which is over and above the value needed to reproduce them. Surplus value is therefore available for the capitalist employer to spend on his own consumption or to reinvest in the employment of additional labour power. The use of surplus for privileged consumption is not remarkable historically; the competitive display for personal use of the fruits of surplus labour is the historically common avenue of rendering evident the exalted stature of living and living well by the work of others' hands.

However, in capitalist society, the status thirst for surplus labour does take a portentous turn in that it becomes channelled toward the expansion of productive wealth *per se*. This simultaneously alters the nature of the process both qualitatively and quantitatively. Quantitatively, the drive to acquire surplus labour is no longer restrained by the limitations of the personal use in kind of the ruling class.

> It is. . . clear that in any given economic formation of society, where not the exchange-value but the use-value of the product predominates, surplus-labour will be limited by a given set of wants which may be greater or less, and that here no boundless thirst for surplus-labour arises from the nature of the production itself. . . (Marx, 1967: I. 235–36).

This implies also a qualitative change in that the nature of production itself now objectively mandates business expansion – to grow or die is a familiar imperative of business. The orientation toward competitive business expansion introduces an unparalleled dynamism into the process of exploitation. The routing of surplus labour toward the growth and development of the social productive plant possesses the capitalist ruling class of the tendency to expand social productiveness toward hitherto unknown levels. The nature-imposed condition that humankind must deal with nature through technological activity receives a qualitative alteration. The scale of the transformation of nature into humanly useful forms is vastly expanded and the passionate possibilities of a previously unimaginable freedom begins to come into focus.

Baran used the economic surplus concept to clarify the expansionary character of the competitive capitalist economy (Baran, 1957: 44–50). Theoretically, in order to maximise growth, an economy must maximise output and the share of output going into capital accumulation (including private, human, and state capital formation). This requirement is divisible into four components: (a) maximum output, (b) minimal consumption, (c) maximum share of the surplus seeking investment outlets, and (d) availability of investment outlets.

The maximisation of output requires full and efficient employment of productive resources. The minimisation of consumption and maximisation of the investment-seeking share of the surplus requires a distribution of income or output claims geared toward accumulation of the means of production. The question of investment outlets requires investment opportunities consistent with the principles which direct investment behavior.

The competitive capitalist economy tends toward full and efficient employment, according to standard equilibrium analysis of relative price adjustments. The minimisation of consumption follows from the logic of classical subsistence wage theory, improved by substitution of Marx's concept of the reserve army of unemployed for the population principle.

The possibility of non-essential consumption for classes other than the proletariat arises with respect to item three, the maximisation of the investment-seeking share of the surplus. In this regard, the pivotal point is the sociological contrast of the medieval aristocratic class's proclivity toward lavish consumption with the ethos of frugality of the nascent capitalist class. The unique character of the competitive capitalist economy is thus revealed by its tendency to produce a maximum economic surplus seeking investment in the expansion of productive wealth.

The fourth item, the availability of investment outlets, is problematic given the possibility of insufficient profit rates to absorb investment of accumulated funds. Even economic crises, however, have a fleeting, self-liquidating character given the fluid adjustment process of competitive capitalism.

THE ECONOMIC SURPLUS AND MONOPOLY CAPITALISM

The accumulation orientation contains the seed of competitive capitalism's self-transcendence since some capitalists 'win' and grow and some 'lose' and have their capital dissolved. Thus the era of competitive capitalism quickly gives way to monopoly capitalism and its central quandaries of power and the quality of human life, macroeconomic instability, and the turmoil of imperialism and uneven development.

The fundamental changes of monopoly capitalism are the decline of competition, the increased role of the state, and the growing internationalisation of the capitalist process. The rise of organised corporate and union interests and state regulatory and demand management activities qualitatively reduced the pressures of competition in product and factor markets. The state's role expanded by a process of interventionist drift as it sought to deal with the manifold dislocations of the capitalist process while simultaneously securing the continuation of that process (Stanfield, 1979b: ch. 5; and 1991). The thirst for exploitable labour power and technological changes that continuously increased and quickened the capitalist's ability to do business over long distances led capital all over the globe.

The surplus analysis of the theoretical maximum-growth society is useful in analysing the impact of imperialism upon the LDCs. Not only is much of the surplus repatriated as profits to the imperialist countries, but the structure of investment is distorted toward pre-industrial branches of production (e.g., raw materials). Then too, the sociological structure is effected and pre-bourgeois elites are perpetuated who combine the attributes of lavish-living aristocrats and bullion-hoarding mercantilists. Much of the available surplus is usurped by the military requirements of perpetuating unpopular regimes and hoarded in foreign accounts for the eventual flight when the regime is toppled by the people or by the imperialist power for whom it has become unwieldy or embarrassing – though it takes a lot to embarrass the imperialist countries' politicians.

The surplus analysis thus reveals that the LDCs are not low-surplus, low-investment economies. The standard lamentations about their excess population, meager living standards and inability to 'save' are severely misleading, indeed obfuscating. Of course the masses live meagerly, but they do not do so from the pressures of population against potential output. Instead they suffer from the ruthless exploitation imposed upon them by their indigenous ruling classes and the imperialist forces that keep these elites in power. The LDCs are high-surplus, low- and distorted-investment economies. Even with severe obstruction of production by corruption, the penury of mass existence generates a relatively large actual surplus that is dissipated in the interests of the indigenous and international power elites.

The familiar imperatives of competitive capitalism are clearly not at work here. Were they present, the actions of entrepreneurs seeking profits would expand the home markets of the LDCs much as they did earlier in the advanced capitalist countries. The stultifying presence of monopoly capital and the strategic insanity of the counter-revolutionary and containment policies of the imperialist states are necessary to account for the perpetuation of uneven development.

The basic concept of necessity becomes problematic in this era of monopoly capitalism. Prices contain administered salaries and the costs of selling which are necessary, if at all, only in an institutional sense. They are required not as a matter of technology but because of a given system of stratification. These expenditures are not required to transform nature into forms more appropriate to human use but to carry out that transformation in a way that maintains the stratification of power and privilege. These 'costs' are embedded in the structure of output in monopoly capitalism and become so habitually accepted as necessary that it is difficult to illustrate the fundamental irrationality of the system in which they are viewed as necessary.

Measurement of the economic surplus thus becomes far more complicated than in earlier capitalism. Accurate accounting of the economic surplus in the sense of a fund for social change requires a shift to the output side (Stanfield, 1973). The use of incomes for such a measurement is primarily of metaphysical interest and provides no accurate indication of the system's ability to pursue a changed future. The price paid for the most essential consumption of the most productive of labourers embodies the systemic waste and distortion of monopoly capitalism. It is therefore not very revealing to divide national income into the necessary wages of productive workers versus the surplus incomes of everyone else. The stratification of labour incomes and degrees of union organisational power further render this procedure suspect as does the obvious necessity for social reproduction of much government expenditures.

The surplus as a fund for social change, especially the systematic waste it contains, becomes the tool for highlighting the surplus repression of the monopoly capitalist order. The enormous social costs of capitalism's development of productivity must become part of the popular consciousness. Much of these costs have the important characteristic of being borne by people who lack the power to decide whether or not to bear them. It is instructive to think of capitalism as a system of institutionalised externalities (Stanfield, 1979b: 82–4). If alienation be that alien powers decide one's fate, then alienated capitalist society is accurately characterised as the institutionalisation of externalities, most especially of external costs. It is this very freedom of the capitalist ruling class virtually to ignore the misery and disruption introduced into the lives of ordinary people by the process of capitalist development that allows its prodigal pace.

The Marxist analysis of the path trodden by capitalism by which renunciation of the rule of capital becomes a manifest possibility is cast in terms of the internal contradictions of the capitalist mode of production. One such contradiction, implicit in the above discussion of alienation and social costs, is the increasing misery of the proletariat. Despite the advance of living standards, much poverty exists in the advanced countries and the deprivation in the LDCs is horrifying. Employment and income insecurity are also systemically obdurate.

Increasing misery is also profoundly important in the sense of the degradation of work and therefore of human beings whose character- istic essence is work. The quality of work is characterised by the development of the human skill and knowledge of work. This development up to a point is thoroughly consistent with increased division of labour and increased productivity (i.e., increased output per unit of labour input). However, obsessive concern within this regard can cause productivity and division of labour to conflict with develop- ment of skill. In the antagonistic capitalist setting, this obsession leads to fragmentation and degradation of work (Braverman, 1974; Stanfield, 1979a). The division of labour is carried to the extremes of the modern assembly line in which the worker is an adjunct to the machine. The human work process is then subordinated to commodities and techniques of production.

Moreover, in order to control alienated labour, the capitalist must remove the knowledge of production from the worker and deposit it in the preserve of management. Knowledge is power and workers whose brains are requisite to production are potentially a much greater threat than workers whose hands only are required. The growth of a managerial, technocratic stratum in contemporary capitalism is a logical outcome of this process. This stratum plans and coordinates the productive activity which is executed by the worker. The human work process – imagination or conception and execution – is thereby divided, which is to say that human life itself is divided and fragmented. This degradation is done to increase productivity and efficiency defined in terms of commodity output and input.

The misery of people in terms of poverty, insecurity, and degradation of work is matched by the havoc created by ecological disruption. The status thirst for surplus labour is likewise a thirst for the resources and amenities of the environment since human work involves transforming the rest of nature. Economic growth in terms of increasing demand upon natural resources and the capacity of ecosystems to service the byproducts of production is a necessary consequence of the status thirst for surplus labour. The social psychology involved in the 'arms race' of nation-states has much in common with the psychology of competitive expansion of commodity production and accumulation of surplus labour. Political organisation to protect ecological balance is again a collective expression for social control of economic activity and it is again fraught with the difficulties of controlling the consequences of the competitive status thirst without removing that institutionalised behavior process itself. It is none the less instructive that this political intervention to curb the excesses of the capitalist mode of production has been ever-present in capitalist history. But, as already alluded to, this interventionist drift is severely distorted by the confines of the capitalist order. Political activity within capitalist society is conditioned by that society and tends to reproduce its contradictions and antagonisms rather than to serve as a collective expression of social purpose and conscience (Stanfield, 1983). Capitalists use the state and nonstate political activity such as cartels or incorporation as instruments in their struggle for surplus labour. New opportunities arise for technocrats, managers, and bureaucrats to join the fray over surplus labour without being capitalists as such in the sense of holding ownership titles. Even labour can associate into unions and organise political power for immediate gains which are in contradiction to their class interests. The struggle for control of surplus labour knows no bounds and will be transcended only by the recognition of the basic communality of human work and the conscious cooperative organisation of that work.

The surplus as a fund for social change is capable of revealing to the popular mind the senselessness of the ecological destruction that they are witnessing and the persistence of alienated and hated toil in their workplaces as conditions of their existence. Only by separation of the necessary and the wasteful in the prices to which they devote their incomes can this be accomplished.

Thus the somewhat neglected Chapter 11 of Baran and Sweezy's classic is perhaps the most important of all. It combines the stagnationist background of Sweezy with the critical theory background of Baran and lays the foundation for a thoroughgoing psycho-cultural critique of monopoly capitalism (Stanfield, 1989). The cultural bankruptcy of the 'ideological wasteland' of late monopoly capitalism is felt by all who struggle to find their essential humanity within its insane social relations.

SURPLUS LABOUR AND THE NEW SOCIETY

Lest the congenital optimism of Marxian social theory be lost sight of, its basis should be made explicit. The strains capsuled above tend to generate both the means and the consciousness necessary for the construction of a new human society. The means for such a society are provided in the abundant material provisions produced by capitalism. These means for abundance are principally the scientific and technological capacity developed under capitalism rather than that system's physical commodities as such because much of these commodities would be useless to a peaceful, rational social system. The knowledge behind them can, however, be reallocated to serve human needs and development in a rationally ordered society. This is true even of the social sciences. The insights of behavioral psychology can be used to serve rather than manipulate human beings. The insights of macroeconomic and microeconomic theory, freed of class antagonism and demystified of commodity fetishism, can likewise serve humanity.

The consciousness necessary for social change can be seen in embryo in worker alienation, disaffection of youth, demands of ethnic minorities and women, and organisation of ecology groups and the underdeveloped nations and subnations. Awareness that more commodities purchased at the price of ecological devastation and human degradation do not increase 'quality of life' is the necessary precondition for social change.

This raises the familiar concept of abundance, upon which radical economics needs to be more precise. William Leiss's discussion (1976) of the ambiguity of human needs and commodities is the type of careful analysis required. Leiss does not argue upon the basis of needs versus wants and refuses to accept any notion of dividing human requirements into objective and subjective categories. Rather, the issue is the competence of people to understand their needs and administer their time and income toward their satisfaction in the 'high-intensity market setting' of monopoly capitalism. The problem is therefore the familiar one of alienation and control of the material process. The systemic tendency in worklife and personal life is to remove from the immediate producer/consumer the competence necessary for control.

Abundance is not infinite resources nor absolute freedom from the restraints imposed by nature. The radical vision embodies an historically, culturally relative concept of abundance. Most importantly, it is freedom from the cultural imperative toward insatiable wants, much of which arises in service to the systemic needs of the commodity production system and not the reasonable needs of self-authentic human beings.

The essence of the radical vision is not in the limits *to* growth but in the limits *of* growth. The limits to growth refers to the question of environmental and resource constraints on further economic growth. The question involved here is essentially: can we continue to grow? The limits of growth on the other hand is concerned with the value of further growth in terms of improving the human life process. Here the question is not: can we grow on like this, but rather: should we? The limits-to-growth argument is no doubt essential in generating the discussion from raised consciousness can develop but it all too quickly reduces to a technocratic wasteland: one group's simulations and projections versus another's. It is all too easy to leave out the cultural realm and to reduce the moral realm to a technological imperative. I know that many scholars involved in creating the limits-to-growth literature are people who are trying to teach that wisdom lies in knowing the limits placed on man by the natural system. None the less the fundamental moral or cultural realm often becomes lost in the process.

The radical vision needs to be based on the limits of growth and the moral imperative derived from understanding the human meaning of material wealth. This advance involves a cultural revolution in which the material realm is demystified as are the social relations surrounding it. Abundance is a major concept in this theory of an impending *gestalt* switch. Abundance in the radical view is not the technological satiation of alienated, insatiable consumers. Obviously this is not possible; hence, abundance must be understood in terms of a cultural revolution which changes the way consumers view commodities in relation to their wants.

This is not to deny that the accumulation of wealth is important in the radical vision. The role of this accumulation is to overcome the very real paucity of resources characteristic of the precapitalist era, thereby paving the way for demystification of the economic process. With the tremendous productivity capitalism makes possible, human beings potentially experience a change in consciousness amounting to a cultural revolution.

Consumers who solve the riddle of material wealth recognise that goods are tools toward life, not life itself. They apply, in other words, standards of instrumental utility to the goods that they buy. As tools, these goods are valuable only in so far as their users possess the skill, imagination, and knowledge to use them. Competent consumers must have craft knowledge and knowledge of the socio-ethical context of their consumption. Such knowledge takes time which *per se* reduces the time spent in the incomes race, chasing a wide array of commodities of dubious instrumental value (Stanfield and Stanfield, 1980).

In other words, as Aristotle taught, wants are limited in the nature of the case by the capacity of the individual (Kern, 1983). It is only unnatural wants, wants which are created by the exchange process itself and have no instrumental utility but merely represent wealth in the abstract, that are infinite. Aristotle taught that conceiving of wealth as a tool meant that the demand for wealth was limited in relation to the ends in view. The finitude of wants then derives from the finitude of the human being to comprehend the use of tools toward ends. Reflections on the ends of life is an essential and time-consuming part of competent, self-authentic consumption.

Perhaps Veblen among all radical scholars put the matter in its clearest form. Commodities have two sorts of usefulness. The first, instrumental utility, is usefulness in terms of the further unfolding of the human life process. This tool orientation toward commodities is satiable in the nature of the case. The individual consumer craftsman can only use so many tools. The second or invidious utility which attaches to goods in predatory societies is insatiable. This secondary utility is entirely relative. It is based on a desire to outdo others. This is a demand for commodities merely to have commodities and not for their instrumental value. Why would someone want to have commodities which have no instrumental utility? To demonstrate pecuniary ability because worth in a market capitalist society has long since become synonymous with one's market prowess, i.e., earnings. This prowess is, of course, based upon the ability to command the surplus labour of others. In this way the means, production, becomes an end *per se*. The economy, properly considered an aspect of human life oriented toward social reproduction and provisioning the further unfolding of the human life process, becomes an end in itself. This is the significance of Aristotle's concept of unnatural wants, as well as Marx's concept of commodity fetishism and Veblen's concept of conspicuous consumption.

This need not conflict with the radical emphasis on class relations. Invidiousness is a phenomenon of class society and abundance implies and requires a classless society. Moreover, class analysis which rises above taxonomy is essentially the examination of *power*. In capitalism, the corporate sellers of commodities have the power to influence consumers at least to the extent of reinforcing an ideology of consumption. The result is self-justifying commodity production (see Stanfield, 1979b: ch. 3).

In sum, radical economics has a highly tenable vision of abundance. The focus on social reproduction and the value of the widest possible cultural participation is sound if in need of synthetic statement. The real challenge of radical economics lies not in natural resources scarcity, but in the development of a psycho-cultural economics that can reveal the pernicious contradictions of monopoly capitalism and the latent possibilities for self-authentic development that these contradictions imply (Stanfield, 1989).

The new society would be organised upon recognition that surplus labour is the basis for the division of labour which allows human beings to develop their skill and productivity. However, the development of human beings would be superior to the growth of output *per se*. Skill, the development of the artistic and scientific potential of humanity, is subject to its own independent criteria of beauty, truth, and intrinsic worth, and productivity and efficiency must be made to serve these criteria rather than vice versa.

For the new society, whether to have economic growth or a stationary state would be a matter of conscious political choice. Growth too must be subordinate not superordinate to the needs of real living human beings. If society chooses to grow, it would marshal a share of surplus labour toward that end. The differential between aggregate surplus labour and aggregate consumption, the fund for social change, would be consciously structured quantitatively and qualitatively toward the collectively agreed-upon growth.

Private enterprise and initiative need not cease to exist in the new society. But such 'entrepreneurship' would look for finance not to an investment banker in accordance with the criteria of profitability but to popular representatives in accordance with the criteria of the social value. Public hearings and other advocacy forums could be established to gather information and opinions on proposed projects. This must stir some feeling even in the heart of the orthodox economists given their concern with external benefits and costs. What better way is there to 'internalise' externalities than by making all people in society, through representative political processes and advocacy hearings, the arbiters of benefits and costs?

The new society would no doubt be unable to dispense with the criteria of productivity and efficiency altogether – even if it wanted to, which is unlikely since functionality and economy of materials and energy exercised toward an instrumental objective have an inherent integrity of their own. Nature will never cease to impose upon its species the condition that they must produce their livelihood or perish. The human species must always first of all *work to exist* before it can achieve its essence of *existing to work.* But humanity can strive to humanise even this necessary work. Socially necessary work in a good society would be an obligation for all members of society to share in to the limits of their abilities. The women's movement demand to 'share the shitwork' transcends the particular interests of women because it is a universal principle. Social coercion to ensure that people are accountable to this obligation would reflect the coercion of nature but it would be nature's coercion humanised by conscious social mediation.

As Pearson indicates, there is much to be developed in the economic surplus concept if it is to pass the tests of social theory. There is also much to be done in developing the radical vision of a new society if it is to meet the challenge indicated by Heilbroner:

> With respect to socialism. . . estimates about the future are worthless unless they consider the underlying substratum of human nature from which socialism. . . will have to draw its energy; unless they describe the main institutional means by which these energies will be shaped and channeled. (Heilbroner, 1985: 207)

The problems of developing a workable model for the new society and a useful concept of the economic surplus are related.

Marx's plunder truism is suggestive rather than definitive. It leaves open the question of why the economic surplus was produced in the first place. Marx started from the fact that humans had produced beyond necessity and thus developed the forces of production. He made this a defining characteristic of the species. This no doubt served as the basis of a powerful social theory but in light of modern anthropology, it is necessary to go further and seek to account for the concrete cultural patterns involved.

Sahlins has demonstrated the antisurplus tendency of the domestic mode of production (Sahlins, 1972: chs 2 and 3). This raises the question of the cultural forces that offset this tendency and induced the generation of the surplus. He suggests the answer lies in the development of political or leadership forces that centralised allegiance and created motives to produce a surplus.

Sahlins' explanation points to the importance of the integrative state as opposed to the repressive state that predominates in the Marxist theory of the state (Stanfield, 1991). Of course, Marx implied the integrative state in his call for planning in a society in which the state was to wither away and in his distinction between coordination or orchestrating versus controlling or ruling (Marx, 1967: I. 329–32).

It is also necessary to account for the evolution of leadership into rulership and this raises issues concerning the new society. Even if leadership and political allegiance, or a prior instinct of workmanship or practical development, is accepted and held to account for the development of productivity, it remains to account for the development of invidious social stratification. Indeed, as Diamond suggests, stratification can account for the expansionary or imperialist character of all but the most primitive of human societies. The psychological insecurity of those who live by usurping the surplus labour of others may well lead to an urge to expand control to ameliorate uncertainty and the eclipse of one's status by a more powerful rival (Diamond, 1974: ch. 1).

But this does not account for stratification. It is plausible that psycho-theory can explain what social theory has yet to adequately treat: perhaps the biological nature of humans and the extended period of dependency that human culture has generated to house its developmental propensity contain an innate tendency toward domination (Heilbroner, 1985: 46–52). The urge to dominate may then account for stratification, given a developmental instinct toward practical progress. The dominative bent may even account for the progress, in the absence of such a bent.

All of this is immensely significant for the task of imaging the future good society. Indeed, it is the political question that reveals the Achilles heel of Marxist-Leninism. If there is an inveterate tendency toward domination, then the phenomenon of alienation is an ever-present threat which requires permanent institutional checks and balances. This goes beyond the problem of transition though it is reflected there. The transition to socialism in Marxist theory, since it presumes that capitalist personality structures still exist, is seen to require repression of counterrevolutionary inclinations. The problem of the transition is how to ensure that the exploitative characters do not establish command. But if there is an inveterate taste for domination, this political question is as eternal as that of social necessary labour. Indeed, the political process becomes an element of social necessity that will not disappear as the personalities of the capitalist era are replaced.

Accordingly, radical proposals for utilizing the economic surplus as a fund for collectively designed social change must be more specific as to the political aspect and more respectful of the classical liberal arguments concerning the respective roles of liberty and democracy in the good society. A radical vision chastened by the political economic dangers of political naivety will be a far stronger critical force and a far safer guide to the future.

REFERENCES

Baran, P. A. (1957). *The Political Economy of Growth*, New York: Monthly Review Press.

Baran, P. A. and P. M. Sweezy (1966). *Monopoly Capital*, New York: Monthly Review Press.

Braverman, H. (1974). *Labour and Monopoly Capital: The Degradation of Work in the Twentieth Century*, New York: Monthly Review Press.

Diamond, S. (1974). *In Search of the Primitive*, New Brunswick, NJ: Transaction Press.

Heilbroner, R. L. (1985). *The Nature and Logic of Capitalism*, New York: Norton.

Hunt, E. K. and Jesse G. Schwartz, eds (1972). *A Critique of Economic Theory*, Baltimore: Penguin Books.

Kern, W. (1983). 'Returning to the Aristotelian Paradigm: Daly and Schumacher', *History of Political Economy*, 15, 501–12.

Leiss, W. (1976). *The Limits to Satisfaction*, Toronto: University of Toronto Press.

Marx, K. (1967). *Capital*, New York: International Publishers.

Pearson, H. W. (1971). 'The Economy has no Surplus: Critique of a Theory of Development', in K. Polanyi, C. M. Arensberg, and H. W. Pearson, eds, *Trade and Markets in the Early Empires*, Chicago: Henry Regnery.

Sahlins, M. (1972). *Stone Age Economics*, Chicago: Aldine Publishing.

Stanfield, J. R. (1973). *The Economic Surplus and Neo-Marxism*, Lexington, MA: Lexington Press.

Stanfield, J. R. (1979a). 'Marx's Social Economics: The Theory of Alienation', *Review of Social Economy*, 37, 295–312.

Stanfield, J. R. (1979b). *Economic Thought and Social Change*, Carbondale, IL: Southern Illinois University Press.

Stanfield, J. R. (1982). 'Toward a New Value Standard in Economics', *Economic Forum*, 13, 67–85.

Stanfield, J. R. (1983). 'The Institutional Crisis of the Corporate-Welfare State', *International Journal of Social Economics*, 10, 45–66.

Stanfield, J. R. (1989). 'Veblenian and Neo-Marxian Perspectives on the Cultural Crisis of Late Capitalism', *Journal of Economic Issues*, 23, 717–34.

Stanfield, J. R. (1991). 'The Dichotomized State', *Journal of Economic Issues*, 25, 765–80.

Stanfield, J. R. and J. B. Stanfield. (1980). 'Consumption in Contemporary Capitalism: The Backward Art of Living', *Journal of Economic Issues*, 14, 437–450.

Veblen, T. B. (1953). *The Theory of the Leisure Class*, New York: New American Library.

9. Economic Surplus and the Market System

Leslie Fishman

INTRODUCTION

The amount of economic surplus generated by an economy, which Joe Phillips estimated, depends crucially on total output, and is the difference between that output and consumption. Under capitalism, production is guided by market prices and private accumulation, with various kinds of competition. This essay develops a new micro paradigm to describe that process. It relates prices to capital values and capital accumulation; it explains price formation and why most market adjustments are quantity adjustments and not price. Capital allocation decisions are made the core of the analysis, and all economic activities (banking, foreign trade, growth, development, inflation) are explained in terms of that capital accumulation framework. Once one truly understands how the market/price process works in capitalism, then one can begin to consider how it might be adapted to socialism. As recent events have shown, none of the socialist economies have ever managed to produce outputs (per capita) comparable to those of the average OECD country, let alone those of Japan. It has become clear the main reason for this was the failure of the socialist economies to make use of the market/price system. Without it, the accounting guides to efficiency and capital allocation and consumer choice and government spending are missing. The ship of the economy is without maps or compasses or a rudder. There are wide variations in productivity, and in the amounts of surplus, between the 'best practice' economies, such as Japan, and the 'worst', such as Britain. With these variations there are differences in behavior (in Japan, for example, firms stress market share and long-term capital accumulation, whereas in Britain the emphasis is on

149

short-term profit). But the essential characteristics of the capitalist market system are the same. Nevertheless, because the socialist economies could not produce at least as well as the average OECD country, they had little hope of surviving. The 'surplus' is not there to be scooped up. It has to be produced. One place to start is to have a realistic paradigm of how the market system works under capitalism. Only after this is appreciated can it then be modified for socialism.

One of Joe Phillips' best known works is his memorable statistical estimates of the United States' economic surplus from 1929 through 1963, and his discussion of the statistical problems which this entailed. It appeared in the Baran and Sweezy volume, *Monopoly Capitalism.* The concept of economic surplus lies at the heart of the Baran and Sweezy work, just as it does of most economic analysis, but since there are so few estimates of the magnitudes involved, Joe Phillips' contribution is especially noteworthy.

In this essay I want to raise questions about the theoretical foundations on which the economic surplus is based, and to relate these questions to the market/price mechanism. In the introduction, Baran and Sweezy (1966: 21) write, 'Our essay-sketch. . . attains its essential unity from one central theme: the generation and absorption of the surplus under conditions of monopoly capitalism'. In the accompanying footnote they refer the reader 'for a discussion of the concept of the economic surplus' to Chapter 2 in Baran's 1957 volume *The Political Economy of Growth.* There Baran begins by defining actual economic surplus as the difference between current output and current consumption. He contrasts this with Marx's surplus value, which is 'the entire difference between aggregate net output and the real income of labour'. Baran also distinguishes a 'potential' economic surplus as the difference between maximum output and 'essential' consumption, which would include 'essential' consumption of capitalists and 'essential' outlays on government 'and the like'. He identifies four kinds or sources of this 'potential' surplus: excess consumption; output lost through unproductive workers; output lost because of irrational and wasteful organisation of production; and output forgone through unemployment. What is involved is contrasting what the United States produces under capitalism with what would be produced under a 'more rationally-ordered society'. Baran quotes approvingly from Marx that in a socialist society the part of the total product

which is destined for the communal satisfaction of needs such as schools, health services, etc. is . . . from the outset . . . considerably increased in comparison with present-day society.

But however interesting and important is the concept of potential economic surplus, it is the 'planned economic surplus [that] is relevant . . . to . . . socialism' (p. 41). This planned surplus is the difference between society's 'optimum' attainable output, given the technology and resources, and some chosen 'optimal' volume of consumption. These 'optima' would not be determined by the fortuitous outcome of a number of uncoordinated decisions, 'but by a rational plan' (p.42). The surplus under socialism might be larger or smaller than under capitalism. The crucial difference is that under socialism the decisions 'represent a considered judgment . . . guided by reason and science', whereas under capitalism they are determined by the anarchy of the market.

In the case of the socialist economy, it must be assumed that the decisions taken to determine the optimum level of consumption and production will have the benefit of prices. Without prices cross-commodity and cross-industry comparisons become exceedingly difficult, if not impossible. Then too, there are the cross-temporal decisions that require prices. Where should these prices come from? How should they be used? Although Marx analysed the drive toward monopoly inherent in capitalism, throughout his writing he used competitive prices. This analysis was effectively carried forward and applied to the United States by the Baran and Sweezy volume that built on Kalecki and Steindl, and this is their conclusion.

> We conclude, then, that with regard to the cost discipline which it imposes on its members the monopoly capitalist economy is no less severe than its competitive predecessor, and that in addition it generates new and powerful impulses to innovation. There can therefore be no doubt about the downward trend of production costs under monopoly capitalism.
>
> On the face of it this would seem to be an argument for monopoly capitalism's being considered a rational and progressive system. And if its cost-reducing proclivities could somehow be disentangled from monopoly pricing and a way could be found to utilise the fruits of increasing productivity for the benefit of society as a whole, the argument would indeed be a powerful one. But of course this is just what cannot be done. The whole motivation of cost reduction is to increase profits, and the monopolistic structure of markets enables the corporations to appropriate the lion's share of the fruits of increasing productivity directly in the form of higher profits. This means that under monopoly capitalism, declining costs simply continuously widen profit margins. And continuously widening profit margins in turn imply aggregate profits which rise not only absolutely but as a share of national product. If we provisionally equate aggregate profits with society's economic surplus, we can formulate as a law of monopoly capitalism that the surplus tends to rise both absolutely and relatively as the system develops. (Baran and Sweezy, 1966: 79–80)

Setting to one side the questions whether a competitive/monopoly capitalism would continue to be a most progressive economic system, or a regulated capitalism that would approximate the competitive model, the underlying query remains: why has socialist economics devoted so little attention to the market system and the relation of prices to planning and efficiency? Although Baran and Sweezy's description of the workings of oligopoly/monopoly markets is still today one of the best in the literature, they did not even consider the problems involved in using the price mechanism in a planned economy.

There are probably many reasons for this. To begin with, the waste and shocking inefficiencies of capitalism are so obvious and pervasive. Both World Wars proved that physical planning was not only possible but worked exceptionally well, albeit under short-run, patriotic pressures. Nationalised industries also worked well and showed what might be accomplished, even when run by capitalist-type managers applying capitalist-type rules. Thus it appeared obvious that science and planning must be superior to anarchy and random market forces. Moreover, the entire field of microeconomics (price theory) and efficiency was always identified with apologies for the status quo and the general position that competition and private property would result in the best of all possible worlds. Marx argued that under capitalism, the rules of the game provide for all commodities exchanging at their competitive values and still result in profits – labour is the one commodity which, in the process of being used up, produces a value greater than the socially necessary labour required to reproduce itself (its standard of living). Thus, the owners of capital are able to buy labour power at its true 'value', but this is less than the product that labour power will produce. Since labour does not own the capital (or the know-how) to employ itself, but must sell its labour power on the open competitive market, the market price system is designed to exploit the workers, even by the most benevolent of employers. The rules of the price/market game are indelibly identified with 'exploitation'. To explore the use of prices for planning was asking to making use of the devil, and best left to old academic theorists like Oskar Lange. Although Lange 'proved' that socialist authorities following proper rules could bring about competitive results, there have been good reasons to ignore his results. The assumptions of his model, just as for the perfectly competitive model, are so extreme as to make it questionable whether either should be applied to the real world and to a real economy. Moreover, the socialist planned economy should work better than the competitive model and should evolve its own rules of the game, untainted by returns to capital, whether owned by individuals, firms, or society. Finally, there has tended to run through much of socialist economic literature a set of themes: since workers actually produce the goods and services, the owners/managers are largely supernumeraries and superfluous; accountants, and accounting are not all that important; monitoring, quality control, design, market analysis, distribution, etc. will largely look after themselves, if the macro overall totals are properly balanced.

Baran and Sweezy, for example, cite Michał Kalecki to show how a socialist authority would deal with the unlikely event of a general glut: 'the simplest and most direct remedy would clearly be to cut prices. This would reduce the amount of surplus at the disposal of the planning authorities and correspondingly raise the purchasing power of consumers. The threatened glut could be quickly and painlessly averted: everyone would be better off, no one worse off' (115–16). The same point is made by Baran in his earlier book, *The Political Economy of Growth* where he quotes from Kalecki's *Theory of Economic Dynamics* at length:

> It is useful to consider what the effect of a reduction in investment in socialist system would be. The workers released from the production of investment goods would be employed in consumption goods industries. The increased supply of these goods would be absorbed by means of a reduction in their prices. Since profits of the socialist industries would be equal to investment, prices would have to be reduced to the point where the decline in profits would be equal to the fall in the value of investment. In other words, full employment would be maintained through the reduction of prices in relation to costs. In the capitalist system, however, the price–cost relationship . . . is maintained and profits fall by the same amount as investment plus capitalists' consumption through the reduction in output and employment. It is indeed paradoxical that, while the apologists of capitalism usually consider the 'price mechanism' to be the great advantage of the capitalist system, price flexibility proves to be a characteristic feature of the socialist economy. (Baran, 1957: 42)

In the original, Kalecki has a footnote: 'It should be noticed that in an expanding socialist economy a reduction in the price–cost ratio will reflect a relative rather than an absolute shift from investment to consumption' (Kalecki, 1965 [1954]: 62) But neither Kalecki nor Baran and Sweezy address themselves directly to the question: what should be the role of market prices under socialism? Kalecki writes that only with socialism will true flexible pricing prevail. But the price adjustment that Kalecki writes about, and that Baran and Sweezy follow, relates to maintenance of full employment under socialism, in the event of a downturn in investment. No discussion takes place on the use of the price/market mechanism in allocation/efficiency. It can be argued that one implies the other, but one looks in vain for an explicit discussion of it. The price mechanism is so closely identified with exploitation and waste and capitalism that creative and constructive use of prices simply does not fit. Yet that is what is required; and to accomplish it a realistic price theory is required.

What is proposed here is a new paradigm for microeconomics, built on the relation of capital accumulation to the price mechanism, and using realistic assumptions about a firm's behavior and costs. The new micro paradigm has drastic implications on the macro side and provides a new way of looking at the workings of a capitalist economy. At a time when socialist economies are attempting to move from systems of physical allocation to the use of market prices, it is important for them to have a realistic model of how the capitalist market-price system actually does work, whether they try to adapt it or strive for something different. Thus, for both 'western'-style economies and 'eastern' economies, a realistic economic theory that relates capital accumulation to the market price system, built on realistic behavioral assumptions, is essential.

THE CENTRAL ECONOMIC QUESTION

Traditional economic theory poses the question, how are scarce resources allocated by the price system among unlimited wants, at a given instant of time? This is the wrong question with which to begin. The right question is: how does the price system allocate capital? In this section I will outline briefly how traditional theory answers these questions and why it has been led into several culs-de-sac. Then I will develop the new paradigm and apply it to several facets of economics.

In traditional theory the two main economic agents are the firm, organizing production and supply, and the consumer, creating the ultimate demand. A firm's decisions are guided by the goal of maximising profit, the difference between sales revenue and cost. An individual consumer's decisions are guided by maximising utility, or the pleasure derived from 'consumption' of goods and services. Firms operating in competitive markets must accept the going price for their products. If costs per unit rise as the rate of production is increased, then the rational profit-maximising firm will produce at that point where the rate of change of cost just equals the price, or where marginal cost equals price (and in this case marginal revenue). If we determine how much each firm will produce of each item, then we have answered the basic question posed by the allocation query. With a rising marginal cost curve, these levels of marginal cost become a supply curve of the firm in the short run. This means that as the price rises, the firm will increase its rate of production until its marginal cost rises to equal marginal revenue. To stop short of MR would mean forgoing profit; to go beyond MR would inflict losses. Thus, the MC curve tells us how much will be produced (how much allocated) at various levels of market prices. If we then add all of the MC curves of firms in the industry, we will have a market supply curve: a curve that tells us how much will be produced at various prices. But where do the prices come from? To answer this we need to turn to our consumer.

The consumer has a limited amount of money to spend, a budget, and, if 'rational', wants to maximise the utility or pleasure to be derived from the purchases, current and future. Or, to put it another way, the consumer wants to support a given level or standard of living at the least possible expense. The consumer knows the approximate prices in the main categories of purchases, such as food and clothing and leisure. He/she will distribute the purchases in such a way so that present and future utility is maximised, which will result when the marginal utility per dollar is equal for all possible purchases. When the price of an item drops, and if its marginal utility remains unchanged, it provides more utility per dollar, and thus more will be demanded. By purchasing more or less, the consumer is casting votes, or expressing preferences on what should be produced (allocated) more of or less of. Aggregating the consumer preferences allows us to obtain a demand curve, which tells us approximately how much consumers will buy of each item at various prices. It can only be approximate because in reality many prices are changing at the same time, not just the one price we are observing, and each price change affects all items and real incomes, however indirectly and however slightly. But for most purposes, and certainly for purposes of exposition, a demand curve emerges which relates the amounts likely to be purchased at various prices.

When we combine the market demand curve, obtained by aggregating the demand curves of all consumers, with the market supply curve, obtained by aggregating the supply curves of all firms in the industry, then a price emerges which will equate the two, clearing the market where supply equals demand. In the event that there is an oversupply, then unwanted inventories will accumulate, and prices will be reduced. This will result in firms producing less and consumers purchasing more, thereby bringing demand into equality with supply. The reverse would occur, according to the theory, if there were to be a favorable shift in demand. Inventories would run down, prices would rise, stores would increase their purchase orders, firms would increase their rate of output, and consumers would lower their purchases until a new equilibrium would emerge where supply and demand were in balance.

Although this traditional economics approach offers important insights, it is deficient in several crucial respects. First, almost all commodities are produced under conditions where average costs are falling and where marginal costs are fairly constant, and considerably lower than average costs. Second, in all but a few exceptional markets, the short-run adjustments which align supply with demand involve primarily quantity adjustments and not price. Moreover, most prices are set by firms, who add a mark-up to average cost, estimated at standard volumes. This is not to deny the key role that price plays in the allocation process; but it must be placed in its proper context. That context emerges when the third deficiency is outlined.

Traditional capital theory has the supply of capital coming from the consumer's decision of how to divide his income between present consumption and future consumption (savings). The price involved is the interest rate. The consumer 'maximises' by shifting expenditure from the present to the future (or vice-versa) until the relative marginal utilities equate with the interest rate. Consumers place themselves in an optimum position when their marginal utility of a dollar's worth of current consumption is just equal to the marginal utility of a dollar's (plus interest) worth of future consumption. The supply curve of capital is thus positively sloped and, consumers save more at higher interest rates. The demand for capital results from the marginal productivity of capital, or the change in total product that results from an additional dollar of investment. This increased productivity is usually attributed to the increased roundaboutness in production which the capital finances, and the additional product covers the interest and profit paid to capital. With diminishing returns to capital, the demand curve for capital will be negatively sloped, and when combined with a positively sloped supply curve, will result in a stable equilibrium at the clearing price for the interest rate. This analysis errs on several crucial points.

In the real world, most of the supply of capital comes from firms, not personal savings. In the U.S.,[1] for example, about 75 percent of all company capital comes from internal sources (reinvested profits and depreciation allowances), about 10 percent from trade credit expansion, and about 5 percent from bank credit. Only about 5 to 10 percent comes from selling new shares and bonds to pension funds, insurance companies, and consumers; and as J.M. Keynes (1936) pointed out, it is not at all clear that households will save more and invest more at higher interest rates. Moreover, traditional theory does not relate capital allocation to the price system. The theory stipulates that capital is allocated to where the expected rate of return (ROR) is highest, which certainly holds throughout; but little attention is devoted to how profit mark-ups and sales turnovers, which are the tools of business, are related to those ROR.

Keynes offered an alternative picture of the savings–investment core of theory, but was deficient in two respects. First, he treated savings as personal savings done by consumers, and did not consider company savings. Second, he had no micro theory on which to base his macro theory. Keynes' great insight was to start with the economy being demand driven. Savings were the residual left over from personal income after consumption spending by the consumer. If this amount of savings was less than the amount firms wished to invest, then demand would exceed supply, and output and employment and economic activity would expand. As output expanded, incomes would expand, and savings would increase. On the other hand, if savings were greater than investment, it would mean that more was being withdrawn from the purchasing-power stream than was being added. Demand would be less than supply, and economic activity would be curtailed. As output and employment fell, so too would consumption, but even more so would savings. The underlying adjustments to the savings–investment imbalances are accomplished by changes in the level of economic activity. Keynes' Marginal Efficiency of Capital (the expected ROR), driven by the 'animal spirits' of entrepreneurs, compared to the cost of capital (the interest rate), determined the levels of investment, and thus income, employment and economic activity. But Keynes was silent on how this related to price determination and the theory of the firm, and his savings were personal savings, the difference between personal disposable income and consumption.

A NEW PARADIGM

What changes are wrought if the starting point is capital accumulation? There are many economic units that accumulate capital, but by far the most important is the firm. The capital value of a firm is estimated in four ways: (a) historical cost less depreciation, (b) replacement cost, (c) resale value, (d) expected earnings discounted to the present. Each of these measures is useful and widely used, with the differences explaining much of the recent merger and acquisition activity.   But by far the most important is the fourth.   To estimate future earnings of a firm, one must estimate expected costs, and especially expected sales and prices.   If the firm is maximising its capital accumulation, then it will through time allocate its capital and invest in those activities with the highest expected ROR.

What are the conditions that enable firms to expect low costs and high prices and volumes?   These turn out to be where the rate of change (increase) in demand is likely to be greater than the rate of change (increase) in capacity.   Thus, the Harrod–Domar balance provides the framework to explain variations in capital accumulation and growth.   The signals for this process work through the price system and the market.

Each industry has a set of key reference prices that broadly reflect the capacity/demand balance at any given time.[2]   Not all sales occur at these reference prices.   Far from it.   Volume discounts, own-brand labels, special discounts and promotions, etc. result in 'special' reductions of the price; but the key reference prices, THE price lists, remain as the standard, as the guide.   The capitalised value of the firm, and the entire industry, depends in large measure on maintaining the reference prices.   If one assumes estimates for standard volumes and costs are constant, then relatively small increases in reference prices result, through the capitalisation formula, in large increases in capital values. And relatively small decreases in expected prices result in substantial decreases in expected profits, and even larger reductions in capital values.   All firms in an industry thus have an enormous vested interest in keeping the reference prices as high as possible, and maintaining solidarity not to cut prices.   This results in channeling competition and adjustments on to the quantity side.

At the same time, there are considerable pressures on the firm to lower or shave the prices, preferably in such ways that do not lower the public reference prices.   First, almost all firms produce in a range where AC is declining and where MC is fairly constant and far below the AC.   Under these circumstances, every increase in the rate of production lowers the cost per unit.   Every sale made at a price above the MC, allows the firm to regain at least some of its overheads and fixed costs.   All firms who are customers of other firms are well aware of this and are eager to take advantage of this situation to improve their own cost and profit position.   Thus, there is always pressure on suppliers to lower prices.   Second, it can be argued, as economists insist on emphasising, that the demand curve is negatively sloped.   Thus, the lower the price, the more will be sold, all other things being equal.

Nevertheless, firms know that the total amount spent in a period is relatively fixed (plus or minus such things as credit expansion) and what counts towards capital accumulation is the profit made per unit of sale. For example, the number of cars sold in a year does not depend to any great extent on the reference prices of cars, although for each consumer the prices of specific cars and models play an important role in determining which specific car is purchased. The number of cars sold by the entire industry depends mainly on such factors as the average age of the car population (i.e., replacement demand and new demand), average number of miles driven by car users, road conditions, credit terms and availability, public transport availability and cost, incomes, parking, spatial distribution of work and homes and leisure activities, accident rates on motorcycles, bicycles and cars, number of new drivers' licenses, and tax provisions for company and fleet cars. Lower or higher prices may affect the timing of new car purchases, and as already mentioned, certainly affect which car and model is finally chosen by each consumer. The car manufacturer balances the tensions of the market and adopts policies to maximise his firm's capital accumulation, but he does not believe he can significantly affect in the short run the total of car sales for the entire industry. Instead, let us trace his crucial decisions and see how they impinge on the firm's capital position.

He has designed a new car model with a given reference price in mind. The huge up-front fixed costs are reasonably well known, as are the expected MC. He knows what his historical market share for this model has been, and on the basis of econometric estimates of the variables listed above, he can estimate the expected total car sales for the coming year, and his model's share, with a plus and minus set of margins. Using these volume estimates, he can see if the mark-up between estimated AC and the reference price is sufficient for him to achieve his target ROR. If it is not, he may modify the design, or the 'extras', or simply rely on higher-than-expected sales volumes to lower per unit cost and thus permit the target ROR to be 'achievable'.

If, when the car model is introduced to the market, demand outruns capacity, then the full reference price would prevail and volumes would exceed standard estimates. Higher ROR than estimated would ensue and the happy situation would result in very rapid capital accumulation indeed. The consumer may, under these circumstances, find his trade-in allowance reduced and he may perhaps even pay the dealer a premium over the listed price; it is very unlikely, however, that the manufacturer will not honor the reference price to the dealer. Instead, with the next price review, higher reference prices may result.

On the other hand, if the new model were not selling up to expectations, if excess capacity was pervasive, various measures might be adopted, but none of them would involve lower reference prices, at least not unless the firm was desperate. Trade-in allowances would be raised. Special credit terms would be made available. Fleet car discounts might be expanded and stretched and made to include 'extras'. Additional advertising campaigns would be mounted. Various 'extras' would be included 'free'. And tie-in 'specials', such as 'free' holidays, might be included. All of these increase the cost to the car dealers and/or the manufacturer, but try to protect the reference price. It can be argued that these extra inducements truly represent price cuts rather than cost increases. And the firms least able to afford the price cuts are often forced by market conditions to make them first. The strongest firms, the price leaders who can most easily absorb price cuts, are usually the last to do so, if at all (unless they indulge in predatory pricing – that is, extreme cuts in prices to drive out competition). But in the real world of capital accumulation what is happening is as follows. Capacity is outrunning demand, as it is wont to do in capitalism, and expected ROR is under pressure. Since the capital value of the firm or industry is a large multiple of expected earnings, say 10×, or a price-earning ratio of 10, firms try to preserve the reference prices at all cost. They channel their competition into innumerable non-reference price paths, thereby protecting the capital values of their firm and industry. Volume and quantity, not price absorb most of the adjustments in most markets. Price wars and price competition do occur, especially when newcomers or NICs or large overhangs of excess capacity are involved; but normally the market signals are transmitted through sales volumes, in the first instance. At the same time, price is crucial in guiding the allocation of capital, through its effect on expected ROR, and thus on capital values.

How is this related to savings and investment? Since most finance for investment comes from re-invested profits, depreciation allowances, trade credit, and bank loans, supply is creating the demand. Firms that are successful generate high levels of internal funds, and can readily attract additional trade credit, bank loans, and also new funds from the stock exchanges, if they do not mind diluting their ownership. These most successful firms are astride those products and services where demand is maintaining a good relation with capacity, where reference prices are strong and strengthening. They thus have the wherewithal to invest and good information on expected ROR. Competition is fierce, however, in searching for the high and relatively secure ROR for the future. The economy seems to generate more capital than good opportunities to invest that capital. The firm must always take care to protect its own core profit centrally by adequate investing that promotes new models, new products, new processes, R&D, better training, etc. But the economy and the world are constantly changing. Areas that were high ROR in the past rapidly become areas of low ROR, unless special monopoly conditions intervene. Thus, firms generating large funds are always under pressure to invest those funds wisely, to search out the high ROR earners of the future – those products where demand is likely to stay ahead of capacity. During a recession profits fall off, as do investment opportunities. During an upswing profits and internal funds increase rapidly, as do investment opportunities. As a result, investment tends to equal savings, not just in the accounting sense, but because the main source of savings (profits) tends to precede investment and to transmit the all-important ROR signals to those responsible for investment.

Hence, with the critical balance of savings and investment, movements in profits (up and down) provide variations in the supply of funds (up and down), just as they provide the key signals (up and down) for investment. There are leads and lags here. When investment is greater than savings, growth in the economy accelerates, and savings tend to increase faster. When savings are greater than investment, growth slows down, and capacity is increasing faster than demand. The underlying adjustments between capacity and demand result from the adjustments made at the micro level by the volume of sales and reference prices. Thus the Harrod–Domar knife-edge problem seldom, if ever, comes into play.

If consumers (and exporters and government) purchase more than expected (more than standard volumes), then sales are buoyant and the weighted average of prices will be at the reference price end of the price spectrum (AC plus full mark-up). If the sales volumes are maintained at the healthy profit margins, profits and company savings soar, and provide the wherewithal to finance increases in investment and expand capacity. If capacity is expanding faster than demand, then sales volume begins to lag behind the *new* standard estimates for sales. Firms try to achieve these new standard volumes by increased sales efforts. If they succeed, then previous growth rates and investment levels can be sustained. If not, they will begin lowering their unofficial prices below the reference price levels and towards the MC levels. Profit margins are squeezed and company savings decline, which in turn slows investment and the rate of expansion of capacity. And the reverse process holds. If demand is expanding faster than capacity, sales volume will tend to exceed standard volume. Actual

AC will be below estimated AC levels, at the same time as more sales take place at reference price levels.   Company profits and savings mount, there is increased pressure to invest more, and these ROR profit signals provide the guides for capacity expansion.

This description of the savings–investment process does not include an explanation of the turning points.   There are various explanations which require discussion; but for purposes of this essay, the point I want to stress is how different the savings–investment process looks when capital accumulation is placed centre stage.   The new capital accumulation paradigm has profound implications for all fields in economics, as well as for political and social institutions.   But in this summary only three will be introduced: the labour market, international trade, and socialist economies.

THE LABOUR MARKET

To apply the capital accumulation paradigm, the three main centres of capital ownership and decision-taking must be defined.   First, there is the individual and the family; then there is the firm; finally, there is the national economy, which can be viewed in at least two significant ways.   Geographically, it is the sum of the capital within its boundaries.   Economically and politically, it is the sum of capital owned and controlled by its nationals, regardless of the physical location of the capital or the nationals.   In addition to these three main capital centres, there are innumerable other organisations and informal groups some of whom own and control capital, but also many others such as industry associations, whose main function is to further the capital accumulation of its members.   Trade unions' main function can be viewed as maximising the capital value of their members, which is largely their expected future earnings, discounted to the present.   Examples of other capital centres are church organisations, governmental units, and charitable societies and clubs.

In the case of the labour market, the four main capital centres involved are the individual (and family), the firm, the industry, and trade unions.   The traditional economic approach traces the demand for labour to the firm, which calculates the marginal product of labour and continues to hire until this negatively sloped (diminishing returns) curve intersects the going wage.   Traditional analysis on the supply side assumes the maximising member of the labour force will work until the marginal disutility of the work is just equal to the marginal utility of the wage.   Aggregating these for the entire work force results in a positive supply curve for labour.   When combined with a negatively sloped demand curve (the aggregate of all firms' demand curves), the intersection gives an equilibrium wage that would clear the market. If there were a perfect market, all those willing to work at the equilibrium wage, or below, would be employed.

There are several glaring shortcomings to this traditional analysis. It provides an inadequate explanation for unemployment: lowering the wage undoubtedly makes additional workers more attractive to employers, but it also lowers effective demand, as Keynes so perceptively developed. To understand involuntary unemployment requires an explanation of why effective demand, and primarily its most volatile element, investment, does not remain sufficiently robust to sustain full employment. Then, too, traditional theory assumes diminishing returns, which provides the rationale for the negatively sloped derived demand curve for labour, when the overwhelming evidence points to constant returns. Constant returns give rise to a horizontal demand curve, which throws the burden of determining 'equilibrium' on to the supply side: that would mean everyone willing to work at the going wage would easily find a job, and this is certainly not true. Finally, and most important, traditional theory has not provided a set of realistic models of labour markets to explain demand and supply.

Keynes highlighted the existence of involuntary unemployment and correctly turned to deficient aggregate demand for an explanation. Nevertheless, he was loath to break with marginal productivity theory. With the flood of involuntary unemployment that came in the Great Depression, 'imperfect labour markets' was hardly a satisfactory explanation. Instead, Keynes devised an ingenious definition for involuntary unemployment, which 'proved' that it could exist in a market economy, where firms and workers were true maximisers.

> Men are involuntarily unemployed if, in the event of a small rise in the price of wage-goods relatively to the money-wage, both the aggregate supply of labour willing to work for the current money-wage and the aggregate demand for it at that wage would be greater than the existing volume of employment. (Keynes, 1936: 15)

This hardly gets us much further in providing a new basic framework within which to analyse supply and demand of labour markets.

For this we need the new paradigm. The capital accumulation paradigm offers a realistic model of the firm on which to build a sensible demand model for labour; it also provides a new set of household models from which realistic supply curves of labour emerge. The firm pursues personnel policies of hiring and firing, of training, of promotions and bargaining, all within the long-run goal of maximising capital accumulation.   Most firms have a manning table for each of their capital centre activities, which depends primarily on the real (as opposed to the money) capital involved.   The manning tables vary with the technology, the management, the work force, and the history of the firm and the industry.   They can be flexible, starting with a core complement of workers, below which the installation cannot function.   If sales warrant it, the core will be supplemented with additional labour, sometimes in steps, reflecting such discontinuities as shift work.   The transition from one level of manning to a higher one is often bridged by overtime work, part-time workers, or temporary additions.   Sometimes extra work will be sub-contracted to other firms, or if technology permits, a putting-out system ban be expanded.   Expansion of the full-time work force is often costly, and taken only if absolutely necessary.   What employers constantly ask themselves is: how many workers do we require to produce the standard quantity we expect to sell, and can we do it at or below our estimated AC, to fulfill our target ROR?   But plans must also be flexible.   If demand exceeds the standard volumes, how might it be best to deal with this at least cost and also to secure the future?   If, on the other hand, demand falls short of expected standard volumes, how can labour costs be minimised, while still preserving the ability to respond to increases in demand, if conditions improve?

The firm may be an acknowledged leader in the industry, able to attract and keep an excellent work force, and able to pay more than the going rate for the jobs.   These jobs might be more secure than the average in the industry, and the 'core' workers are likely to be exceedingly valuable to the firm in terms of experience, training, and identification with the interests of the firm.   The 'core' workers know that their own capital value (primarily consisting of future earnings discounted to the present) is in large part dependent on the firm's future as a capital accumulator.   It is this identification of the interests of workers and firm that is emphasised by the Japanese, German, and cooperative models.

The identification is reinforced if the share-out of the capital fruits, and the hardships, are to be equitable, and if participation and responsibility are recognised, encouraged, and rewarded.   But this involves taking the long-term capital accumulation view, as opposed to the short-term profit-maximising view.   Nevertheless, the tension between these two approaches exists in all firms, to some degree.

In sharp contrast, the firm may be a new, marginal, small firm trying to gain a foothold, hiring the minimum number of workers, and anxious (and able) to pay the least they can get away with.   These rates might be considerably below the going rates, and the identification of the workers with the firm may be minimal. Workers and trade unions try to protect their own capital by establishing going rates for the job, raising them as fast as possible, and protecting them against competitive pressures, just as firms protect the value of their capital by protecting reference prices. It is to the interest of both trade unions and established firms to police these 'unfair' shops and ensure that they do not gain an 'unfair' advantage by not paying the going rate.

Nevertheless, far from there being a single wage, which traditional theory predicts, and which trade unions and industry associations strive to regularise, in reality a spread of wage rates usually exists, around a central tendency. All kinds of variations tend to persist, such as those cited above, and revolve around security, age of firm and worker, expanding or contracting work force, technological change, safety, transport allowances, perks, etc. Overall, it is demand, derived from final markets, which dominates most labour markets, modified usually in a muted sense by such supply conditions as educational requirements, apprenticeship, and trade unions. The level of final demand is also best analysed in terms of capital accumulation. In addition, however, the way various firms translate this demand into demand for labour also lends itself to such capital analysis.

The underlying tension in the firm–employee situation is best approached from a capital standpoint. The workers are only too aware that their outlook for future earnings is dependent on the capital accumulation outlook of the firm. The more successful the firm, the more likely it will be that they will also prosper. On the other hand, workers are in no position to evaluate how their future wage increases (or lack of them), their intensity or flexibility of work (or lack of it), will be made use of by management. If they were to moderate their wage demands or increase their work rate, would management increase their efficiencies too, and would more of the profits be reinvested or put into R&D to brighten the firm's future capital accumulation outlook? Or will the additional profits be shared by management and shareholders, with the workers and the future of the firm being left to take care of themselves? Would the first lucrative takeover bid be accepted, once the price had been raised as much as it could, with little thought of how it might affect the future of the work force? Thus, often the safest and most reliable course is simply to ensure the going rate is adhered to, and is raised as fast as the market and the trade union can achieve.

On the employer side, each employer wants to keep the best workers, but at the same time there is considerable pressure for solidarity in maintaining wages at the minimum going rate, and not breaking ranks, or at least not doing so publicly.   Once the going rate is breached, all other things being equal, the result will be lower profits and lower capital values of the firm.   In the event the wage increase spreads throughout the industry, then no firm in the industry will enjoy a competitive advantage, but the entire industry's capital would suffer relative to all other industries.   At the same time, each firm would benefit greatly if its employees believed they were special and were receiving more than the going rate, even if only in low-cost luncheons, extra days off, special purchases or credit arrangements, special allowances, or other ingenious non-wage benefits.

In the Japanese post-war context, lifetime employment in large firms, and the proliferation of sub-contracting with small firms, made a great deal of sense in capital accumulation terms.   With lifetime employment and large profit-sharing bonuses paid semi-annually, the accumulation of capital by the workers and managers was aligned with the capital accumulation of the firm.   Shareholders, who were often banks and related firms, such as suppliers, found their capital goals also aligned through the huge increases in stock prices and the large increase in custom.   But complete alignment of interests is impossible because the share-out problem will always exist.   Simply nationalising industry did not accomplish this.

In the Russian experiment, once the New Economic Policy was replaced by Stalin with physical allocation under the five-year central plans, they lost the essential accounting and statistical guides to capital allocation.   It is unclear what would have happened if the NEP had been followed up, but in such countries as Sweden and Germany, the nationalised sectors have tended to be service industries (health, transport, education) where capital accumulation criteria are difficult to apply.   In British manufacturing there has been a notable lack of success in aligning the aims of capital accumulation by the firm and the work force, with significant exceptions.   As a result, early on Britain adopted the unusual policy of inviting foreign firms to take advantage of British workers and markets – first U.S. and Dutch firms, and then more generally German, Swiss, Japanese, South Koreans, and others.   This open-door policy to foreign capital has spread, but the British are the most welcoming among the industrial nations.   Many of these 'foreign'-owned plants in Britain, and especially the Japanese, report ROR at least equal to those in their home country.   In capital accumulation terms this means that British governments have been willing to give Japanese capital the opportunity to employ (and spread) their management skills, taking advantage of British (and EC) markets, and thereby adding to the demand for British labour and helping the British balance of trade, at least in the short-run. In return, Japanese capital accumulation is sustained, perhaps in place of British capital.

What is abundantly clear from the above brief analysis of the demand side of the labour market is that the new paradigm provides a far richer and more realistic framework for analysis than does traditional theory. This is particularly evident on the supply side of the labour market. For several decades economists have applied capital analysis to estimates of returns to education and training; and it has often appeared in models about unemployment and vacancies, and women's employment. The main capital centre involved on the supply side is the individual (or the family or household). Each adult in the household has a set of expected capital values for various time horizons. Age, family circumstances, work history, education, geographic location, level of savings, friends, housing, transport, pension, and unemployment benefits, union affiliation, social security entitlements, health, will all influence a person's attitude towards entering and remaining in the work force, how they go about the job search, and their attitude towards further education and training and part-time employment, etc. For many, the immediate wage and circumstances will dominate most decisions. But for many others, they will only be some factors among others to be considered in the decision. The capital approach enables all factors to be related in a significant fashion.

To explore whether the capital approach is helpful, let us apply it to a segment of the labour market that is growing in importance, the young single mother with a pre-school child. Traditional analysis searches for reservation wages that would reveal the following important information: at what wage various members of these mothers would actively join the labour force and what hours they would be willing to work. The capital approach, on the other hand, stimulates models that explore the immediate situation and the longer term. The immediate situation, for example, stresses current and future welfare entitlements, cost and quality of child-care provisions, extra costs of going to work (dress, transport, extra food cost, etc.), and increased future losses that result from extending the period of non-working: in other words, the short-run capital position of the family with and without the various possible jobs. In the longer term, the analysis broadens to include such variables as more education and training. Both the traditional and the capital approaches have their usefulness; but by viewing the household as a capital centre, one is able to appreciate the multi-dimensional nature of the supply decision.

Important as the supply side is, the demand side is decisive. It is the demand side that structures the alternatives available, that is proactive. The supply side then reacts. It maximises the individual capital centre positions, given these alternatives. Few workers are faced with a smooth demand curve, as pictured by traditional analysis. Most workers work 40 hours a week (plus overtime) or zero or a fixed number of part-time hours. If work is slack then they will be asked to work a fixed number of hours less than 40, but it will be a fixed amount. It is true that there is always the ultimate alternative open to the household centre, that of becoming self-employed. Important though this is, for most of the work force at any one time this is not a significant demand factor, although it lends itself very much to capital analysis.

All in all, the traditional supply and demand analysis is greatly enriched by the addition of the capital approach. The demand side takes its rightful dominant position, but with the emphasis on the degree of success of the firm pursuing its proper goal of capital growth. The reactive supply side throws the spotlight on the multi-faceted household capital position and outlook, where the wage is important, but is far from being the only, or even the decisive, variable involved in the work decisions.

CAPITAL ACCUMULATION AND INTERNATIONAL TRADE

In international trade, the main centres of capital accumulation involved are firms, national economies, banks, and central banks. Wealthy individuals and families, as well as 'foreign' workers, and others, such as tourists, are also involved, but for a first, main model, they can be ignored. The capital value of a country can be estimated as the sum of the capital values of all of its nationals; alternatively, it can be estimated as the sum of the capital values within its borders, including the capital value of the work force. As in the case of labour markets, the new paradigm stresses how capital centres cooperate and compete with one another. One nation competes with all other nations, and at the same time cooperates; just as one firm competes with all other firms in the same industry, and yet cooperates to maintain the capital values of the entire industry. Similarly, each central bank attempts to maximise the 'wealth of (its) nation', while at the same time cooperating to maintain an orderly global capital market.

The reason why international trade takes place is because capital centres, usually firms, believe they can accumulate more capital in so doing. The value of the capital in one country is linked to the value of the capital in a second country by the exchange rate. Just as in the case of a domestic market, the higher the price (the exchange rate), the greater is the capital value of the nation. But the higher the price (the exchange rate), the more expensive are both the capital and the sale price of all of its goods and services involved in international trade; and the cheaper are the purchases of imported goods and services, and foreign capital purchased by home firms and banks. A tension thus exists similar to that between the firm and the industry in the domestic economy. Importers of goods and services and exporters of capital want a strong domestic currency, which will maximise their capital accumulation. Exporters of goods and services and importers of capital prefer a weak currency to maximise their capital accumulation. All international transactions involve at least two prices: the price of the good or service or capital good, and the price of the money in which the settlement must be made, the exchange rate.

Exchange rates respond to the forces of supply and demand in the foreign exchange markets. These forces can be broken down, on the supply side, into exports of goods and services, exports of capital, loans by banks, and gifts and remittances. Similarly for the demand side, but involving imports instead of exports. What the capital accumulation approach adds to the analysis is that it enables each of these transactions to be related to the capital centres involved, and enables us to trace the impact of the transactions on the capital positions of the centres. For example, the national economy has a net worth in yen, which could be defined as the sum of the net worths of its citizens and those in permanent residence. Or it could be defined as the sum of the net worths of all capital centres domiciled within its borders. Under the first definition Japanese firms owning and operating large plants in Britain would be included in Japan, but in the second definition, in the U.K. It is this sum which is the wealth of the nation, and which the nation tries to maximise. The larger this sum, the more powerful and influential and productive is the nation. The higher the exchange rate, the greater is this sum in money terms, but the more expensive are its exports. To maximise capital accumulation for the nation, one would strive for a rising exchange rate plus enough technical progress and increased efficiency to more than offset the rise, and thus maintain or even increase exports. The capital centre approach allows us to shed new light on this process.

The traditional economic theory approach to international trade emphasises comparative advantage as the underlying rationale for all trade. Japan with natural comparative advantages in seaweed and earthquakes, illustrates the limitations of the traditional theory. Of course, such factors as skilled management, highly trained and cooperative labour, excellent education and R&D, sensitive and adaptable design and marketing, etc. can be interpreted as 'comparative advantage', but that is like saying success is what the successful do. In contrast, the capital accumulation approach provides a theory to explain why some firms are more profitable than others, why some nations are more successful than others. The process of capital accumulation is placed under the microscope to be studied and dissected. A dramatic example of the kind of benefit that results is in considering how one would define 'the Japanese economy'. With the capital approach it is natural to start with the sum of the capital owned by Japanese individuals and Japanese firms throughout the world, regardless of their physical location. In contrast, traditional trade theory uses the geographical definition for exchange rate and national economic policy. All trade statistics are gathered on this geographic basis, although it has been obvious for several decades that the interpenetration of capitals and plants by transnational firms has made it imperative to supplement this with the capital approach. In recent years ever more attention has been devoted to measures of 'net foreign indebtedness' and 'net foreign capital investment', but these aggregate measures have lacked the solid micro anchor that the capital accumulation theory can provide.

Why, for example, did the Japanese government and the Bank of Japan protect, encourage, and support the fledgling motor car industry in post-World War II Japan? Traditional theory characterises such infant industry strategy as misguided economic subsidies paid for by consumers, taxpayers, and other industries. Capital accumulation theory, in contrast, analyses: (a) why MITI and the Ministry of Finance and the Bank of Japan based their policies on the foresight and judgment that the expected ROR for cars could be enormous in two or three decades; (b) how the industry was structured so that the five or six firms competed bitterly with each other, while at the same time they cooperated to share the best practices learned from the United States and Europe; (c) and why, despite having to import all of the materials going into the car from long distances (except glass) and exporting the finished cars long distances, the Japanese car industry is such a fairy-tale success story; (d) and finally, when it reaches the pinnacle as the dominant national car industry in the world, why does it embark on a massive foreign investment, foreign plant decentralisation/joint venture activity, while continuing to accelerate certain central functions, such as R&D and design?

At the same time, the theory should be universal. It should provide a good framework with which to analyse the decimation of the indigenous British car industry over this same period. The capital accumulation theory does just that.

SOCIAL DEMOCRACIES AND SOCIALIST ECONOMIES

The final example in this introduction of the application of the capital theory approach is to social democratic and socialist economies. At one level of abstraction it can be argued that social democratic and communist parties address similar ills of society: unemployment, poverty, inequalities, waste, inefficiencies, pollution, lack of social provision for such things as sanitation, health care, education, planning, and housing. The social democrats approach these ills through reform programs stemming from democratic political movements that accept the market and the price system. The reforms seek to use government powers to curb or correct the excesses of capitalism; or to take advantage of the externalities available, usually to government, but also to other organisations; or to meet social needs; or to promote full employment, productivity, growth, stable prices, and a strong international position. Maximising social capital accumulation is seldom, if ever, explicit as a goal. (Conservative parties, however, do implicitly seek to maximise private capital accumulation.) But if the broader definition of capital is used, one that includes the skills and health and culture and well-being of the entire population, as well as the total environment, then a different perspective is necessary. And therefore a new capital theory is required: one that enables us to estimate and monitor the ROR of various policies, and one which is not ideologically imprisoned by a *laissez-faire* mentality or, at the other extreme, an anti-market, anti-price fixation. Rather, we need a theory which will enable the maximisation of social capital, making use of new market and new price techniques, and constantly searching for new ways of accumulating social capital and making the best use of it. Ideally, this would mean aligning individual capital accumulation with that of society's.

In the case of a housing estate, for example, the conservative historical cost estimate of its capital value would consist of the cost of building the estate, including the land value, minus depreciation. If the houses were individually owned, there would be an apportionment of costs, including some *pro rata* method of distributing the cost of common spaces and equipment (lifts, halls, heating, garden space, and play area, etc.). The aim would be to maximise the individual's capital, and thereby maximise the total capital value. A truly optimising owner would invest as little as possible in improvements, but try to convince his neighbors to invest as much as possible, thereby maximizing his own capital position. A social democratic approach might well respond to the needs of low-income families and political pressures. Their evaluation of the estate might run more in terms of the improvement in general living conditions and the political support this generates. In contrast, the social capital accumulation approach would try to align the individual family interest with that of the estate and community, an approach which unfortunately is often absent from housing estates in Britain today. This is not easy to achieve and requires constant adaptation and monitoring. Innovative forms of capital ownership should be explored, such as share-ownership of the total estate where only occupants are eligible. To estimate the social capital value of the estate, one must measure the total expected returns from the property, including better health, reduction of crime and vandalism, neighborliness, better care of the elderly and handicapped, ease of transport and shopping, improved environment, etc. Making these estimates with the estate occupants and owners would be part of a learning process, and they should be projected into the future, along with their costs. The sum might well be greater than (or less than) the simple addition of the parts. But by placing the emphasis on the future (the entire expected life of the estate) and estimating monetary values for all important character-istics, both for the individual and the community, full recognition is given to the social nature of the value of capital.

It is far more difficult to apply the new capital theory to communist societies. Marx 'proved' that playing by the capitalist market rules of the game, labour would be paid its full competitive value as a commodity – the socially necessary amount required for its reproduc-tion – and profit would result, because the work which labour accom-plished always exceeded its value. Marxists are thus inclined to identify prices and the market system totally with exploitation. They find it difficult to see how the market system can be used, in fact must be used, if they are to succeed in approximating the kind of society they idealise.

In the Soviet Union, however, the rejection of the price mechanism as a major allocation tool took place historically, and primarily for political reasons, not economic. The 1917 revolution was followed by some three and a half years of war communism, and then over half a decade of the NEP (New Economic Policy). The war communism period was characterised by a series of crises that necessitated rationing, confiscation, sequestration, requisitioning, commandeering, and what Alec Nove calls extreme communisation. Although the

Supreme Council of National Economy (VSNK$_H$, or Vesenkha) was created in mid-December 1917 to plan 'the economic life of the country', there is little doubt that most allocation during this period was done by local markets (and black markets especially) coupled with all of the various physical seizing of goods and labour that accompanied a revolution, the ending of a devastating world war, invasion by foreign armies across vast distances, civil counter-revolutionary war, followed by a war with Poland. The durability and resilience of the market-price system was shown when the NEP was introduced in desperation in 1921. Despite severe famine and enormous industrial difficulties, the economy responded well to monetary reforms and incentives, and the evolving 'mixed' forms of direction from the market and the VSNK$_{II}$ and its various subordinate bodies. Nevertheless, serious problems arose. Severe shortages and inflationary pressures persisted along with the 'scissors crisis' – industrial prices getting far out of balance with agricultural prices. Then, too, these existed the usual market problems of profiteers, of growing inequalities, and of the numerous examples of unfairness that inevitably accompany shortages and price expansions. Against this backdrop, after Lenin's death in 1924 the party debated the crucial issues of how to industrialise, whether socialism can be built in one country, and the way to accumulate enough capital (extract enough surplus) from the over 95 percent of the work force involved in peasant agriculture. By 1928 the many great debates were over. Stalin had triumphed. The kulaks would be squeezed and squeezed again (poor though they were) and the surplus would be extracted. Heavy industry, extra-rapid industrialisation, unbalanced growth would be physically planned and effected. Price and market tools would be shunted aside, largely ignored for policy, and mainly restricted to households balancing their budgets, and firms and banks noting aggregate costs to be covered by income and subsidies from the state. Physical central planning would rule. The party would make the key allocation decisions. It is ironic that they chose the path of accumulating capital by confiscation instead of encouraging firms to use the price mechanism for the accumulation. Confiscation gave them a minute sum compared to the cumulative, compound interest sum they could have gained using the market system.

Now, some 60 years later, we see the Soviet Union fumbling in its attempt to reintroduce prices (competitive, 'socially necessary' prices?) and make use of the market as the effective allocator of capital. Can it possibly give rise to a progressive economy where consumer and producer preferences are allowed free rein, but coordinated and structured to produce a balanced, consistent, and fair society? One approach to the answers to these questions is through understanding how the price and market system truly works in advanced capitalist economies. This understanding of capital accumulation can then be examined on its adaptability, or lack of it, for so-called socialist economies, and then another estimate of the economic surplus might be in order.

CONCLUSION

Writing in the mid-sixties, Baran, Sweezy, and Phillips developed their critique of monopoly capitalism by highlighting the waste and irrationality of the U.S. economy. The success of an economy depends in large measure on how great a surplus is generated and how wisely that surplus is used. This essay has argued that although Baran and Sweezy included the usual *caveat* that prices and the market system would be needed during the transition from socialism to communism, they, along with most theorists on the left, completely underestimated and misjudged the role of prices in determining the size of the surplus and in society coming to grips with how best to use that surplus.

In a crucial footnote, Baran and Sweezy (1966: 235) wrote:

> Marx emphasised in his *Critique of the Gotha Programme* that the principle of equivalent exchange must survive in a socialist society for a considerable period as a guide to the efficient allocation and utilisation of human and material resources. By the same token, however, the evolution of socialism into communism requires an unremitting struggle *against* the principle, with a view to its ultimate replacement by the ideal 'From each according to his ability, to each according to his need'. In a fully developed communist society, in which social production would be organised as in one vast economic enterprise and in which scarcity would be largely overcome, equivalent exchange would no more serve as the organizing principle of economic activity than at the present time the removal of a chair from one's bedroom to one's sitting-room requires charging the sitting-room and crediting the bedroom with the value of the furniture. This is obviously not to imply that the communist society of the future can dispense with rational calculation; what it does indicate is that the nature of the rationality involved in economic calculation undergoes a profound change. And this change in turn is but one manifestation of a thoroughgoing transformation of human needs and of the relations among men in society.

The reader, however, looks in vain for an analysis of how capital is truly allocated in the U.S. economy, and how a transition economy might improve on this process, while moving to a more rational schema. This essay has proposed that a theory relating prices to capital values is the proper starting point for the analysis, and has applied the theory to industrial market analysis, to the labour market, to international trade, and to socialist and social democratic economies.

This essay has suggested that the American economy has not become much more rational since Joe Phillips made his estimates of the economic surplus. What has changed, and changed dramatically, is our perception the role of prices. The evolution of the market system is going forward, and to appreciate that evolution requires a realistic price theory. It would be convenient to believe that an economy could make a leap directly from capitalism to physical planning, and forget about markets and prices and personal accumulation of capital. Apparently society does not change in that fashion. What is required is that we agree democratically how large a surplus we want to create and how to allocate it, while simultaneously recognising the price and market adaptations needed to accomplish it.

NOTES

1. See Table B-92, 'Sources and Uses of Funds, Non-farm, Non-financial Corporate Business', *President's Economic Report*, 1988.
2. For supporting data, see Franck and Quint, eds, 1947.

REFERENCES

Baran, Paul A. (1957). *The Political Economy of Growth*, New York: Monthly Review Press.

Baran, Paul A.and Paul M. Sweezy (1966). *Monopoly Capital*, New York: Monthly Review Press.

Franck, Peter G. and Milton Quint, eds (1947). *Problems in Price Control: Pricing Techniques*, Washington D.C.: Office of Price Administration.

Kalecki, Michal (1965 |1954|). *Theory of Economic Dynamics*, London: George Allen & Unwin.

Kalecki, Michal (1969). *Introduction to the Theory of Growth in a Socialist Economy*, Oxford: Basil Blackwell.

Keynes, John M. (1936). *The General Theory of Employment, Interest and Money*, New York: Harcourt, Brace.

Lange, Oskar (1938). *On the Economic Theory of Socialism*, Minneapolis: University of Minnesota Press.

Nove, Alec (1969). *An Economic History of the U.S.S.R.*, London: Penguin Books.

Nove, Alec (1983). *The Economics of Feasible Socialism*, London: George Allen & Unwin.

President's Economic Report (1988). Washington D.C.: Government Printing Office.

Steindl, J. (1952). *Maturity and Stagnation in American Capitalism*, Oxford: Basil Blackwell.

10. Industrial Integration, East and West: Planning the Market Economy

Keith Cowling

The integration of the industrial economies of Eastern and Western Europe is now at the top of the economic and political agenda. However, the presumption appears to be, consciously or by default, that the market should be left to achieve such integration. This is not to say that governments fail to recognise their interest and relevance within the process of organising new institutions located round the edge of the industrial economy – for example, institutions related to the currency – but there seems to be neither interest nor concern with the involvement of governments in the actual processes of industrial integration and restructuring, certainly in the West, and it seems increasingly in the East. In contrast to this present reality, this paper advances the view that leaving the market to achieve such integration will inevitably generate global inefficiency. The process has to be planned at a level beyond that of the individual corporation, the principal actor in the present reality: collective strategy is required, informed by a collective vision nurtured by a strong democratic base. I will argue that if we seek dynamic efficiency and a full democracy then our vision for the new Europe will be one of relatively small-scale production, but one where the state, acting at various levels, provides a supportive environment to ensure technological progressiveness. This sort of structure will not be the outcome of an unfettered market process of industrial integration given that large-scale enterprise, although not guaranteeing efficiency, certainly guarantees power.

I will start by explaining and describing the present process of integration orchestrated by the giant corporations. I will then proceed to consider the planning imperative and the broad nature of strategy. Then I will consider a vision of a new Europe which will turn on the

177

reemergence of the region or city region as a meaningful entity. I will end by considering what needs to be done to move us toward that view. A broad-brush approach to a broad canvas!

THE PRESENT PROCESS

Current industrial restructuring within Europe is being affected by two sets of forces that are unique to Europe – the forces unleashed by the approach of 1992 and those unleashed by the opening-up to the East. The latter development can be seen as redirecting the forces of 1992, but also amplifying them. The combination of these two sets of forces will increasingly produce an integrated continental economy with a growing similarity to that of the United States. We may expect to observe that the evolution of such an economy may replicate at least some of the experiences of the United States economy in its recent history.

Theory

In order to understand the present restructuring within Europe, and its implications, we have to dig below the surface phenomena to uncover the essence of the modern corporation and the related reasons for its changing transnational base – we have to go back to square one to consider the nature of the firm.

The orthodox view is that the firm is the means of coordinating production without market exchange (Coase, 1937). Obviously such a view is concerned with the type of exchange, yet the crucial issue is the essential qualities, the nature, of exchange. Whether it is effected through the market or not should be of lesser interest. In looking for the distinctive feature bringing an exchange within a firm I shall focus on control. I shall take this to imply the ability to determine broad corporate objectives despite resistance from others – the ability to make strategic decisions. Thus the notion of a center of strategic decision-making goes to the heart of the matter and provides a clear basis for defining a firm: a firm is the means of coordinating production from one center of strategic decision-making. This, for example, puts much sub-contracting and joint-venture within the ambit of the firm – provided control is established. The transnational firm is then the means of coordinating production from one centre of strategic decision-making when this coordination takes the firm across national boundaries (see Cowling and Sugden, 1987b). I now want to pose the question: why should firms seek to organise or reorganise themselves across national boundaries? As we shall see later, this is the dominant process of integration we are observing – it is not arms' length trading! Where trade increases it is largely within the control of the dominant firms which are choosing to extend their influence and control across national frontiers.

The key to understanding the emergence of transnationals lies in the oligopolistic environment within which they operate. Whilst, if circumstances allowed it, a firm would not hesitate to become a pure monopolist by driving rivals from the industry, more generally it cannot do this and will therefore accommodate their presence. Thus we have the superficially paradoxical coexistence of rivalry and collusion, with rivalry as the cement of collusive arrangements. Retaliatory power is the lynch-pin in such a world: positions have to be defended but the positions of others can also be attacked. This suggests two reasons for moving transnational, for reasons of defense or attack. Thus transnationals arise because they are a means of maintaining or increasing profit in an oligopolistic world. Whether or not the welfare of employees within the firm, or the local community, increases or not is not the central issue.

An important reason for going transnational is lower labour cost – there are, of course, many others, but this particular reason would appear most fundamental. Costs of different types of labour vary substantially across countries and firms will take advantage of this, wherever they are able, and 1992 and the opening-up to the East facilitates such behavior. But this is too restrictive a view because it depicts firms as passive reactors to given cost conditions. Costs depend on the bargaining power of labour and its employers, and this is endogenous to a firm's strategic decisions. Transnationals arise to divide and rule. The bargaining power of workers depends very much on their ability to act collectively and is very difficult when people work in different countries due to organisational problems and deep-rooted cultural factors. The latter pose the more fundamental problems and reveal a basic asymmetry between labour and its employers (Cowling and Sugden, 1987a). Collective action by labour requires cooperation – pursuing profits across the globe simply (?) requires hierarchical organisations into which people can be slotted. This puts it too starkly, but the asymmetry is real enough.

Thus a firm may decide to produce in various countries so that it can face a divided workforce, thereby reduce labour's bargaining power, and therefore lower labour costs. Similarly a firm contemplating new investment may bargain with divided *potential* employees.[1] The choice between market and non-market exchange may be especially interesting in this context. For example, sub-contracting may be particularly appealing in that it can provide an extreme division of a militant, or potentially militant, workforce. Imagine the problems of workers dotted across Europe in small workshops, operating under different names, of actually organising collective action.

Thus divide and rule implies manufacturing operations spread across different countries. Those parts of the process requiring skilled labour may be concentrated in the older industrialised economies, but unskilled activity knows no bounds. Moreover, divide and rule gives an impetus to the development of technology which deskills most, or all, operations. The whole of Europe (and beyond) will be opened up to more and more manufacturing (and other) activities. However, there may be important differences between eastern Europe and 1992 developments in southern Europe, and also within eastern Europe, between north/central and south, given their different industrial traditions. Putting 1992 and the opening-up to the East together and we can expect to see a movement of production from north-west Europe towards the south-west (the Mediterranean Rim) and the east, but there will be imposed on this a *qualitative* distinction in the production received between the north-east and south.

These predictions differ from those in a recent paper by Krugman and Venables (1990). In the presence of economies of scale, they argue, local firms in peripheral economies will lose out as barriers to trade fall – there are strong forces at work pulling manufacturing towards the central economies, but they also point out that these centripetal tendencies are strongest at some intermediate level of barriers. With the total elimination of barriers production will shift to lowest-cost production sites.

My main problem with the Krugman and Venables model is that it focuses entirely on national rather than transnational firms. Of course there are important centripetal tendencies within the system I seek to describe, but they lie within the realm of the location of strategic decisions, rather than at the level of production. It is important to recognise that the shift in production in a transnational world does not imply a similar relocation in strategic decision-making. Divide and rule leads to locating manufacturing throughout the world – there is no reason for strategic decision-makers to move as well. Cities like New York, Tokyo, Frankfurt, Paris, and London will remain the key cities of the world, alongside a renaissant Berlin! Indeed their joint dominance will grow with the growth of the transnationals whose headquarters they contain. The world being depicted is characterised by firms with a global spread of production, but controlled from a handful of locations.

Observation

The industrial restructuring within Europe that hit the headlines prior to the dramatic events of autumn 1989 demonstrated the battles and arrangements between the giant corporations as they positioned themselves for the 1990s. We can see such moves as attempts to defend or attack within the generally ubiquitous oligopolistic environment. This continues as merger, takeover, and joint venture and has extended its remit into Eastern Europe as barriers to economic integration are progressively removed. The processes of 1992 have been significantly augmented by the process of East–West integration orchestrated by the same major players. The process can be seen most vividly in the case of East Germany.

The financial press is full of the news of chairmen of the major West German companies – for example, Daimler-Benz, Volkswagen, Thyssen, Metallgesellschaft – proceeding collectively to East Germany to discuss economic partnership.[2] An important criticism of the then East German administration appeared to be the 49 percent limit on foreign participation in joint ventures. The pressure was on to achieve the dominance which is implicit in the 'market'. And the basis of their interest was clear: Heinz Dürr (CEO, AEG) was quoted as saying, 'we would benefit from a reduction in costs '.[3] But the process is not entirely one-sided—the managerial hierarchy within the Kombinate (giant, vertically integrated, state enterprises) see great opportunities for themselves (see *Financial Times*, January 15, 1990). It is clear that those able to establish powerful positions in East German industry will have much to gain from the process of integration, and much to lose from any restrictions imposed on it. The East German government at that time quickly fell into line, with Professor Christa Luft (then Minister of Finance) proclaiming the end of the middle way (between capitalism and central planning) and offering almost complete independence for the Kombinate.

It is also interesting to see Carl Hahn (CEO: Volkswagen) likening Eastern Europe to the Pacific Rim economies,[4] with similar growth prospects – presumably for similar reasons, particularly an elastic supply of low-waged, skilled, educated, and disciplined workers. The largest company in the world probably has a similar view. GM recently announced a joint venture with Raba (Hungary) relating to engines and car assembly. The President of GM Europe described it as a 'strategic partnership', but notice that GM has 67 percent of the equity and appoints the management. This is just the economic colonisation of Eastern Europe.[5]

Alongside these mergers, takeovers, and joint ventures involving the giants, and in some cases tied up with it, is a rather quieter development. The major Western European corporations have been steadily moving towards a more fragmented production base for some time – and this could receive added impetus with the approach of 1992 and the quickening pace of East–West integration.

Production within these firms has been, and is being, progressively shifted from large plants in the older industrialised regions and countries to smaller plants in those regions or countries which are beginning the process of industrialisation, in some cases via non-market exchange, in other cases via market exchange, but typically subject to strategic control from the center. We have already seen lots of evidence of this in the case of Eastern Europe, for example major clothing firms in the West, manufacturers and retailers (e.g. Next in Britain) are putting out production to firms in the East, but controlling design and marketing.[6]   The pace of such integration is likely to quicken and some of the joint ventures (already described) represent an extension of this mode of integration.   Increasingly we may observe the Kombinate developing in this way, or being circumvented by Western capital, as in the case of BMW, working directly with smaller enterprises, including cooperatives.

There remains the possibility of significant growth in sectors of the economy lying outside the orbit of the giant eurocompanies. We shall return to this after considering whether or not the present system of integration – the unfettered market process – warrants a significant degree of government intervention.

THE CASE FOR PLANNING

The essence of the argument about the inefficiencies of the market and the need for the imposition of a community-based economic planning system, whether local, regional, national, or supranational, relates to the displacement of the pure market (Walras) by command economies, that is giant firms, which are no longer guided by democratic decision-making. This has a spatial context (i.e., centripetalism and transnationalism) and a class context (i.e., dominant and subordinate groups). The development of capitalism has led to a concentration and centralisation of decision-making and relevant parts of the constituency are being left out of the process of decision-making. Increasingly communities are losing their capacity to determine their own futures – the essence of democracy. Thus economic democracy is fundamental to maximising a community's economic welfare. If portrayed in terms of a community's welfare function, then its maximization requires that a community makes its own choices. Obviously principal-agent problems will remain but the principle is clear. If others make these choices, there is no reason why they should correspond to the community's optimum – and every reason why they should not. In theory, this requirement for economic democracy fits very easily within neoclassical economics, which is all about individuals making choices. In practice, it cuts across the grain of neoclassical analysis, which assumes an even distribution of power, ignores power asymmetries, and therefore fails to grasp the democratic/undemocratic distinction.

I have identified three proximate reasons for imposing on the market – the private system of planning – coherent, community-based economic planning systems within which these processes are allowed to operate (Cowling, 1990). They are transnationalism, centripetalism, and short-termism, and they are each related to an underlying concentration of power/decision-making. These are not new factors but they now assume such significance that economic policy must be fundamentally realigned to fully account for them, and 1992 and East–West integration serve to dramatically sharpen the issues. I would, quite briefly, like to describe these forces and assess their implications.

The fundamental issue posed by transnationalism is that of the asymmetry of power between corporation and community: the flexibility of transnationality confronting the inevitable locational rigidity of community. To achieve its own objectives the transnational corporation can switch investment and production – or threaten to do so – whenever conditions in any one country appear disadvantageous. To protect itself the community has to intervene in the strategy-making of the transnationals, or accept their dominance in its own affairs. To do so is to admit that a community has no real autonomy.

This is a perfectly general phenomenon. National communities in general can suffer from the unrestricted activities of transnationals. Any community considering a tax or wage increase will be faced with the possibility that capital will migrate. The general system effect is that wages and taxes will be held down against the wishes of each national community and, similarly, subsidies to investment or production will be raised. Of course, I am predicting this result on the assumption that communities are chasing scarce investment rather than that capital is chasing scarce labour. But, barring a few specialist skills, this is the reality at the close of the twentieth century.

Thus we have a basis for regulation, a matter for both East and West as the transnationals extend their activities into the previously centrally planned economies, but also a basis for establishing a role for a community economic strategy at national and supranational level – a pan-European strategy – a point at which the (Western) European Community should get together with the countries of Eastern Europe to establish a European coherence to national policy-making. It is surely important to try and resolve pan-European problems by voice, in a common arena, rather than by exit via 'market processes' which are themselves controlled by the private strategies of powerful agents. Transnationals are not a threat if their strategies are harmonised with the economic strategy of the community, but a necessary condition is the existence of a community strategy. Having established such a strategy, cultural, political, and economic pressure will be needed to ensure harmony is achieved and maintained.

Centripetalism is a systemic feature of transnationalism, with the control of the use of an ever-increasing share of the world's economic resources being drawn into the ambit of the key cities of the world. For example, in 1984 fifty-nine of the world's biggest transnational corporations were headquartered in New York, whereas one Third World country, South Korea, had a city which headquartered more than two, Seoul with four (see Smith and Feagin, 1987). All the world's major transnationals are headquartered in a small minority of the world's cities – Glasgow and Manchester, Marseilles and Lyons, Vienna and Budapest, seem not to count. Strategic decisions, with major implications for many local, regional, and national communities, are being taken outside those communities and the same centralising forces are siphoning off resources to the centre and thereby reducing the capacity of the periphery to sustain its own economic, political, and cultural development, on which future self-determination is based. This is what will happen to Eastern Europe with existing processes, but it is important to recognise the dynamic inefficiency of the whole process for East *and* West. With production and jobs going one way and decision-making the other, communities on *either* side are losing control over their futures.

The third basis for requiring an industrial strategy is the systemic short-termism of the market as it has developed in the twentieth century. This is partly related to transnationalism, given the limited commitment to production at any one location, and partly related to centripetalism, given that the withdrawal of strategic decision-making from huge swathes of the world's surface implies a wider infection: investment in broader and deeper aspects of the community within the regions will not command serious attention. The growth of the forces of transnationalism and centripetalism implies an increasing failure to internalise various dynamic external economies, perhaps somewhat paradoxically. Previously locally based industry could recognise the importance for them of cultural investment: this link has been substantially broken. But short-termism is not purely a consequence of these forces: it is also promoted by the concomitant development of other organisational forms and institutions. The development of M-form corporations has raised the problem of the efficient conception and implementation of long-term strategy. The existence and development of an active market for corporate control also pushes long-term thinking from center-stage.

The implication of short-termism is that incremental change can be handled quite well by market institutions, but more fundamental changes, involving quantum leaps in product, process or structure will not be handled so well. The market hardly seems the sort of institution to offer the job of perestroika following a major political revolution encompassing half a continent. Within both the existing market economies and the formerly centrally administered economies we need mechanisms and institutions within which long-term planning is facilitated.

Summing up at this point I would argue that the central tendencies within modern market economies, when taken together, point to the need for community economic planning in order to achieve dynamic efficiency, but although planning is seen to be essential for reasons of efficiency, the nature of planning is all-important. In this regard I believe we have much to learn from Japan. Japan appears to have been able substantially to transcend the forces I have analysed by purposive national action. I do not want to go into the Japanese experience in this present context; people who are interested should read Chalmers Johnson (1982); but drawing the appropriate lessons would require in the case of Western Europe a move from *ad hoc* intervention towards a coherent strategic policy, with a proactive stance replacing a reactive one. In the case of Eastern Europe it certainly requires a greater devolution of control to the market, but coupled with the establishment of strategic planning by the state in certain key sectors. But strategy has to be informed by vision: what sort of vision might we have of a future Europe?

CREATING A SMALL-ENTERPRISE ECONOMY

The central point, of which we should be clear, is that the development of giant European champions would be inappropriate. The collapse of the industrial economy of Eastern Europe provides further dramatic evidence that the pursuit of bigness has failed. It appeared that central 'planning' favored industrial concentration, presumably for reasons of scale economies in production, but also for administrative convenience and control. Certainly giant monopolies were created and are now seen to be dinosaurs.

It could, of course, be argued that it was not the monopolisation of production that led to the inefficiency and lack of dynamism of these organisations; rather, it was the excessively detailed, and in many cases arbitrary, control imposed by the central administrative structure of the so-called 'planning' agencies which led to the poor performance. And that indeed is the view now being strongly represented by the management of these monopolies as they engage in negotiations over joint-venture arrangements with the giants of the West.

These arguments may prove difficult to assess in the context of the experience of Eastern Europe, since we have limited observation of either a hands-off central administration (although some might suggest Hungary offers a case in point – a position challenged by many Hungarian observers!) – or an unconcentrated industrial structure: the recent development of cooperatives has been primarily in areas of enormous excess demand where profit performance has had more to do with very high prices than with gains in efficiency. It is therefore important to remember that research in the West has demonstrated convincingly that the creation of the Western European industrial giants as a result of the merger boom of the late 1960s and early '70s was, to a large extent, disastrous in efficiency terms. The most recent and comprehensive assessment was provided by Adams and Brock (1988) in an important survey article. They in fact use the evidence to try and dissuade the United States from following a similar path in response to the Japanese challenge, who they reveal have followed a deconcentrating strategy, contrary to popular mythology.

Giantism has not delivered the goods in the East and has revealed severe deficiencies in the West. The problems posed by the dominance of the giants have to be addressed as issues of regulation, but also as issues of development. We need to avoid the perhaps too-easy transition from state socialism to monopoly capitalism (see Newbery, 1990). We need to react to the accumulated power of the giant corporations in terms of regulations: we also need to act strategically to counterpose our own vision of the future. I have suggested elsewhere (Cowling, 1990) that perhaps a fruitful way forward would be to create the conditions necessary for a significant extension of the system of flexible specialisation (see Piore and Sabel, 1984). This implies the modern re-creation of many of the characteristics of traditional craft production. The basic unit of production tends to be small-scale, in some cases incorporated into larger enterprises, but typically organised as networks defining geographical, industrial districts. Piore and Sabel argue that these structures have some superior properties and achieved superior performance in the 1970s and '80s. Many expect the system to increasingly crowd out the system of mass production operated by the giants. But this would appear unlikely, as a generality, unless and until a supportive environment is provided by the national, regional, and local state. Without this support, successful experiments are likely to succumb to the powerful advances of the giants, manifest via acquisition or predation. Sabel (1988) makes the interesting point that the supportive environment must also incorporate some form of insurance to cover changes in the composition of demand. Specialist firms have to be allowed time to achieve conversion in the face of changing demand. He suggests a confederation of industrial districts to pool resources, and to avoid a local narrowness. Thus regional policies should come much more to the fore and industrial strategy should be articulated at that level. Strategy has to be devolved and decentralised, but with a national coherence. We need to create the conditions for expanding circles of prosperity. We need policies which will allow the re-emergence of the (city) region (Sabel, 1988). Finally, given the span of control of the transnationals, we need a European coherence to our strategic planning. This will require a pan-European council with democratic roots and an associated agency on the lines of MITI, to develop vision and strategy for the whole federal structure.

NOTES

1. GM's recent agreement with Merseyside unions about a new engine plant was recently described as 'the most flexible union arrangements in Europe' (*Financial Times*, April 6, 1990). The unsuccessful unions in this case were those in Kaiserslautern, West Germany.
2. I am reminded at this point of the similarities with the movement of the political giants of West Germany into East Germany for the recent elections – something that was eloquently described by a New Forum spokesperson as the Day of the Elephants.
3. Non-West German industry sees similar opportunities. Asea-Brown Boveri (Swedish–Swiss power engineering company) were taking control of Zemech (Poland) with the aim of becoming 'the world's lowest cost producer'.
4. Notice, however, that the United Nations Economic Commission for Europe in its 1989/90 annual report comes to a very different conclusion, arguing that the monopolistic structure of the East European economies has to be addressed as a first priority.

5. I am reminded of Sydney Pollard's description of the process of industrialisation of Britain over the century beginning around 1750 as 'the inner colonisation of labour'(Pollard, 1978).
6. BMW is planning direct investment in small-scale workshops in the East, producing tools and components, arguing that this offers them maximum control—'a vital feature for a company known for its hands-on management style and exacting technical requirements' (*Wall Street Journal Europe*, April 18, 1990, p.8).

REFERENCES

Adams W. and J. Brock (1988). 'The Bigness Mystique and the Merger Policy Debate: An International Perspective', *Northwestern Journal of International Law and Business*, 9, 1–48.

Coase, R.H. (1937). 'The Nature of the Firm', *Economica*, 4.

Cowling, K. (1990). 'A New Industrial Strategy: Preparing Europe for the Turn of the Century', *International Journal of Industrial Organisation*, 8, 1.

Cowling, K. and R. Sugden (1987a), *Transnational Monopoly Capitalism*, Brighton: Harvester Press.

Cowling, K. and R. Sugden (1987b). 'Market Exchange and the Concept of a Transnational Corporation: Analyzing the Nature of the Firm', *British Review of Economic Issues*, 9, 57–69.

Johnson, C. (1982). *MITI and the Japanese Miracle: The Growth of Industrial Policy 1925–75*, Stanford: Stanford University Press.

Krugman, P.R. and A. J. Venables (1990). 'Integration and the Competitiveness of Peripheral Industry', Centre for Economic Policy Research, Discussion Paper 363.

Newbery, D. (1990). 'Tax Reform, Trade Liberalisation and Industrial Restructuring in Hungary', Centre for Economic Policy Research, Discussion Paper 371.

Piore, M. and C. Sabel (1984). *The Second Industrial Divide*, New York: Basic Books.

Pollard, S. (1978). 'Labour in Great Britain', in P. Mathias and M. M. Postan, eds *The Cambridge Economic History of Europe*, Cambridge: Cambridge University Press.

Sabel, C. (1988). 'The Re-emergence of Regional Economies', *Papers de Seminari*, 29–30, 71–140.

Smith, M.P. and J. R. Feagin, eds. (1987). *The Capitalist City*, Oxford: Basil Blackwell.

Index

Printed and bound by CPI Group (UK) Ltd, Croydon, CR0 4YY

23/04/2025

14661004-0001